Tennessee Tables

presented by

The Junior League of Knoxville, Inc.

The purpose of the Junior League is exclusively educational and charitable and is to promote voluntarism; to develop the potential of its members for voluntary participation in community affairs, and to demonstrate the effectiveness of trained volunteers.

Proceeds from this Junior League of Knoxville publication will benefit organizations that serve our community.

Cover Design and Illustrations
by
Marsha Shelley

Additional Copies may be obtained by writing
Tennessee Tables
The Junior League of Knoxville, Inc.
6701 Baum Dr.
Suite 255
Knoxville, Tennessee 37919
or
www.jlknoxville.org

ISBN 0-9608174-0-9

First Printing - April 1982 - 20,000 copies
Second Printing - August 2002 - 2,500 copies

WIMMER
COOKBOOKS
ConsolidatedGraphics
1-800-548-2537

Foreword

With the proposal of the 1982 World's Fair in Knoxville, our league foresaw a need to provide a collection of table fare reflecting the area.

Tennessee Tables is the combined effort of Junior League members and friends. It is a culmination of three years of submitting and soliciting over 1800 recipes, triple testing, editing, and proofing. We regret that we were unable to use all of the recipes, but similarity and lack of space prevented this. Brand names of ingredients have been used only when necessary. These recipes are our favorites and are equally challenging to the novice and the expert.

Suzanne Fletcher
Co-Chairman

Marti Hobson
Co-Chairman

Cookbook Committee

Co-Chairmen	Suzanne Fletcher
	Marti Hobson
Public Relations and Research	Geri Muse
Recipe Chairman	Beth Stivers
Recipe Assistants	Anne Hillmer
	Rusha Sams
Design Coordinator	Floweree Galetovic
Testing Coordinators	Karen Henry
	Jeanne Hyatt
	Anne Walters
Testors	Janice Allen
	Jennifer Brown
	Ann Browning
	Candy Brownlow
	Lin Christenberry
	Alice Clayton
	Nancy Dickson
	Ginger Hall
	Vicki Keller
	Ena Kirkpatrick
	Debbie Ledbetter
	Dale McCarley
	Margaret McKinnon
	Jane Milner
	Mary Moore
	Gail Pettit
	Janey Sterchi
	Suzanne Stowers
	Patsy Wright
Special Section	Ena Kirkpatrick
	Geri Muse
	Anne Walters
Typists	Marie Alcorn
	Ann Brownlee
	Donna Clark
Proofreaders	Donna Clark
	Emily S. Fuller
Index	Melissa Gill
Sustainer Liaison	Sara Ann Cantrell

Table of Contents

Table Trends 'n' Menus

Table Trends and Menus

The mood for entertaining is enhanced not only by the taste appeal of fine foods but equally by the eye appeal of an enticingly set table. The trend in entertaining has shifted to less emphasis on etiquette and formalities, enabling people to feel free to entertain in any number of casual ways that simplify the process.

In Tennessee, we are fortunate to have three full months of each season which give us the opportunity to enjoy and take advantage of the surrounding freshwater lakes and the Great Smoky Mountains. These blessings of nature greatly influence the way we live, relax, and entertain. Many Tennessee Tables are anything *but* tables, as our entertaining lends itself to informal settings.

The Spring of Tennessee is welcomed with blooming dogwoods, azaleas, and rhododendron. In Knoxville, the Dogwood Arts Festival is an annual event in April which provides two weeks of fascinating events, parades, and tours. On Market Square Mall, the hub of the Festival's events, visitors can find such regional delicacies as Apple Stack Cake (page 203), Funnel Cakes (page 99), and the featured lunch of the day provided by local restaurants. East Tennesseeans love to entertain during the Festival and many Tennessee Tables are done "garden style" while nature's blooms are at their peak.

Summer comes to Tennessee precisely on time. Casual entertaining becomes the focus, and hostesses like to discover new menus for boating and hiking. A summer Tennessee Table is usually on deck, at poolside, or beside a mountain stream.

Fall finds the Great Smoky Mountains ablaze with color and revolves around trips to the mountains and football festivities. Mountain picnics, brunches, and tailgating become Tennessee fare.

In Winter, Tennessee Tables offer hearty soups, stews, and "stick-to-the-bone" meals. Ski excursions to neighboring slopes are a favorite getaway and food is carried "in tow."

Across our state and particularly in Knoxville, people love to be invited to a *Tennessee Table!*

Menu Suggestions from Tennessee Tables

The recipes in the following menus can be found in the index except when indicated with an asterisk (*).

Spring

Dogwood Arts Festival Luncheon

White Sangria
Shrimp, Mushroom, Artichoke Casserole
Baked Tomatoes
Lemon Bread
Strawberries Romanoff

For Spring parties, early blooms, flowering fruit trees, or colorful vegetables are accessible sources for centerpieces. For a special touch fold your napkins in the Lobster fold.

LOBSTER

A — Fold top half of napkin down to bottom of napkin.

B — Fold both right and left hand corners down to center.

C — Fold both right and left hand corners up to center.

D — Hold napkin at bottom and turn napkin over (flip bottom toward top).

E — Lift the upper layer of the bottom of napkin to top.

F — Lift top layer of napkin in the middle. Lift bottom legs up over napkin as shown. Bottom legs will rest on lifted edges.

Rack of Lamb Dinner

Cream of Broccoli Soup
Spinach Salad
Rack of Lamb
Carrots with Orange
Potatoes Alexandre
Dorothy's Popovers
Cold Lemon Soufflé

Place four or five small pots of flowering bulbs in a glass bowl. Cover pots with oriental garden stones or small shells. Fold your napkins in the Bishop's Miter for an elegant dinner.

BISHOP'S MITER

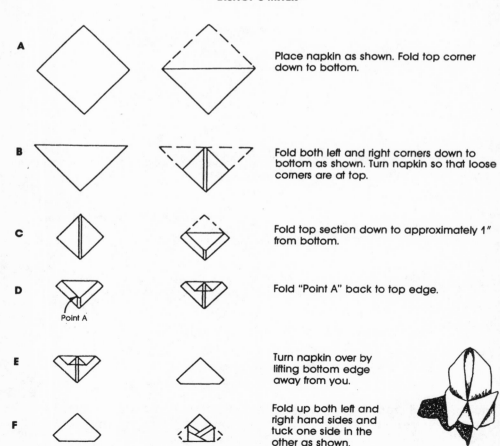

A — Place napkin as shown. Fold top corner down to bottom.

B — Fold both left and right corners down to bottom as shown. Turn napkin so that loose corners are at top.

C — Fold top section down to approximately 1″ from bottom.

D — Fold "Point A" back to top edge.

Point A

E — Turn napkin over by lifting bottom edge away from you.

F — Fold up both left and right hand sides and tuck one side in the other as shown.

Mother's Day Brunch

Muse's Orange Julius
Beef-Sausage Quiche
Marinated Tomatoes and Artichokes
Feather Muffins
Frozen Toffee Dessert

Place fresh eggs of varying hues in an old basket and fill in with fresh baby's breath. Napkins can be gracefully placed in the Upright Fan fold.

UPRIGHT FAN

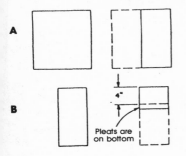

A Fold left half of napkin to right edge.

B Fold in 1" accordion pleats starting at the bottom. Stop pleats approximately 4" from top. (Decrease 4" to 3" or 2" if using small napkins.)

Pleats are on bottom

Pleats are now showing

C Fold left side of napkin to right edge.

D Fold complete right corner down and tuck under pleats.

Center Section

E Pick up napkin by center section and place on table. Pleats will open to form a fan.

Summer

Picnic in the Smokies

Creamy Cucumber Soup
Sausage and Chicken Pâté en Croûte
*Fresh Fruit in Season**
Homemade Bread
Lemon Cookies

Place your homemade bread in a basket tied with a bow and streamers. Roll your silverware in individual napkins and tie tightly with grosgrain ribbon. Ribbon can be cut 13 inches long and tied in a square knot.

Poolside or Terrace Dinner

Fresh Peach Daiquiri
Herb Cheese   Assorted Crackers*
Jacksonville Shrimp Scampi
Dill Vegetables
Processor French Bread
Raspberry Ice Cream
Scotch Shortbread

As a centerpiece, float a single flower blossom in a shell or use a large piece of coral. Mirror the shell or coral for a special effect. Fold your napkins in a Sailboat pattern.

SAIL BOAT

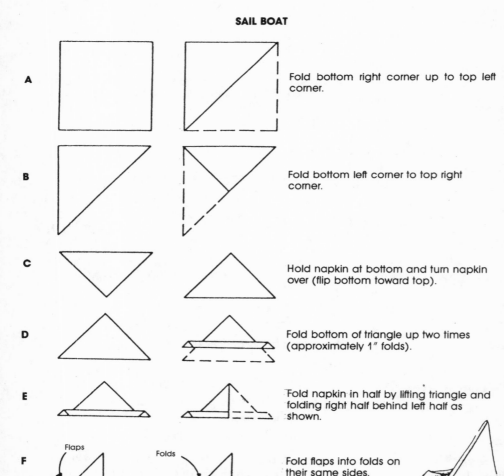

A   Fold bottom right corner up to top left corner.

B   Fold bottom left corner to top right corner.

C   Hold napkin at bottom and turn napkin over (flip bottom toward top).

D   Fold bottom of triangle up two times (approximately 1″ folds).

E   Fold napkin in half by lifting triangle and folding right half behind left half as shown.

F   Fold flaps into folds on their same sides.

Fourth of July Buffet

*Beer**
Ready-to-drink Iced Tea
Muse's Nuts and Bolts
Pork Barbecue or Beef Barbecue
Artichoke Rice Salad
Don's Genuine Corn Pone
Royal Stuart Ice Cream
Aunt Jo's Brownies

Use a drum surrounded with greenery and flowers for a simple and fun centerpiece. For a large buffet, two duplicate lines speed service. Fold your napkins in the Rocket fold.

ROCKET

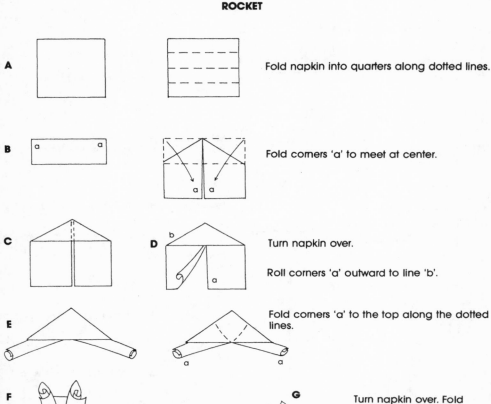

A Fold napkin into quarters along dotted lines.

B Fold corners 'a' to meet at center.

C D Turn napkin over.

Roll corners 'a' outward to line 'b'.

E Fold corners 'a' to the top along the dotted lines.

F Napkin after stage E.

G Turn napkin over. Fold point down and arrange on the table with the point toward the diner.

Fall

Before-the-Game Brunch

Tomato Soup Piquant
Bleu Cheese Wafers
Make-Ahead Breakfast
Curried Fruit
Sally Lunn Muffins
Angel Toffee Roll

Before-the-game brunches are a tradition in "Big Orange Country." Fresh oranges are favored as a centerpiece for this type of Tennessee Table; however, a football helmet or pumpkin filled with Autumn flowers are alternatives. If serving buffet, fold your napkins to hold the silverware.

BUFFET

A   Fold bottom half of napkin up to top edge.

B   Fold upper layer of top back down to bottom. (Bottom section is now three layers.)

C   Flip napkin over from left to right.

D   Fold left and right corners down to center.

E   Fold down outer left and right edges as shown.

F   Fold both left and right sides in to center.

G   Repeat Step 'F'.

Pockets for silverware

Tailgate Picnic

Bloody Mary Mix
Beer Cheese   Assorted Crackers*
Gourmet Fried Chicken
Marinated Salad
Whole Wheat Cheese Biscuits
Chess Squares

Use a festive stadium blanket as a tablecloth on the tailgate or hood of your car. Have napkins and silverware ready to go, folded in the Carry-all fold.

CARRY ALL

A Fold bottom half of napkin up to top edge.

B Fold left half of napkin to right side.

C Turn napkin so loose corners are at the top and fold the top layer in half.

D Fold the second layer and tuck under the top layer. Leave about an inch showing.

E Fold sides under equally. Place silverware in resulting pockets.

Homecoming Buffet

Frozen Margaritas
Assorted Cheeses and Fruits*
Filet of Beef Roll
Rice Supreme
Caesar Salad
Refrigerator Rolls
Chocolate Mousse Pie

A pastry cornucopia made from refrigerator crescent rolls is a unique centerpiece. Make a cornucopia form from aluminum foil. Roll the crescent dough out and cut into strips. Holding the foil form over your arm, wrap the strips of dough around the form. Brush with egg-yolk and bake in the oven until golden. Remove foil when cornucopia has cooled. Glaze fresh fruit with an egg white - sugar mixture and arrange spilling from the cornucopia. The pastry cornucopia will freeze for later use. Fold napkins in the Swirl pattern so your guests can pickup their glasses and napkins at the same time.

SWIRL

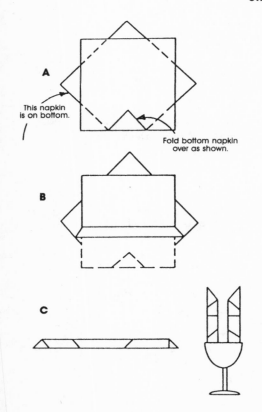

A

This napkin is on bottom.

Place two napkins as shown. Contrast napkin colors as desired.

Fold bottom napkin over as shown.

B

Roll napkin starting at bottom, rolling all the way to the top.

C

Fold rolled napkin in the middle and place in fancy glass.
Note: Small napkins are better for this style.

Winter

40th Birthday Bash

Fried Camembert
Joe's Goose
Wild Rice with Mushrooms
Yellow Squash Boats with Spinach
Pickled Peaches
All Bran Rolls
Black Forest Cake

Depending on the attitude of the celebrant, this may be a time for mourning or a time for celebration. If mourning is the case, a styrofoam funeral wreath with plastic flowers from the dime store, or a cake shaped like a headstone, would make a whimsical centerpiece. Roll your napkins in the Candle pattern.

CANDLE

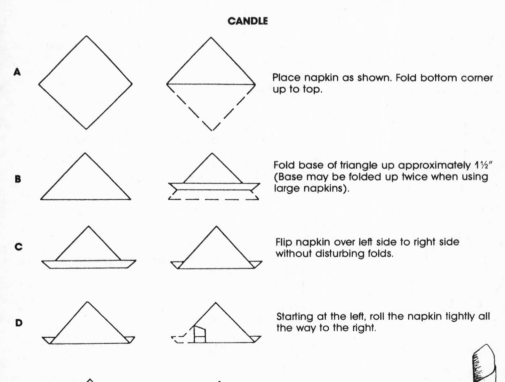

A Place napkin as shown. Fold bottom corner up to top.

B Fold base of triangle up approximately 1½" (Base may be folded up twice when using large napkins).

C Flip napkin over left side to right side without disturbing folds.

D Starting at the left, roll the napkin tightly all the way to the right.

E Fold corner of the napkin into the flap to hold in place.

Ski Excursion Dinner
Red Flannel Grog
Spiced Nuts
Lutie's Soup
Mercedes Salad with Dressing
Emma Gene's Corn Bread
Sour Cream Apple Pie

This is the perfect time to use available ceramics as centerpieces. For this soup dinner, a soup tureen is the logical choice. A wooden bowl or basket piled with apples is also effective. Use the Triangle pattern for a napkin fold.

TRIANGLE

A   Fold bottom half of napkin up to top edge.

B   Fold left half of napkin to right side.

C   Fold bottom left corner to upper right corner.

D   Turn napkin counterclockwise to position shown.

E   Lift center of napkin up until napkin stands upright.

Valentine Luncheon
Kir
Sauté of Lemon Chicken
Buttered Rice with Parsley*
Strawberry Nut Mold
Mashed Potato Rolls
Tea Punch
Regas' Red Velvet Cake

Take pots of red tulips and put several in a basket. Cover the tops of the pots with dampened dried moss so the tulips appear to be "growing" out of the basket. Have your napkins folded in the Arrowhead pattern.

ARROWHEAD

A

Fold top and bottom edges under along dotted lines.

B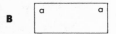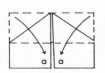

Fold corners 'a' in to meet at center.

C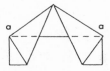

Fold back corners 'a'.

D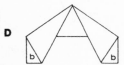

Keeping the two sides ('b') flat on the table, press them toward the middle; this will make the center line stand up. Fold sections 'b' under at the dotted line. Open out the center fold and arrange on the table with the point away from the diner.

Cocktail Buffet

Open Bar*
Beef Tender   Oriental Turkey Breast
Assorted Breads and Condiments*
Crab Dip   Curry Pâté
Melba Rounds*   Fish Wheat Crackers*
Marinated Mushrooms and Broccoli Buds
Fried Sweet Potato Chips
Round Chocolate Éclairs

Traffic flow around the table is an important consideration for the cocktail buffet. To facilitate this, separate the bar from the food table—in different rooms if possible. Another concern is the quantity of liquor to buy for an open bar. Below is a chart indicating how many drinks you should get from bottles of liquor or wine. However, if serving wine with dinner, figure on fewer glasses to a bottle, about 5 or 6 to a liter and 3 or 4 to a 750-milliliter.

How Much to Buy

	No. Drinks per Bottle	
	liter	750-milliliter
whiskey, gin, vodka (mixed drinks, highballs, 1½-oz. servings)	22	17
table wines (red, white, rosé, 4- to 5-oz. servings)	6-8	5-6
sherry (3-oz. serving)	11	8
cordials (1-oz. serving)	33	25
champagne, sparkling wine (4- to 5-oz. servings)	6-8	5-6

As a general rule, figure two drinks per person for the first two hours, 1½ per person for the third hour, and one drink per person per hour after that. Have extra on hand.

Appetizers

Bleu Cheese Wafers

6 ounces sharp Cheddar cheese,
  grated
3 ounces bleu cheese
1 cup margarine, softened
2¾ cups all-purpose flour
1 tablespoon Worcestershire sauce

½ teaspoon garlic salt
½ teaspoon celery salt
¼ to ½ teaspoon paprika
1 cup chopped pecans
Dash cayenne

Combine all ingredients and shape into log rolls. Wrap in waxed paper and refrigerate to chill. Slice thin and bake 10 minutes or until slightly brown at 375°.

Yield: 3 dozen   Jennifer Brinner (Mrs. Richard)

Whole Wheat Cheese Biscuits

½ cup butter
½ cup corn oil margarine
1½ cups whole wheat flour
½ cup all-purpose flour

3 cups grated sharp Cheddar cheese
½ teaspoon crushed red pepper
⅛ teaspoon cayenne pepper
2 cups Special K cereal

Preheat oven to 350°. Cream butter and margarine. Add flours, cheese, and peppers; mix thoroughly. Add cereal and mix. Roll into small balls and place on greased cookie sheet. Flatten with fork. Bake 10 minutes or until lightly browned.

Yield: 6 dozen   Donna Dahlen Kerr (Mrs. David B.)

Microwaved Hot Holiday Dip

1 (8-ounce) package cream cheese
¼ cup sour cream
2 tablespoons milk
2 tablespoons grated onion
2 tablespoons chopped green pepper

⅛ teaspoon salt
½ teaspoon pepper
1 (2½-ounce) jar dried beef,
  chopped
½ cup English walnuts (optional)

Place cream cheese in 1-quart glass dish, and put in microwave on full power about 30 seconds. Add sour cream and milk. Blend and microwave on full power 30 seconds. Add remaining ingredients and microwave on full power 1½ to 2 minutes. Serve immediately with Fritos.

Note: Add 2 tablespoons additional milk and serve chilled, if desired.

Yield: 2½ cups   Theresa Gibson Carnathan (Mrs. Ralph)

Curry Dip

1 cup salad dressing or mayonnaise
4 teaspoons curry powder (or to taste)
1 tablespoon Worcestershire sauce
3 tablespoons catsup
1 clove garlic, crushed
1 teaspoon minced onion
Salt to taste

Combine all ingredients and chill. Serve with raw vegetables.

Yield: 1½ to 2 cups   Retta Finley Wood (Mrs. Van H.)

Green Goddess Dip

2 (3-ounce) packages cream cheese,
    softened
1 cup mayonnaise
1 cup sour cream
2 tablespoons lemon juice
¼ cup tarragon vinegar
1 tablespoon garlic salt
½ cup chopped green onions with tops
⅔ cup chopped fresh parsley

Mix all ingredients. Let flavors blend. Serve as a dip with fresh vegetables.

Yield: 3 to 4 cups   Catherine Webb Angel (Mrs. Richard W.)

Hot and Creamy Mustard Dip

¼ cup dry mustard
2 tablespoons vinegar
1 tablespoon water
¼ cup sugar
1 egg yolk
1 (8-ounce) package cream cheese

In a small saucepan combine mustard, vinegar, water, and sugar. Cook on
low heat a few minutes then slowly add egg yolk and cream cheese. Cook
until cheese is melted and mixture is creamy. Place in a fondue pot or small
chafing dish and serve with large pretzels or bread sticks.

Yield: 1½ cups   Joyce Zirkle Tapscott (Mrs. Jack L.)

Artichoke Heart Dip

1 (8½-ounce) can artichoke hearts,
    drained
1 cup mayonnaise
1 cup Parmesan cheese

Preheat oven to 350°. Slice hearts into bite-size pieces. Combine
mayonnaise and cheese in mixing bowl. Add sliced hearts and mix well.
Pour into 1-quart baking dish. Bake 30 to 45 minutes or until it begins to
brown around edges. Serve warm with rye party slices or crackers.

Yield: 8 servings   Rose "Posey" Stewart Congleton (Mrs. Joseph)

Broccoli Dip

1 cup chopped onion
¼ cup margarine
2 (10-ounce) boxes frozen chopped
  broccoli, cooked and drained
1 cup chopped almonds

1 (10½-ounce) can cream of
  mushroom soup, undiluted
1 (6-ounce) tube Kraft garlic
  cheese spread
Tabasco sauce to taste

Sauté onions in margarine. Add remaining ingredients and simmer 3 to 5 minutes. Serve with Fritos or crackers.

Yield: 12 servings   Ellen Hardwick Tipton (Mrs. Joseph Maugham)

Spinach Vegetable Dip

1 (10-ounce) package frozen
  chopped spinach
1½ cups mayonnaise
½ cup sour cream

½ cup chopped parsley
½ cup chopped green onions
Dash Worcestershire sauce
Salt and pepper to taste

Cook spinach slightly; drain well. Combine mayonnaise, sour cream, parsley, green onions, Worcestershire sauce, salt, and pepper; add drained spinach to this mixture. Serve with raw vegetables or chips.

Yield: 4 cups   Cordy Wiley Arnold (Mrs. Arch V., III)

Mexican Dip

4 (10¾-ounce) cans chili
  beef soup, undiluted
2 green peppers, chopped
1 medium onion, chopped
1 (15-ounce) can tomato sauce
½ teaspoon oregano
½ teaspoon tarragon
½ teaspoon onion salt

½ teaspoon garlic powder
½ teaspoon sweet basil
1 (1¼-ounce) package onion dip
2 tablespoons chili powder
1 tablespoon crushed hot pepper
1 (8-ounce) package grated
  sharp Cheddar cheese

Combine all ingredients and simmer. Transfer to chafing dish and keep warm. Serve with corn chips.

Yield: 20 servings   Sue Arnold Herrmann (Mrs. Milo)
                                       Boggy Bayou, Florida

Crab Dip

3 (8-ounce) packages cream cheese
2 teaspoons confectioners' sugar
½ cup mayonnaise
2 teapoons dry mustard

Dash garlic salt
1 teaspoon onion juice or grated onion
⅔ cup dry white wine (Sauterne)
1 pound fresh backfin crabmeat

Melt cheese in double boiler until smooth. Add remaining ingredients except crab. When ready to serve, add crab, reheat, and transfer to chafing dish. Serve with melba toast.

Yield: 25 servings   Donna Dukes Trimble (Mrs. William Scott, Jr.)

Shrimp Dip

1 envelope unflavored gelatin
¼ cup water
1 (10½-ounce) can tomato soup
3 (3-ounce) packages cream cheese,
   softened
1 cup chopped celery

1 tablespoon chopped green pepper
1 tablespoon chopped onion
2 cups shrimp, mashed
1 cup mayonnaise
1 cup sour cream
Dash Tabasco sauce

Dissolve gelatin in cold water. Bring tomato soup to boil. Add cream cheese and gelatin. Blend well. Add all remaining ingredients and chill. Serve with chips.

Yield: 7 cups   Doris Thompson Ellison (Mrs. Billy)
                                             Lexington, Mississippi

Smoked Oyster Dip

2 (8-ounce) packages cream cheese,
   softened
1 teaspoon Worcestershire sauce
2 teaspoons fresh lemon juice

1 cup sour cream
1 (3¾-ounce) can smoked oysters,
   undrained

Blend cream cheese with Worcestershire, lemon juice, and sour cream. Combine with undrained oysters. Serve with corn chips.

Yield: 12 to 14 servings   Jeanne Holmes Hyatt (Mrs. Hugh C.)

Bleu Cheese Ball

3 (8-ounce) packages cream cheese,
  softened
2½ pounds bleu cheese
¼ cup bourbon

3 tablespoons Worcestershire sauce
2 teaspoons onion powder
Ground nuts, paprika, or parsley

Combine cream cheese, bleu cheese, bourbon, Worcestershire, and onion powder. Shape into a ball and roll in nuts, paprika, or parsley.

Letty Bartlett Taylor (Mrs. George C.)

Coconut Cheese Ball

3 (8-ounce) packages cream cheese,
  room temperature
¾ cup grated Cheddar cheese
2 tablespoons mayonnaise
2 tablespoons confectioners' sugar

½ cup finely chopped pecans
Cinnamon and nutmeg to taste
Coconut
Fresh fruit

Combine all ingredients except coconut and fruit. Form a ball and roll in coconut. Serve with apple, pear, and peach wedges, pineapple chunks, and other fresh fruit. Also good on snack crackers.

Yield: 1 cheese ball

Mary Adair House Crossley (Mrs. Robert)

Herb Cheese

4 cloves garlic, crushed
2 tablespoons dry vermouth
1 teaspoon snipped parsley
¾ teaspoon salt
½ teaspoon basil
¼ teaspoon tarragon

¼ teaspoon minced chives
¼ teaspoon thyme
¼ teaspoon sage
Dash white pepper
1 (8-ounce) package cream cheese,
  softened

Combine ingredients. Form into ball and chill. Serve with crackers.

Yield: 6 servings

Suzanne L. McMillen

Fried Camembert

1 (8-ounce) round ripe Camembert
2 tablespoons all-purpose flour
1 egg, beaten
1 tablespoon milk

1 cup dry bread crumbs
½ teaspoon salt
¼ cup melted butter or margarine

Cut Camembert in half horizontally, forming 2 thin rounds; do not remove rind. Coat each round in flour. Combine egg and milk; set aside. Combine bread crumbs and salt; set aside. Dip cheese rounds in egg mixture, then in bread crumbs. Repeat process. Cook in butter over medium heat 1 minute on each side or until brown and crisp.

Yield: 2 brunch servings or several appetizers   Tinque Blakely

Bleu Cheese Asparagus Rolls

1 loaf white bread
1 (8-ounce) package cream cheese
1 (4-ounce) package bleu cheese
2 eggs

1 (16-ounce) can asparagus
    spears, drained
½ cup butter, melted

Trim crust from bread and roll flat with rolling pin. Combine cheeses and eggs, blending well. Spread mixture on bread. Place 1 asparagus spear to one side of bread and roll up. Dip rolls in melted butter and freeze. To serve, slice and bake 45 minutes to 1 hour at 350°.

Yield: 12 to 15 servings   Lynne Greek Fain (Mrs. Walter D.)

Cheese Puffs

1 loaf unsliced bread
1 (3-ounce) package cream cheese
¼ pound sharp Cheddar cheese

½ cup butter
2 egg whites, stiffly beaten

Remove crust from bread and cut into 1-inch cubes. Melt cheeses and butter. Fold in egg whites. Dip bread cubes into mixture and scrape off excess. Chill or freeze.

Defrost cheese puffs 30 minutes before baking. Heat oven to 400° and bake 10 to 12 minutes until lightly browned. Serve hot.

Yield: 3 to 4 dozen   Jennifer Logan Brown (Mrs. L. Daniel)

Fresh Tomato Hors D'Oeuvre

Thin sliced bread, cut in rounds
Homemade mayonnaise (recipe follows)
Tomato slices
½ cup Worcestershire sauce

1 teaspoon Beau Monde seasoning
2 dashes Tabasco sauce
Fresh parsley or dill (optional)

Spread rounds of bread with mayonnaise. Place tomato slice on bread. Brush with mixture of Worcestershire sauce, Beau Monde, and Tabasco. Garnish with parsley or dill.

Homemade Mayonnaise:

1 egg
⅛ teaspoon cayenne pepper
⅛ teaspoon paprika
½ teaspoon dry mustard

½ teaspoon onion flakes
2 tablespoons lemon juice
1 cup vegetable oil

Put all ingredients except oil in blender. Blend on medium speed for a few seconds. Add oil gradually. Blend until oil is mixed thoroughly. Refrigerate.

Yield: 1½ cups   Sissy Law Wilson (Mrs. George Ed, III)

Beer Cheese

1 pound Cheddar cheese, grated
1 pound Swiss cheese, grated
1 clove garlic, crushed

1 tablespoon dry mustard
2 teaspoons Worcestershire sauce
1 cup beer

Combine all ingredients and mix well. Store in a covered jar in refrigerator. Serve with crackers.

Yield: 2½ cups   Priscilla Brandau Siler (Mrs. Tom A.)

Fiesta Cheese Mix

1 pound (approximately) extra-sharp
   Cheddar cheese, grated
⅓ cup chopped ripe olives
⅓ cup chopped green olives

⅓ cup chopped onion
⅓ cup chopped green pepper
Catsup

Combine cheese, ripe olives, green olives, onion, and green pepper. Add catsup to taste. Serve as hot or cold spread on crackers, or spread on sliced French bread and heat as loaf.

Yield: 4 to 5 cups   Silent Butler
                                                          Ann Bond
                                                        Alice Clayton
                                                           Di Wall

Sombrero Spread

½ pound ground beef
½ cup chopped onion, divided
¼ cup extra hot catsup
  (or catsup with cayenne)
1½ teaspoons chili powder
½ teaspoon salt

1 (15-ounce) can red kidney beans
  with liquid
½ cup grated American cheese
¼ cup chopped stuffed olives
King-size corn chips

Brown meat and ¼ cup onion. Stir in catsup, chili powder, and salt. Mash in beans and heat. Place meat mixture in chafing dish. Garnish top with cheese in center and olives and ¼ cup onion encircling cheese. Serve with king-size corn chips.

Note: Meat mixture can be prepared ahead and frozen. Thaw and reheat before serving.

Yield: 8 servings   Jeanne Holmes Hyatt (Mrs. Hugh C.)

Henry Bain's Sauce

1 (12-ounce) bottle chili sauce
1 (14-ounce) bottle tomato catsup
1 (11-ounce) bottle A-1 Sauce

1 (10-ounce) bottle Worcestershire
  sauce
1 (12-ounce) bottle Major Gray's
  Chutney

Combine all ingredients and refrigerate at least 24 hours. Serve over cream cheese with crackers.

Note: By adding ½ cup bourbon, this sauce can be used as a marinade for beef, pork, or chicken.

Yield: 2 quarts   Gale Cifers Pettit (Mrs. Michael)

Jezebel Sauce

1 (18-ounce) jar apricot preserves
1 (18-ounce) jar apple jelly
1 (5-ounce) jar horseradish

1 (1-ounce) can dry mustard
1 teaspoon coarse pepper

Combine all ingredients in blender. Serve over cream cheese and with crackers.

Note: Keeps indefinitely when refrigerated.

Yield: 6 cups   Gale Cifers Pettit (Mrs. Michael)

Stuffed Mushrooms

1 pound fresh mushrooms
1 tablespoon chopped scallions
1 tablespoon butter
1 cup whipping cream

1 tablespoon sherry
½ teaspoon salt
⅛ teaspoon pepper

Wash and dry mushrooms. Remove stems and chop very fine. Sauté minced mushroom stems and scallions in butter. Add cream, sherry, salt, and pepper. Cook until mixture thickens, about 10 minutes. Fill caps and broil until brown and bubbly.

Yield: 4 to 6 servings   Gale Cifers Pettit (Mrs. Michael)

Liver Stuffed Mushrooms

14 to 16 medium to large
   mushrooms
Garlic powder to taste
6 parsley sprigs, leaves only,
   minced
2 chicken livers, minced
2 tablespoons seasoned bread crumbs

½ medium onion, minced
4 slices ham, finely chopped
4 heaping tablespoons sour cream
¼ cup butter, softened
Salt and pepper to taste
3 tablespoons olive oil
Sauce (recipe follows)

Preheat oven to 300°. Grease oven-proof dish with olive oil. Wash and pat dry mushrooms. Cut out stems and reserve. Chop stems and combine with remaining ingredients except oil and sauce. Mix well with fork. Stuff caps and place in oven-proof dish. Drizzle oil over tops of mushrooms and bake 45 minutes. Serve immediately after pouring 1 teaspoon of following sauce over each mushroom.

Sauce:

6 tablespoons olive oil
⅛ teaspoon garlic powder
2 tablespoons wine vinegar
½ lemon, squeezed (juice only)
1 teaspoon salt

1 teaspoon coarse ground
   black pepper
2 scallions, chopped
Oregano to taste

Combine all ingredients and blend well. Pour 1 teaspoon over each mushroom.

Yield: 16 mushrooms   Annie Parrott Lansky (Mrs. Hal)
                                             Los Angeles, California

Pepperoni Stuffed Mushrooms

12 large fresh mushrooms
2 tablespoons butter
1 medium onion, finely chopped
½ cup diced pepperoni
¼ cup finely chopped green
  pepper
1 small clove garlic, minced
½ cup finely crushed rich
  round crackers

3 tablespoons Parmesan cheese
1 tablespoon finely chopped
  parsley
½ teaspoon seasoned salt
¼ teaspoon crushed oregano
⅛ teaspoon pepper
⅓ cup chicken broth

Wash mushrooms. Remove and finely chop stems. Melt butter in skillet; add onion, pepperoni, green pepper, garlic, and chopped mushroom stems. Cook until tender. Add cracker crumbs, cheese, parsley, seasoned salt, oregano, and pepper. Mix well. Stir in chicken broth. Spoon stuffing into mushroom caps. Place in shallow pan with ¼-inch water in bottom of pan. Bake 25 minutes at 325° or until heated through.

Yield: 12 servings   Beverly Binkley Hogin (Mrs. John H.)

Caviar Pie

4 hard-cooked eggs
Finely chopped onion
2 (4-ounce) jars black caviar

1½ cups sour cream
Chopped parsley

Finely chop yolks and whites of eggs. Add sufficient amount of onion to flavor eggs. Pat firmly into pie pan with back of fork. Layer caviar on top of egg mixture. Cover entire pie with sour cream. Make a ring around outside edge with chopped parsley for color. Serve with party rye or crackers.

Yield: 10 to 12 servings   Cynthia Zierer

Cocktail Hour Crab Mold

1 pound crabmeat
1 (8-ounce) package cream cheese
Dash Tabasco sauce
Freshly ground pepper to taste

1 teaspoon chives
Dash Worcestershire sauce
Cocktail sauce

Mix all ingredients except cocktail sauce and mold in 4-cup ring mold. At serving time, unmold and fill center with cocktail sauce. Serve with crackers.

Yield: 8 to 10 servings   Kaye McIntyre Littlejohn

Layered Cheese Appetizer

2 cups sour cream
½ cup finely chopped green pepper
½ cup finely chopped celery
4 tablespoons finely chopped
  stuffed olives
4 tablespoons finely chopped onion

2 teaspoons lemon juice
1 teaspoon Worcestershire sauce
Dash paprika
3 to 6 drops Tabasco sauce
32 cheese crackers, crushed
  and divided

Combine all ingredients except cracker crumbs. Line 3-cup mold with plastic wrap. Spread 1 cup mixture in bottom of mold. Add ⅓ cup crumbs. Repeat layers. Cover and chill overnight. When ready to serve, turn out onto serving plate. Garnish with remaining crumbs. Serve with crackers.

Yield: 10 to 20 servings   Jane Crumpler DeFiore (Mrs. Joseph C.)

Sara Vestal's Taco Ring

2 (16-ounce) cans refried beans
1 (1¼-ounce) package taco mix
1 small onion, finely chopped
1 small dried red pepper,
  finely chopped
6 avocados, pared and finely
  chopped
1 teaspoon salt
2 tablespoons lemon juice
2 tablespoons mayonnaise
1 teaspoon vegetable oil
4 drops Tabasco sauce

2 (6-ounce) cans pitted black
  olives, finely chopped
1 (9-ounce) jar green olives,
  finely chopped
1 bunch green onions, finely
  chopped
1 (3-ounce) can jalapeño peppers,
  finely chopped
Cherry tomatoes, sliced and
  drained
8 ounces Cheddar cheese,
  grated

Mix beans with taco mix and form into ring on serving dish. Combine onion, red pepper, avocados, salt, lemon juice, mayonnaise, oil, and Tabasco sauce to make guacamole. Spread thick layer on ring, reserving what is not used. Combine black and green olives, green onions, and jalapeño peppers. Spread in layer over guacamole. Arrange layer of tomatoes over olive layer. At this point, spread reserved guacamole over tomatoes. Sprinkle with cheese and refrigerate. Serve with Doritos.

Note: May be prepared 1 to 2 days ahead.

Yield: 50 servings   Cassandra (Candy) Johnson Brownlow (Mrs. William G.)

Shrimp Mold

1 envelope unflavored gelatin
1 (8-ounce) can minced clams,
  reserve juice
1 cup mayonnaise
1 (8-ounce) package cream cheese,
  softened
2 (4-ounce) cans shrimp, drained

½ cup minced onion
1 cup finely chopped celery
1 teaspoon lemon juice
Tabasco sauce to taste
Salt and pepper to taste
Curry powder to taste

Soften gelatin in clam juice. Dissolve over low heat. Cream mayonnaise and cream cheese. Combine all ingredients. Pour into lightly oiled fish mold.

Yield: 12 servings   Anne Rogers Killefer (Mrs. Robert)

Curry Pâté

2 (3-ounce) packages cream cheese,
  softened
1 cup grated extra-sharp
  Cheddar cheese
2 tablespoons dry sherry
½ teaspoon curry powder

¼ teaspoon salt
1 (8-ounce) jar mango chutney,
  finely chopped
⅓ cup finely sliced
  green onions with tops

Thoroughly blend cream cheese, Cheddar cheese, sherry, curry powder, and salt. Spread on serving platter or 8-inch quiche dish to ½-inch thickness. Chill until firm. At serving time, spread with chutney and sprinkle with green onions. Serve with Pepperidge Farm Fish Wheat Crackers.

Yield: 8 servings   Ena Taylor Kirkpatrick (Mrs. David M.)

Chinese Barbecue Spareribs

4 pounds spareribs
1 cup soy sauce
½ cup water
3 tablespoons red wine

1 tablespoon sugar
1 teaspoon salt
1 clove garlic, crushed

Score meat between ribs but do not cut through. Place meat in large bowl. Combine all other ingredients and pour over ribs. Let stand 1 hour. Cook ribs on grill or bake 1½ hours at 350°. Turn often and baste. Cut into individual ribs and serve on warm platter.

Yield: 8 to 10 servings   Kaye McIntyre Littlejohn
20 to 30 appetizers

Sausage and Chicken Pâté en Croûte

½ pound mild or hot sausage
¾ pound boned chicken breast
½ cup bread crumbs
1 egg
¼ cup whipping cream
2 tablespoons dry sherry
¼ pound mushrooms, cut in half

¼ teaspoon tarragon
2 to 4 parsley sprigs
1 tablespoon fresh or dried chives
½ teaspoon salt
1 can crescent rolls
1 beaten egg

Preheat oven to 350°. Grease 8½- x 3⅝-inch loaf pan. Place sausage and chicken in food processor fitted with knife blade and grind into smooth paste. Add all other ingredients except rolls and beaten egg. Process thoroughly. Spoon smooth mixture into prepared pan. Bake 1 hour. Let cool and remove from pan.

Preheat oven to 400°. Roll out crescent rolls and place pâté loaf in center. Fold over and tightly tuck in pastry around edges. Decorate loaf with cut-outs, if desired. Brush pastry with beaten egg and bake 10 minutes or until brown.

Note: Pâté can be frozen after first baking and before wrapping in pastry. Loaf can be frosted with following frosting instead of wrapping in pastry.

Frosting:

1 (8-ounce) package cream cheese, softened
1 tablespoon mayonnaise
1 tablespoon Parmesan cheese

Sliced ripe olives (optional)
Grated hard-cooked egg (optional)
Fresh parsley (optional)

Blend cream cheese, mayonnaise, and Parmesan cheese thoroughly. Frost pâté loaf with mixture and garnish with olive slices, grated egg, and fresh parsley. Serve with buttered and toasted Italian bread rounds.

Note: Frosting spreads best if almost to room temperature.

Yield: 1 loaf

Silent Butler
Ann Bond
Alice Clayton
Di Wall

Marinated Shrimp

2 pounds shrimp
¾ cup catsup
½ cup vegetable oil
½ cup wine vinegar
1 teaspoon sugar

1 teaspoon salt
1 tablespoon Worcestershire
  sauce
½ teaspoon pepper
Sliced onions

Boil and clean shrimp. Combine remaining ingredients for marinade and pour over shrimp. Marinate 48 hours.

Yield: 8 servings   Martha Bacon Hemphill (Mrs. James L.)

Sautéed Shrimp

1½ pounds uncooked shrimp,
  shelled and deveined
½ cup light rum
¼ cup butter

½ teaspoon garlic salt
⅓ cup grated Parmesan cheese
Ground pepper

Marinate shrimp in rum several hours. Melt butter in large skillet. Add shrimp and rum mixture with garlic salt. Sauté 8 to 10 minutes or until shrimp cook through. Sprinkle cheese and pepper over shrimp. Broil 2 to 3 minutes or until cheese browns. Serve hot.

Yield: 12 servings   Scott Davis Wilson (Mrs. Don)

Bu-Ja-Su Salami

2 pounds ground beef
1 cup water
2 tablespoons Morton Tender
  Quick Salt (fast cure salt)
2 tablespoons liquid smoke
1 tablespoon garlic juice

1 tablespoon onion powder
1 tablespoon cracked pepper
1 tablespoon peppercorns
1 tablespoon whole mustard seed
1 teaspoon ground cumin
1 teaspoon crushed red pepper

Thoroughly combine ground beef, water, and salt. Add remaining ingredients and mix thoroughly. Shape into 3 rolls about 2 inches around. Cover and refrigerate 24 hours. Bake on a rack 1 hour at 300°. Turn rolls over halfway through.

Yield: 3 rolls   Jan Griffith Hanna (Mrs. Ross, III)
                                                 Lenoir City, Tennessee

Spiced Nuts

2 cups pecan halves
1½ tablespoons melted butter
1 teaspoon salt
2 teaspoons soy sauce

⅛ teaspoon Tabasco sauce
Dash Worcestershire sauce (optional)
Dash nutmeg (optional)

Preheat oven to 300°. Combine pecan halves and melted butter. Place in 9-inch pan. Toast 30 minutes, stirring often. Add remaining ingredients and stir until well coated. Serve hot or cold. Can be frozen.

Yield: 1 pint   Mary Ann Durst Cochran (Mrs. Robert B.)

Muse's Nuts and Bolts

2 tablespoons garlic salt
1½ tablespoons seasoning salt
2 cups buttery flavored
  vegetable oil
3 tablespoons Worcestershire sauce
1 (12-ounce) box Rice Chex
1 (15-ounce) box Wheat Chex
1 (15-ounce) box Cheerios

1 (10-ounce) box very thin
  pretzels, broken
1 box sesame stix
3 (12-ounce) cans deluxe
  mixed nuts
1 (12-ounce) can cashew nuts
1 (12-ounce) can peanuts
1 pound pecan halves

Combine garlic salt, seasoning salt, oil, and Worcestershire. Mix remaining ingredients in roasting pans and drizzle oil mixture over all, stirring gently. Roast 2 hours at 250°, stirring every 15 minutes. Cool and store in air-tight containers.

William S. Muse, Jr.

Cove Mountain Gorp

A high energy snack for hikes and vigorous mountain air.

1 pound M&M's
1 (12-ounce) can cashew nuts
1 (12-ounce) can peanuts
1 (9-ounce) package raisins

1 (8-ounce) package banana chips
1 (8-ounce) package mixed
  dried fruit, snipped

Combine ingredients. Store in air-tight container.

Yield: 4 pounds   Geri Carmichael Muse (Mrs. William S., Jr.)

BEVERAGES

MARU '80   © I. DEZINE, inc.

Ready To Drink Iced Tea

3 cups boiling water
8 tea bags
¾ cup to 1¼ cups sugar
  or to taste

1 cup water
Juice of 4 lemons
4 cups cold water

Pour boiling water over tea bags and steep 3 to 5 minutes. Discard tea bags. Boil sugar and 1 cup water until sugar is well dissolved and slightly syrupy. While hot add to tea mixture and blend. Add lemon juice and lemon halves and let stand 5 minutes. Remove lemons. Add 4 cups cold water. Serve over ice in tea glasses.

Yield: 10 to 12 servings   Ann Dooley

Tea Punch

1 quart boiling water
2 cups sugar
7 (regular size) tea bags

1 (6-ounce) can orange juice
  concentrate
6 ounces lemon juice or 1 (12-ounce)
  can lemonade concentrate

Pour boiling water over sugar and tea bags. Let steep for 10 minutes. Remove tea bags. Add frozen orange juice and lemon juice. Add enough water to make one gallon.

Note: When using lemonade, reduce sugar by ½ cup.

Yield: 1 gallon   Kathryn Wilson Cockrill (Mrs. William G.)

Aunt Julia's Spiced Tea

3 quarts water
1 tablespoon whole cloves
2 sticks cinnamon
5 regular size tea bags
1 cup sugar

1 (6-ounce) can orange juice
  concentrate
1 (6-ounce) can lemonade concentrate
2½ cups pineapple juice
1 cup 7-Up or Sprite (optional)

Combine water, cloves, and cinnamon sticks; bring to a boil. Remove from heat, add tea bags, and steep 5 minutes. Add remaining ingredients. Serve hot or cold.

Yield: 1 gallon   Sharon Kelley Thomas (Mrs. William M.)

Hot Buttered Lemonade

4½ cups water
¾ cup sugar
¾ cup lemon juice
1½ teaspoons grated lemon peel

6 cinnamon sticks
6 teaspoons butter, divided
Rum (optional)

In a saucepan combine water, sugar, lemon juice, and peel. Cook until hot and sugar has dissolved. Serve in mugs with a cinnamon stick stirrer and top with 1 teaspoon butter per mug. Add ½ jigger of rum per mug, if desired.

Yield: 6 servings   Betsy Snyder Roberts (Mrs. Clark M.)

Banana Sunrise

1 (12-ounce) can apricot
    nectar, chilled
1 (6-ounce) can pineapple
    juice, chilled

6 ounces milk, chilled
2 bananas, quartered
¼ teaspoon nutmeg
¼ teaspoon almond extract

Put all ingredients into blender and blend on high speed until well blended, 15 to 30 seconds.

Yield: 2 to 3 servings   Lynne Greek Fain (Mrs. Walter D.)

Muse's Orange Julius

1 (6-ounce) can frozen orange
    juice concentrate
1 teaspoon vanilla

6 ounces water
6 ounces milk
12 to 14 ice cubes

Place all ingredients in blender and blend to desired consistency.

Note: Can be made ahead and placed in freezer. Blend again when ready to serve.

Yield: 6 servings   William S. Muse, Jr.

Spiced Mocha

½ cup whipping cream
1 teaspoon instant coffee
1 tablespoon sugar

¼ teaspoon cinnamon
6 tablespoons chocolate syrup
Hot coffee for 6

Beat cream with instant coffee, sugar, and cinnamon until stiff peaks form. Set aside. Into each of 6 coffee cups place 1 tablespoon chocolate syrup. Pour in hot coffee. Top with whipped cream mixture.

Yield: 6 servings

Jayne Crumpler DeFiore (Mrs. Joseph C.)

Hot Crabby Punch

5 cups sweet apple cider
4 cups cranberry juice cocktail
¼ cup firmly packed light
   brown sugar
1 cinnamon stick

½ teaspoon whole allspice
½ teaspoon whole cloves
Apple slices and cinnamon
   stick (garnish)

In large saucepan, combine all ingredients except garnishes. Heat uncovered to boiling, reduce heat, and simmer 20 minutes. Remove spices before serving. Serve hot and garnish with apple slices and cinnamon stick.

Yield: 9 servings

Dale Reid McCarley (Mrs. Thomas H.)

Red Flannel Grog

*"A fireplace has warmth and cheer
But red flannel grog atmosphere.
Red flannel grog, warm and bright
Is bound to be all guests' delight!"*

1 quart apple cider
3 cinnamon sticks
6 whole cloves

2 whole nutmeg
1 cup light rum

Combine cider, cinnamon, cloves, and nutmeg in chafing dish. Heat until very hot. Reduce heat to simmer and add rum.

Yield: 6 servings

Carolyn Arwood Miller

Summertime Coffee Punch

1 gallon water
11 tablespoons instant coffee
1 pint half and half cream,
   sugared to taste

1 quart chocolate milk
1 gallon vanilla ice cream

Combine water, coffee, cream, and chocolate milk. Add ice cream immediately before serving. If desired, make ice cubes from additional chocolate milk and water. Add at serving time.

Yield: 50 small punch cups

Donna Peters Clark (Mrs. Steven A.)

Bloody Mary Mix

1 (46-ounce) can tomato juice
1 cup bottled lemon juice
¼ cup Worcestershire sauce
Beau Monde
Celery salt

Tabasco sauce
Basil
Oregano
Marjoram
Gin or vodka

Combine tomato juice, lemon juice, and Worcestershire. Sparingly sprinkle Beau Monde, celery salt, and Tabasco. Liberally add basil, oregano, and marjoram. Refrigerate. When ready to use, mix 3 parts tomato mixture with 1 part gin or vodka.

Yield: 7 cups

Connie Bell Taylor (Mrs. Alexander M.)

Tomato Soup Piquant

2 (8-ounce) cans tomato sauce
2 (10½-ounce) cans beef bouillon
5¼ cups water
2 (1-pint) cans tomato juice
½ teaspoon prepared horseradish
4 drops Tabasco sauce

1½ teaspoons salt
1¼ teaspoons pepper
¼ teaspoon basil
Lemon slices
Vodka (optional)

Combine all ingredients except lemon slices and vodka. Simmer 10 minutes. Serve with lemon slice and vodka if desired.

Note: This is a delicious warm drink for cold pre-game days.

Yield: 6 to 8 servings

Rusha Kinard Sams (Mrs. Bert E.)

Border Buttermilk

3 (6-ounce) cans lemonade
   concentrate or 2 (12-ounce) cans
   orange juice concentrate
1 (6-ounce) can limeade concentrate

¼ cup sugar
5 (6-ounce) cans water
3 (6-ounce) cans tequila
Crushed ice

Combine all ingredients except ice in pitcher. Blend half of mixture at a time in blender with crushed ice.

Yield: 8 to 10 servings

Sandy Mourfield Goode (Mrs. Gerald)
Canyon Lake, Texas

Frozen Margaritas

1 (6-ounce) can limeade concentrate
¾ cup tequila
¼ cup Triple Sec
Crushed ice

Lime wedge
Salt
Lime slices (optional)

Combine limeade, tequila, and Triple Sec in a blender. Fill blender with ice and blend. Rim glasses with lime wedge and salt. Fill with limeade mixture and garnish with lime slice.

Note: Can be made ahead and stored in air-tight container in freezer. Spoon into glasses when needed.

Yield: 4 servings

Geri Carmichael Muse (Mrs. William Scott, Jr.)

Fred's Frozen Daiquiris

1 (6-ounce) can frozen lemonade
   concentrate
1 (6-ounce) can frozen limeade
   concentrate

10 to 12 ounces ginger ale,
   7-Up, or Sprite
16 ounces rum
16 ounces water

Combine above ingredients in plastic pitcher and place in freezer. If a "weaker" drink is desired, reduce amount of rum and water to 12 ounces each.

Note: Must be made the day before!

Yield: 6 to 8 servings

Alix Frincke Dempster (Mrs. Donald)

Fresh Peach Daiquiri

½ cup bottled daiquiri mix
½ cup light rum
3 fresh peaches, peeled and
   quartered

½ teaspoon almond extract
Juice of ¼ lime
1 tablespoon sugar

Place all ingredients in blender with ice. Blend until smooth.

Yield: 5 servings   Suzanne Wood Fletcher

Red Sangria

1½ (⅘ -quart) bottles dry red wine
½ cup rum or gin
3 lemons, divided

½ to 1 cup sugar
1 (28-ounce) bottle club soda,
   chilled

In a large container combine wine and rum. Add juice and rind of 2 lemons.
Cut third lemon into slices and add. Stir in sugar to taste. Mix well and chill
8 to 10 hours. Taste and add more sugar if desired. Just before serving add
chilled club soda. Serve very cold.

Yield: approximately ½ gallon   Suzanne L. McMillen

Sangria Slush

1 (12-ounce) can frozen lemonade
   concentrate, thawed
1 (6-ounce) can orange juice
   concentrate, thawed
1½ cups water

Orange, lemon, and lime
   slices
Dry red, dry white, or rosé
   wine, chilled

Combine juice concentrates and water. Place in ice trays and freeze until
firm. Scoop frozen mixture out and place in small bowl. Fill larger bowl with
ice; insert bowl of slush in ice-filled bowl and surround with fruit. To serve,
place spoonful of slush mixture into glass and pour in selected wine. Add
slice of fruit.

Note: For non-alcoholic drink, substitute soda, 7-Up, or ginger ale for wine.

Yield: 4 cups slush   Pamela Young Richardson (Mrs. Charles Franklin)

White Sangria

24 ounces dry white wine,
   chilled
1 (10-ounce) bottle bitter lemon,
   chilled
2 tablespoons orange-flavored liqueur

1 large peach, sliced
1 large nectarine, sliced
1 large orange, sliced
1 cup seedless grapes

Combine all ingredients in a 2-quart pitcher. Chill at least 2 hours.

Yield: 4 to 6 servings   Jeanne Holmes Hyatt (Mrs. Hugh C.)

Kir

1 cup white wine
½ ounce Cream de Cassis

Twist of lemon

Combine ingredients and chill. Rub rim of wine glass with slice of lemon before serving.

Note: Adjust quantity of each ingredient according to number of people to be served. Quantity of Cream de Cassis can vary to taste.

Yield: 1 serving

Kahlua

2 cups water
3 cups sugar
7 tablespoons instant coffee
   dissolved in ½ cup
   hot water

2 teaspoons vanilla
3 teaspoons glycerin
1 (⅘ -quart) bottle vodka

Combine water and sugar. Heat until clear. Add remaining ingredients and pour into bottles.

Yield: 2 fifths   Doris Thompson Ellison (Mrs. Billy)

Bay Point Milk Punch

Vanilla ice cream
¾ cup brandy
¼ cup light crème de cacao

Ice
Nutmeg

Fill blender ¾ full with ice cream. Add brandy and crème de cacao. Fill with ice and blend. Pour into glasses and sprinkle each with nutmeg.

Yield: 4 servings   Cordy Wiley Arnold (Mrs. Arch V., III)

"Bowle A La Kumpa"
Festive German Wine Punch

3 liters white wine, divided
2 pints fresh strawberries

1 liter champagne

Ten to twelve hours prior to serving, pour 1 liter of wine over fresh strawberries in large pitcher. Place in refrigerator. Three hours prior to serving, place 2 liters of wine and champagne in freezer. Immediately prior to serving, add these to strawberry-wine mixture. Pour all in large punch bowl.

Yield: 4 liters punch   Karlyn Riggsby Wold (Mrs. Steven)

Christmas Punch

16 ounces cranberry juice
   cocktail
1 (6-ounce) can orange juice
   concentrate, thawed
2 cups water

1 tablespoon sugar
¼ teaspoon ground allspice
1 (⅘-quart) bottle dry white wine
Red food coloring (optional)
Whole cranberries (optional)

Bring cranberry juice, orange juice, water, sugar, and allspice to simmer. Add wine and heat but *do not boil*. Add red food coloring, if desired, for brighter color. Chill thoroughly and serve icy cold with cranberries afloat.

Note: To serve 50 to 65 people, increase quantity of each ingredient 15 times. Can be made a day ahead.

Yield: 12 to 16 servings   Carolyn Dew Pearre (Mrs. Courtney N.)

Elegant Champagne Punch

1½ cups sugar
2 cups freshly squeezed
   lemon juice
2 (⅘-quart) bottles Sauterne
   wine, chilled

1 (⅘-quart) bottle champagne,
   chilled
½ cup brandy
½ cup Cointreau
1 lemon, sliced
1½ cups sliced strawberries

Combine sugar and lemon juice; stir until sugar is dissolved. Chill. Just
before serving, pour over ice in punch bowl. Gently pour in Sauterne and
champagne. Add Cointreau and brandy. Garnish with lemon slices and
strawberries.

Yield: 26 servings

Karen Brown Henry

Copper Penny

3 ounces Amaretto
3 ounces Crème de Cacao

3 cups softened vanilla
   ice cream

Combine all ingredients in blender and mix until smooth. Serve in wine
glasses.

Note: Alcoholic content can be varied to taste.

Yield: 4 servings

Copper Cellar Restaurant
Knoxville, Tennessee

Nikolai's Coffee

From Nikolai's Roof in Atlanta

Hot coffee
½ ounce Stolichnaya Vodka
1 ounce Grand Marnier

Whipped cream
½ teaspoon honey
Ground cinnamon

Fill tall wine glass with coffee; add vodka and Grand Marnier. Top with
whipped cream and pour honey over cream. Sprinkle with cinnamon and
serve.

Yield: 1 serving

Suzanne L. McMillen

soup

Chilled Cantaloupe Soup

1 (3-pound) ripe cantaloupe
¼ cup sugar

½ cup dry sherry
1 tablespoon lime juice

In a blender combine cantaloupe meat with remaining ingredients. Blend until smooth. Cover and refrigerate until very cold.

Yield: 4 servings   Anne Walters Pittenger (Mrs. Gaines Sherman)

Spring Fruit Soup

1 (46-ounce) can orange-pineapple
  flavored fruit drink, divided
6 whole cloves
1 (2-inch) piece stick cinnamon
4 tablespoons cornstarch
2 tablespoons lemon juice

1 pint fresh strawberries,
  washed, hulled, and halved
2 cups sliced bananas
1 cup halved green grapes
Fresh mint (optional)

Reserve ½ cup fruit juice. Pour remaining juice in large saucepan. Add cloves and cinnamon. Heat to boiling. Reduce heat and simmer 5 minutes. Blend cornstarch into reserved juice to make smooth paste. Stir into hot mixture. Cook, stirring constantly, until mixture thickens and bubbles (approximately 1 minute). Remove from heat and stir in lemon juice. Pour into large bowl and chill completely. Remove spices with slotted spoon. Just before serving, pour liquid into large glass bowl. Fold in strawberries, bananas, and grapes. Ladle into small bowls or cups. Garnish with fresh mint, if desired.

Yield: 10 servings   Ann Dooley

Russian Gazpacho

1 (8½-ounce) can beets,
  with liquid
1 cup beef broth or consommé
½ small onion, chopped
½ cup sour cream
Juice of ½ lemon

Dash tarragon vinegar
Pepper to taste
Sour cream, chopped chives, and
  finely chopped hard-cooked
  egg for garnish

In blender, blend thoroughly beets with liquid, beef broth, onion, ½ cup sour cream, lemon juice, vinegar, and pepper to taste. Chill. Garnish with sour cream, chopped chives or chopped egg before serving.

Yield: 2 servings   Jeanne Holmes Hyatt (Mrs. Hugh C.)

Gazpacho

1 clove garlic, minced
4 tomatoes, peeled and quartered
½ green pepper,
    seeded and sliced
½ small onion, sliced
1 cucumber, peeled and
    thickly sliced
1 teaspoon salt

¼ teaspoon black pepper
2 tablespoons olive oil
3 tablespoons wine vinegar
½ cup tomato juice
Dash red cayenne
¼ teaspoon horseradish
Dash Tabasco sauce

Blend garlic, tomatoes, green pepper, onion, cucumber, salt, black pepper, olive oil, vinegar, and tomato juice in a blender 4 to 5 seconds. Add cayenne, horseradish, and Tabasco sauce. Blend and adjust seasonings. Chill.

Yield: 1 quart   Rhys Jones Swan

Cheddar Cheese Soup

4 tablespoons butter or
    margarine
½ cup diced carrots
½ cup diced green pepper
½ cup chopped onion
½ cup chopped celery

⅓ cup all-purpose flour
1 quart well-seasoned
    chicken stock
12 ounces Cheddar cheese, grated
3 to 4 cups milk
Salt and pepper to taste

Melt butter in 3-quart saucepan. Add vegetables and saute until tender, not browned. Blend in flour; cook and stir 1 minute. Add stock and cook, stirring until thickened. Add cheese and cook until melted. Add enough milk to thin to cream consistency. Season to taste.

Yield: 12 servings   Ann McCallum Brownlee (Mrs. Wylie M.)

Creamy Cucumber Soup

1 (10¾-ounce) can cream
    of celery soup
1 cup milk
1 small cucumber
1 small green pepper, seeded

¼ cup sliced pimiento-
    stuffed olives
Dash hot sauce
1 cup sour cream
1 tablespoon lemon juice
Cucumber slices (optional)

Combine soup, milk, cucumber, green pepper, olives, and hot sauce in bowl of food processor. Blend. Add sour cream and lemon juice. Refrigerate at least 4 hours. Garnish with cucumber slices.

Yield: 5 servings   Geri Carmichael Muse (Mrs. William Scott, Jr.)

Cream of Broccoli Soup

8 cups fresh or frozen broccoli
1 quart chicken stock
½ cup butter
1 cup all-purpose flour
1½ quarts milk

Dash Tabasco sauce
Dash Worcestershire sauce
2 teaspoons white pepper
½ cup whipping cream

Cook broccoli in chicken stock. Remove broccoli and reserve stock. Purée broccoli in blender or food processor and set aside. In heavy pan melt butter. Add flour to form roux, and cook over low heat 5 minutes. Gradually add milk while beating with whisk. Add stock, seasonings, and puréed broccoli. Simmer 15 minutes. Adjust seasonings to taste. To serve, add 1 tablespoon cream to each serving.

Yield: 8 to 10 servings

Copper Cellar Restaurant
Knoxville, Tennessee

Cream of Cauliflower Soup

1 large head (2 pounds) cauliflower
2 tablespoons butter
¼ cup diced celery
2 tablespoons minced onion
1 clove garlic (optional)
2 tablespoons all-purpose flour

1½ cups half and half cream
½ cup chicken broth
¾ teaspoon salt
White pepper to taste
¼ teaspoon nutmeg
½ cup sour cream

Trim cauliflower and break into flowerets. Cook in small amount of water 15 minutes or until tender. Drain. Purée cauliflower, reserving ½ cup flowerets. Melt butter and sauté celery, onion, and garlic. Stir in flour to make smooth paste; blend in half and half cream, broth, and puréed cauliflower. Add salt and pepper and heat just to boil. Stir in nutmeg, sour cream, and reserved cauliflower. Heat and serve.

Yield: 4 to 5 servings

Judith Stephens Frost (Mrs. Robert B.)

Cream of Spinach Soup

2 (10-ounce) packages frozen
  chopped spinach
1 onion, chopped
3 cups chicken stock
4 tablespoons butter
5 tablespoons all-purpose flour

1 teaspoon tarragon
1 scant teaspoon salt
⅛ teaspoon pepper
1 cup milk
Bacon bits

Cook spinach and onion in stock until tender. Make a roux using butter and flour. Cook 3 minutes, stirring constantly. Add spinach mixture, tarragon, salt, and pepper. Thin with milk to desired consistency. Soup should be thick and creamy. Serve warm. Garnish with bacon bits.

Yield: 6 to 8 servings

Joelyn von Haam Yoder (Mrs. Milton G.)

Cream of Zucchini Soup

8 small zucchini (2 pounds),
  sliced
1 cup water
2 tablespoons instant minced onion
4 chicken bouillon cubes, divided
2 teaspoons Season-All
1 teaspoon parsley flakes

4 tablespoons butter
4 tablespoons all-purpose flour
2 cups milk
1 cup half and half cream
Sour cream
Paprika

Combine zucchini, water, onion, 2 bouillon cubes, Season-All, and parsley. Cook until zucchini is tender. Purée mixture in blender. In saucepan melt butter, add flour and remaining bouillon cubes, and blend well. Add milk and cream. Simmer and stir until thickened. Stir in puréed zucchini, mix well. To serve, garnish with spoonful of sour cream and paprika.

Yield: 8 servings

Corinne Spinelli Patrick (Mrs. Edward P.)

Vichyssoise

2 tablespoons minced dry onion
⅓ cup butter
4 cups chicken stock
2 cups thinly sliced potatoes

1 cup whipping cream
1 teaspoon salt
½ teaspoon white pepper
Chives (optional)

Sauté onion in butter 5 minutes over low heat. Add chicken stock and potatoes. Cook until tender. Process in blender or food processor. Add cream, salt, and pepper. Garnish with chives.

Note: Can be doubled or tripled successfully, and freezes well.

Yield: 4 servings   Judith Stephens Frost (Mrs. Robert B.)

Lutie's Soup

1 cup dry navy beans
Water
2 (14½-ounce) cans condensed
  chicken broth
2 teaspoons salt
1 small head cabbage, shredded
4 carrots, pared and sliced
2 medium potatoes, pared
  and chopped
1 (28-ounce) can Italian tomatoes

2 medium onions, thinly sliced
¼ cup olive oil
1 rib celery, sliced
2 zucchini, sliced
1 large fresh tomato,
  peeled and chopped
1 clove garlic, minced
¼ cup snipped parsley
1 cup spaghetti (optional)
Pasta Sauce (recipe follows)

Cover beans with cold water and place in refrigerator overnight. Drain beans. Add water to chicken broth to make 1 quart. Place beans, stock mixture, 2 additonal quarts water, and salt in large pot. Bring to boil, reduce heat to simmer, and cook covered 1 hour. Add cabbage, carrots, potatoes, and Italian tomatoes; cover and cook ½ hour. Meanwhile, sauté onions in olive oil. Add celery, zucchini, fresh tomato, and garlic to onions. Cook slowly uncovered 20 minutes. Add to bean mixture. Add parsley and spaghetti, cover, and cook 30 minutes. To serve, add 1 tablespoon Pasta Sauce to each serving of soup.

Pasta Sauce:

¼ cup butter, softened
¼ cup Parmesan cheese
½ cup snipped parsley
1 clove garlic, minced

1 teaspoon basil
½ teaspoon marjoram
¼ cup olive oil
¼ cup chopped nuts

Combine and use as directed.

Yield: 8 to 10 servings   Mary Culver Spengler (Mrs. Joseph)

Minestrone

¼ to ⅓ cup olive oil
1 clove garlic, minced
½ cup chopped onion
2 stalks celery with leaves, chopped
2 medium carrots, pared and diced
1 (16-ounce) can tomatoes, undrained
3 beef bouillon cubes
2 cups diced potatoes
1 cup chopped cabbage
2 tablespoons chopped parsley or to taste

2 teaspoons salt
½ teaspoon pepper
1 teaspoon dried marjoram leaves
¼ teaspoon dried rosemary leaves
6 cups water
1 cup ditalini macaroni, uncooked
1 (10-ounce) package frozen peas
1 (17-ounce) can red kidney beans, undrained
Grated Parmesan cheese

Heat oil in a 6-quart kettle. Add garlic, onion, and celery. Sauté until tender, about 4 to 6 minutes. Add carrots, tomatoes, bouillon cubes, potatoes, cabbage, parsley, salt, pepper, marjoram, rosemary, and water. Bring to a boil. Reduce heat, cover, and simmer about 40 minutes. Add ditalini, peas, and kidney beans; bring to a boil. Reduce heat and simmer an additional 20 minutes. Serve with cheese sprinkled over each serving.

Yield: 8 to 10 servings   Sheila Prial Jacobstein (Mrs. Richard)

San Juan Black Bean Soup

1 pound dried black beans
2 quarts water
1 tablespoon salt
4 cloves garlic, crushed
1½ teaspoons cumin
1½ teaspoons oregano
4 tablespoons white vinegar, divided

10 tablespoons olive oil, divided
1 large onion, chopped
1 large green pepper, chopped
Juice of ½ lemon
½ cup rice, cooked
¼ cup minced onion

Soak beans in water and salt overnight. Cook until tender (about 2 to 2½ hours). Combine garlic, cumin, oregano, and 2 tablespoons vinegar in food processor with steel blade, or crush with mortar. Heat ½ cup olive oil in Dutch oven. Add onion and green pepper and fry until light brown. Add crushed seasonings and fry slowly. Drain some water off cooked beans before adding to Dutch oven. Add lemon juice. Cook slowly until ready to serve. Mix cooked rice and remaining onion and marinate in remaining 2 tablespoons olive oil and 2 tablespoons vinegar. To serve, top each serving of soup with one large spoonful of marinated rice.

Yield: 6 servings as main course; 10 as appetizer   Suzanne Wood Fletcher

Hearty Turkey Soup

¼ cup butter
2 tablespoons chopped onion
1 teaspoon curry powder (optional)
1 cup diced potatoes
½ cup diced carrots
½ cup celery, sliced diagonally
3 cups turkey or chicken broth
Salt and pepper to taste

½ (10-ounce) package frozen
  french green beans
1 cup diced cooked turkey
1 teaspoon minced fresh oregano
  or ½ teaspoon dried
1 tablespoon minced parsley
1 (14½-ounce) can evaporated milk
2 tablespoons all-purpose flour

Melt butter in a 3- to 4-quart oven-proof dish and cook onion until transparent. Add curry powder, cooking mixture 1 to 2 minutes longer. Stir in potatoes, carrots, celery, broth, salt and pepper, and bring to boil. Transfer to 300° oven for 10 to 15 minutes or cook on top of stove on low heat. **Stir in green beans, turkey, oregano, and parsley. Continue baking 15 minutes or until vegetables are tender-crisp. Combine milk and flour; stir until well blended. Adjust seasonings. Soup should be slightly thick.**

Yield: 4 to 6 servings   Millie Stubley Johnson (Mrs.Merle)

Turkey Soup

This soup is an excellent way to use leftovers from Thanksgiving or Christmas dinner.

Turkey carcass
2 bay leaves
Salt and pepper to taste
Pinch each of thyme, marjoram,
  and basil
3 to 4 quarts water
4 tablespoons butter, divided
3 tablespoons all-purpose flour

½ cup uncooked rice, washed
½ cup minced fresh parsley
1 cup chopped celery
½ pound fresh mushrooms,
  whole or sliced
Leftover gravy and dressing
3 tablespoons Madeira

Remove meat from carcass and set aside. Break up carcass and put in large pot with bay leaves, salt, pepper, thyme, marjoram, and basil. Cover with 3 to 4 quarts water and simmer 3 to 4 hours. Remove bones and strain liquid. Chill to remove all fat. Melt 2 tablespoons butter in pot. Stir in flour and cook until smooth. Gradually add stock and bring to boil. Add rice, parsley, and celery. Season with salt and pepper. Simmer 30 minutes or until rice is cooked. Sauté mushrooms in remaining butter and add to stock. Add diced turkey, gravy, and dressing. Simmer gently. Before serving, add Madeira.

Yield: 8 to 10 servings   Ena Taylor Kirkpatrick (Mrs. David M.)

Harvest Salmon Chowder

1 (7¾-ounce) can salmon
1 clove garlic, minced
½ cup chopped onion
½ cup chopped celery
½ cup chopped green pepper
3 tablespoons butter
1 cup diced potatoes
1 cup diced carrots

2 cups chicken broth
1 teaspoon salt
½ teaspoon pepper
½ teaspoon thyme
½ cup frozen peas
1 (17-ounce) can cream style corn
1 (13-ounce) can evaporated milk
Minced parsley

Drain salmon (reserving liquid), bone, and flake. Set aside. Sauté garlic, onion, celery, and pepper in butter. Add potatoes, carrots, reserved salmon liquid, broth, and seasonings. Cover and simmer 20 minutes. Add peas and cook 5 minutes. Add salmon, corn, and evaporated milk. Heat but *do not* boil. Sprinkle with parsley and serve with cornbread.

Yield: 4 to 6 servings

Sandra Whittaker Shumaker (Mrs. Richard)
Johnson City, Tennessee

New England Clam Chowder

3 slices bacon
1 cup diced sweet onion
2 (8-ounce) cans minced clams
1 (8-ounce) bottle clam juice
1 pound potatoes, pared
    and diced

3 cups half and half
    cream, divided
4 tablespoons all-purpose flour
1 teaspoon salt
Pepper to taste
1 cup milk

In large saucepan, fry bacon until crisp, drain on paper towel, crumble, and set aside. Fry onion in drippings until golden brown. Drain clams and reserve liquid. Add clam liquid, bottled clam juice, and potatoes to drippings. Boil gently until potatoes are tender. Gradually, stir 1 cup cream into flour until smooth. Add to potato mixture along with remaining cream, clams, and seasonings. Cook over low heat, stirring constantly until thickened. Stir in milk and bacon. Heat and serve.

Yield: 8 to 10 servings

Ethel Baumann Skaggs (Mrs. William C., Jr.)

Southern Gumbo

1 cup vegetable oil
1 cup all-purpose flour
8 stalks celery, chopped
3 large onions, chopped
1 green pepper, chopped
2 cloves garlic, minced
½ cup chopped parsley
1 to 2 pounds okra, sliced
2 tablespoons vegetable shortening
2 quarts chicken stock
2 quarts water
½ cup Worcestershire sauce
Tabasco sauce to taste
½ cup catsup

1 large, ripe tomato, chopped,
    or 1 (1-pound) can tomatoes
2 tablespoons salt
4 slices bacon, or 1 large
    slice ham, chopped
1 to 2 bay leaves
¼ teaspoon thyme
¼ teaspoon rosemary
Red pepper flakes to taste
2 cups cooked chicken, chopped
1 to 2 pounds cooked crabmeat
4 pounds shrimp, uncooked
Lemon juice
Cooked rice

Heat oil in heavy iron pot over medium heat. Add flour very slowly, stirring constantly with wooden spoon until roux is medium brown, 30 to 45 minutes. Add celery, onion, green pepper, garlic, and parsley. Cook additional 45 minutes to 1 hour. Fry okra in shortening until brown. Add to gumbo and stir well over low heat for a few minutes. (At this point mixture may be cooled, packaged, and frozen or refrigerated for later use.) Add chicken stock, water, Worcestershire, Tabasco, catsup, chopped tomato, salt, bacon or ham, bay leaves, thyme, rosemary, and red pepper flakes. Simmer 2½ to 3 hours.

About 30 minutes before serving time, add cooked chicken, crabmeat, shrimp, and a squeeze of lemon juice. Simmer 30 minutes or until shrimp are done. Check seasonings. Ladle gumbo over hot cooked rice.

Yield: 15 to 20 servings

Debbie Van Mol (Mrs. John)
Nashville, Tennessee

Shrimp and Crab Gumbo

½ cup bacon fat
3 tablespoons all-purpose flour
½ cup chopped onion
½ cup chopped green pepper
½ cup chopped celery
1½ teaspoons salt
½ teaspoon mixed pickling spice
½ teaspoon pepper
5 cloves
1 bay leaf
1 clove garlic, crushed

4 cups canned whole tomatoes
4 cups water
1½ cups sliced okra
1 pound shrimp, shelled
  and deveined
1 pound king crab meat
1 teaspoon Tabasco sauce
1 teaspoon Worcestershire sauce
½ teaspoon salt
1½ teaspoons filé powder
½ cup rice, cooked

In a kettle melt bacon fat; stir in flour, and cook over moderate heat, stirring 1 minute. Add onion, green pepper, and celery; cook, stirring 4 minutes or until vegetables are light brown. Add salt, pickling spice, pepper, cloves, bay leaf, and garlic; combine mixture well. Add tomatoes, water, and okra, bringing liquid to boil over moderately low heat, stirring. Cook 1½ hours on low. Add shrimp and well-picked crabmeat and simmer until shrimp is just cooked, about 10 minutes. Add Tabasco, Worcestershire, and salt to taste and simmer for 1 minute. Remove from heat and stir in filé powder. Do not cook again after filé has been added since the gumbo will become stringy. Place heaping tablespoon of cooked rice in bowl and ladle gumbo over it.

Yield: 8 servings   Jeanne Holmes Hyatt (Mrs. Hugh C.)

Italian Stew

2 pounds boneless beef, cubed
2 tablespoons vegetable shortening
1 medium onion, chopped
¼ teaspoon garlic powder
1 (1-pound, 13-ounce) can tomatoes
½ cup water
1 cup diced celery
2 tablespoons parsley flakes

1 teaspoon mixed Italian seasoning
1 teaspoon salt
½ teaspoon basil
¼ teaspoon pepper
3 large carrots, pared and cut
  into 2-inch pieces
3 medium potatoes, pared and
  quartered

Brown beef in shortening in large skillet or Dutch oven. Add onion, garlic powder, tomatoes, water, celery, parsley flakes, Italian seasoning, salt, basil, and pepper. Cover and simmer 1 to 1½ hours until meat is tender. Add carrots and potatoes and simmer 30 minutes longer until tender.

Yield: 8 servings   Betty McAfee Greene (Mrs. Clayton)

Chili

1 large onion, chopped	3 whole cloves
1 green pepper, chopped	1 bay leaf
1 cup chopped celery	2 tablespoons chili powder
1 pound ground beef	2 (15½-ounce) cans Joan
3½ cups canned tomatoes	of Arc kidney beans
1½ teaspoons salt	2 (15½-ounce) cans water
⅛ teaspoon paprika	1 to 2 (3-ounce) cans
⅛ teaspoon pepper	mushrooms (optional)

Brown onion, pepper, celery, and meat. Add tomatoes and seasonings.
Simmer 2 hours. Add beans, water, and mushrooms. Simmer 15 minutes.

Yield: 4 servings   Nancy Tombras Faulkner

Pat's Chili

2 tablespoons butter	¼ cup Worcestershire sauce
2 yellow onions, chopped	2 cubes beef bouillon
4 pounds ground beef	Red wine
2 teaspoons salt	1 (28-ounce) can tomatoes
2 cloves garlic, minced	1 to 2 jalapeño peppers
4 to 6 tablespoons chili powder	(optional)
1 to 2 tablespoons cumin	2 (15-ounce) cans kidney beans,
2 teaspoons garlic powder	drained (optional)

In large skillet, sauté onions in butter; transfer to Dutch oven. Brown meat
in skillet and transfer to Dutch oven. Add salt, garlic, chili powder, cumin,
garlic powder, and Worcestershire. Mash bouillon cubes in enough red wine
to make a paste. Add to meat mixture with tomatoes. Add jalapeño peppers
and kidney beans, if desired. Cook 3 hours on low heat in Dutch oven or
overnight in crock pot.

Yield: 8 to 10 servings   J. Pat Roddy, III

salad

IDEZINE 80
MARU 80

Caesar Salad

1 clove garlic, crushed
1 head Romaine lettuce, torn
Juice of 1 lemon
1 egg
2 tablespoons olive oil
¼ teaspoon dry mustard

Pepper to taste
Croutons
Parmesan cheese to taste
1 (2-ounce) tin anchovies
  (optional)

Rub wooden bowl with garlic, leaving small portion in bowl. Add lettuce and set aside. Combine lemon juice, egg, and olive oil, stirring quickly. Pour over lettuce. Add mustard, pepper, and croutons. Sprinkle heavily with Parmesan cheese and toss. Separate anchovies and lay individually on salad.

Yield: 4 to 6 servings   Gale Cifers Pettit (Mrs. Michael)

Mandarin Salad

¼ cup sliced almonds
1 tablespoon plus 1 teaspoon sugar
½ head iceberg lettuce,
  torn into pieces
½ head Romaine lettuce,
  torn into pieces

1 cup chopped celery
2 green onions, thinly sliced
1 (11-ounce) can mandarin
  oranges, drained and chilled
Dressing (recipe follows)

Cook almonds and sugar over low heat, stirring until sugar is melted and almonds are coated. Cool and break apart. Store at room temperature. Place greens in plastic bag, and add celery and onion. Fasten bag securely and refrigerate. Five minutes before serving, shake and pour dressing into bag. Add oranges and almonds. Fasten bag securely and shake well.

Dressing:

½ teaspoon salt
¼ teaspoon pepper
2 tablespoons sugar
2 tablespoons vinegar

¼ cup vegetable oil
Dash Tabasco sauce
1 tablespoon snipped parsley

Place all ingredients in covered jar, shake, and refrigerate.

Yield: 8 to 10 servings   Jean L. Nichols Alsentzer (Mrs. John S.)

Mercedes Salad with Dressing

Lettuce
Spinach
Avocado slices
Artichoke hearts
Hard-cooked egg slices

Onion slices
Cucumber slices
Tomato wedges
Mercedes Dressing
  (recipe follows)

Make a tossed salad with mixture of above vegetables and top with dressing. Toss lightly and serve.

Mercedes Dressing:

1 cup oil
¼ cup wine vinegar
2 tablespoons lemon juice
¼ cup chopped green onion
¼ cup chopped parsley
¼ pound Roquefort cheese,
  crumbled

1 (2-ounce) can anchovies
½ teaspoon coarsely ground
  pepper
½ teaspoon salt
⅓ teaspoon garlic
  powder

Combine all ingredients.

Yield: 8 servings   Jennifer Logan Brown (Mrs. L. Daniel)

Lemon-French Spinach Salad

1½ quarts fresh spinach,
  washed and torn,
  with heavy stems removed
½ cup vegetable oil
2 tablespoons lemon juice
2 tablespoons vinegar
1 teaspoon sugar
1 teaspoon grated lemon rind

½ teaspoon salt
½ teaspoon dry mustard
Fresh mushrooms, sliced (optional)
Cherry tomatoes (optional)
Bacon, fried crisp (optional)
Mandarin orange segments (optional)
Fresh grapefruit sections (optional)
Hard-cooked eggs, sliced (optional)

Chill spinach until serving time. Combine oil, lemon juice, vinegar, sugar, lemon rind, salt, and dry mustard in jar. Shake dressing well and toss with spinach. Add several or all garnishes and toss again.

Yield: 6 servings   Jo Ann Cattlett McCallen (Mrs. Perry)

Spinach Salad

1½ pounds spinach, washed
   and drained
½ pound mushrooms, sliced
1 small Bermuda onion, sliced,
   with rings separated
3 hard-cooked eggs, chopped

½ to 1 pound bacon, fried
   crisp and crumbled
½ to 1 (14-ounce) can
   artichoke hearts, quartered
Sour Cream Dressing
   (recipe follows)

Place spinach in salad bowl. Top with mushrooms, onion, eggs, bacon, and artichokes. Serve with Sour Cream Dressing.

Sour Cream Dressing:

4 tablespoons sour cream
6 tablespoons red wine vinegar
½ teaspoon prepared mustard
2 teaspoons chopped parsley
Minced garlic to taste

1 teaspoon sugar
1 cup vegetable oil
¼ teaspoon pepper
Salt to taste

Mix in blender and chill at least 2 hours.

Yield: 8 to 10 servings   Priscilla Brandau Siler (Mrs. Tom A.)

Spinach-Avocado-Orange Salad

½ teaspoon grated orange peel
¼ cup orange juice
½ cup vegetable oil
2 tablespoons sugar
2 tablespoons wine vinegar
1 tablespoon lemon juice
¼ teaspoon salt

6 cups spinach or other greens,
   torn into bite-size pieces
1 small cucumber, thinly sliced
1 (11-ounce) can mandarin
   oranges, drained
2 tablespoons sliced green onions
1 avocado, sliced

Combine orange peel, orange juice, oil, sugar, vinegar, lemon juice, and salt, and shake until thoroughly blended. Mix remaining ingredients in a bowl and pour dressing over all. Toss lightly.

Yield: 8 servings   Caroline Monckton Smith (Mrs. David F.)

Special Salad

Juice of 1 lemon
1 to 2 cloves garlic, crushed
Salt and pepper to taste
¾ cup vegetable oil
¼ pound bacon, diced
2 heads Romaine lettuce, torn
   into small pieces

2 cups cherry tomatoes, halved
1 cup coarsely grated
   Swiss cheese
⅔ cup slivered almonds, toasted
⅓ cup freshly grated Parmesan
1 cup croutons

Combine lemon, garlic, salt, and pepper. Add oil in stream, beating with fork. Let stand covered 3 hours. Sauté bacon until crisp and drain. In salad bowl, combine Romaine, tomatoes, Swiss cheese, almonds, Parmesan, and bacon. Toss with dressing. Adjust salt and pepper and garnish with croutons.

Yield: 8 servings

Jeanne Holmes Hyatt (Mrs. Hugh C.)

Taco Salad

1½ to 2 pounds ground beef
1 (1.25-ounce) package Ortega
   Taco Seasoning Mix
½ cup water
1 (15-ounce) can red kidney
   beans, drained
1 (8-ounce) bag plain tortilla
   chips, crushed

2 ripe tomatoes, chopped
1 medium mild onion, chopped
1 to 1½ cups grated
   Cheddar cheese
1 small head lettuce, chopped
2 to 3 tablespoons Basic French
   Dressing (recipe follows)
Ortega Taco Sauce (optional)

Brown ground beef and drain. Add taco seasoning, water, and drained beans. Simmer for 15 to 20 minutes. In large bowl, layer in this order: tortilla chips, hot meat mixture, tomatoes, onions, cheese, and lettuce. Pour Basic French Dressing over all and toss. Serve immediately with Ortega Taco Sauce if desired.

Basic French Dressing:

½ cup vegetable oil
¼ cup olive oil
¼ cup red wine vinegar
Juice of ½ lemon

1 teaspoon Pommery mustard
Salt
Freshly ground pepper
Garlic to taste

Combine ingredients and let stand 1 day before serving.

Yield: 4 to 6 servings

Martha Bacon Hemphill (Mrs. James L.)

Gourmet Asparagus Salad

1 (10-ounce) package frozen asparagus
   spears, cooked and drained
1 (14-ounce) can artichoke hearts,
   drained and halved
Freshly ground pepper
⅓ cup olive oil or vegetable oil

¼ cup lemon juice
1 clove garlic, halved
½ teaspoon salt
4 lettuce cups
¼ cup sliced ripe olives

Combine asparagus and artichokes. Sprinkle with freshly ground pepper. Thoroughly combine oil, lemon juice, garlic, and salt; pour over vegetables. Cover and chill several hours, tossing once or twice. Drain and remove garlic. Arrange vegetables in lettuce cups and top with ripe olive slices.

Yield: 4 servings

Cissie Stewart White (Mrs. Frank)
Atlanta, Georgia

Marinated Asparagus

1 (15-ounce) can asparagus, drained
½ cup sugar
¼ cup white vinegar
¼ cup water

3 whole cloves
1 cinnamon stick
½ teaspoon celery seed
½ teaspoon salt

Place asparagus in dish. Combine remaining ingredients, bring to boil, cool, and pour over asparagus. Cover and refrigerate at least 12 hours before serving. Keeps well.

Yield: 4 servings

Georgia Walker Seagren (Mrs. Richard D.)

Calico Salad

4 to 6 tomatoes, chopped
3 medium onions, chopped
3 green peppers, chopped
5 cucumbers, chopped

½ cup mayonnaise
1 tablespoon water
Vinegar
Salt and pepper to taste

Combine vegetables. Make a dressing of mayonnaise, water, and enough vinegar to thin. Add salt and pepper. Chill. When ready to serve, pour dressing over vegetables and toss lightly.

Yield: 8 servings

Sandie Kohlhase Bishop (Mrs. Archer)

Marinated Mushrooms and Broccoli Buds

3 bunches broccoli
1 pound fresh mushrooms
1 cup cider vinegar
1 tablespoon sugar
1 tablespoon dill

1 tablespoon Accent
1 teaspoon freshly ground pepper
1 teaspoon garlic salt
1½ cups vegetable oil

Remove and discard stems from broccoli and mushrooms. Combine remaining ingredients and pour over broccoli buds and mushroom caps. Refrigerate for 24 hours, turning occasionally. Drain before serving.

Yield: 20 servings   Karen Herndon McWilliams (Mrs. William B.)

Marinated Tomatoes and Artichokes

6 medium tomatoes, sliced
1 (14-ounce) can artichoke
  hearts, quartered
2 cups sliced onions
1 cup pitted ripe olives
¼ cup minced parsley
1 teaspoon salt

2 teaspoons sugar
⅛ teaspoon turmeric
¾ teaspoon cumin
¼ teaspoon pepper
6 tablespoons olive oil
4 tablespoons lemon juice

Alternate layers of tomatoes, artichokes, onions, olives, and parsley in glass salad bowl. Combine remaining ingredients and pour over vegetables. Marinate 2 hours or longer and serve chilled.

Yield: 6 to 8 servings   Ena Taylor Kirkpatrick (Mrs. David M.)

Marinated Zucchini and Tomatoes

1 pound zucchini, thinly sliced
½ cup cream-style cottage
  cheese with chives
¼ cup sour cream
1 tablespoon lemon juice

½ teaspoon garlic salt
¼ cup chopped green pepper
2 medium tomatoes, sliced
Endive

Steam zucchini until tender-crisp (2 to 3 minutes). Combine cottage cheese, sour cream, lemon juice, and garlic salt. Add zucchini and green pepper to cottage cheese mixture and toss to coat. Chill. Serve on tomato slices and garnish with endive.

Yield: 4 to 5 servings   Lou Bennett (Mrs. Bill)

Marinated Salad

½ cup vegetable oil
½ cup vinegar
⅓ cup sugar
2 teaspoons prepared mustard
3 teaspoons salt
1 teaspoon oregano
Black pepper
1 head cauliflower or 2 large
   broccoli, broken into flowerets
1 green pepper, sliced thinly

4 carrots, cut into sticks
4 stalks celery, cut into sticks
3 to 4 green onions, sliced,
   or 1 large purple onion, sliced
½ pound mushrooms, sliced
2 small yellow or zucchini
   squash, sliced
2 tomatoes or 1 cup cherry
   tomatoes, sliced
1 cucumber, sliced

One day before serving, combine oil, vinegar, sugar, mustard, salt, oregano, and pepper to make a marinade. Add cauliflower or broccoli, green pepper, carrots, celery, onions, mushrooms, and squash. Marinate at least 24 hours. Before serving add tomatoes and cucumber. Drain and serve as an appetizer or on lettuce leaves as a salad.

Yield: 8 to 10 servings   Carolyn Dew Pearre (Mrs. Courtney N.)

Greek Village Salad

1 clove garlic, cut in half
5 tomatoes, peeled and
   quartered
2 medium green peppers, sliced
4 green onions with tops,
   chopped
2 cucumbers, seeded and cubed

16 to 18 pitted ripe olives
1 cup Feta cheese, crumbled
2 to 3 tablespoons olive oil
3 to 4 tablespoons wine vinegar
Salt
Freshly ground pepper
Oregano to taste

Toss garlic with tomatoes, green peppers, onions, cucumbers, olives, and cheese. Discard garlic. Season with oil, vinegar, salt, and pepper. Toss and sprinkle with oregano.

Yield: 6 to 8 servings   David M. (Pete) Kirkpatrick

Broccoli and Cauliflower Salad

½ cup sour cream
1 cup mayonnaise
1 tablespoon sugar
1 tablespoon vinegar
Dash Tabasco sauce
Dash Worcestershire sauce
Salt and pepper to taste

1 medium head cauliflower,
  cut in flowerets
1 medium head broccoli,
  cut in flowerets
Several green onions, diced
Cherry tomatoes (optional)

Mix sour cream, mayonnaise, sugar, vinegar, Tabasco, Worcestershire, salt, and pepper. Combine remaining ingredients and pour dressing over all. Refrigerate 1 hour before serving.

Yield: 5 to 6 servings   Sally Corsi Lynn (Mrs. Jerry)

Fresh Broccoli Salad

1 head fresh broccoli,
  cut in flowerets
1 very ripe tomato, chopped
2 hard-cooked eggs, chopped

10 slices bacon, cooked
  and crumbled
Mayonnaise
Salt and pepper

Combine broccoli, tomato, eggs, and bacon. Add mayonnaise to moisten. Add salt and pepper to taste. Refrigerate 3 to 4 hours before serving.

Yield: 4 servings   Courtney Carmichael Jackson (Mrs. J. Presley)
                                       Little Rock, Arkansas

Cauliflower Bacon Salad

Medium head cauliflower, broken
  into pieces
Small head lettuce, finely
  torn
1 pound bacon, cooked and
  crumbled

2 to 4 tablespoons sugar
¼ cup grated Parmesan cheese
1 cup mayonnaise
Swiss cheese or Cheddar cheese
  (optional)

Layer ingredients in order given, spreading mayonnaise on top. Refrigerate 3 to 4 hours before serving. Toss lightly. Top with grated Swiss or Cheddar cheese if desired.

Yield: 10 to 12 servings   Cheryl Arnhart Child (Mrs. Charles)

Harvest Coleslaw

1 cup mayonnaise
¼ cup French dressing
1 teaspoon salt
Dash freshly ground pepper
4 cups shredded cabbage
½ cup chopped celery

¼ cup chopped green onions
¼ cup sliced radishes
¼ pound sharp Cheddar
  cheese, cubed
1 cup diced unpeeled tomatoes

Combine mayonnaise, French dressing, salt, and pepper. Set aside. Put remaining ingredients in a large bowl and lightly toss with mayonnaise mixture.

Note: If this is prepared early in the day, add tomatoes just before serving.

Yield: 6 to 8 servings   Sharon Kelly Thomas (Mrs. William M.)

Green Pea Salad

2 (10-ounce) packages frozen
  peas, thawed
4 slices crisp bacon, crumbled
Dash salt and pepper

Dash garlic powder
¼ cup scallions, chopped
1 cup sour cream
Lettuce leaves

Combine all ingredients except lettuce and refrigerate several hours before serving. Serve on lettuce leaves.

Yield: 6 servings   Karen Herndon McWilliams (Mrs. William B.)

Cucumbers in Sour Cream

3 cucumbers
2½ teaspoons salt
1 cup sour cream or yogurt
2 green onions with tops,
  thinly sliced

2 tablespoons capers, drained
1½ teaspoons snipped fresh dill
1 teaspoon sugar
½ teaspoon pepper

Trim skin from cucumbers at ½-inch intervals.Slice cucumbers thinly, sprinkle with salt, and let stand 1 hour. Drain and pat dry on paper towel. Combine sour cream, green onion, capers, dill, sugar, and pepper. Toss cucumbers with sour cream mixture. Refrigerate, covered, 1 hour. Garnish with additional dill to serve.

Yield: 4 servings   Margaret McKinnon

Salad Niçoise

3 cups French Potato Salad
  (recipe follows)
1 head Boston lettuce
3 cups green beans, cooked
  tender-crisp and chilled
3 tomatoes, quartered
½ cup black olives

3 hard-cooked eggs, quartered
12 anchovies
1 (7-ounce) can white tuna, drained
Sliced red onion (optional)
Sliced green pepper (optional)
Fresh mushrooms (optional)
1 cup oil and vinegar dressing

Prepare French Potato Salad and chill several hours or overnight. At serving time arrange lettuce on large platter. Arrange French Potato Salad and remaining ingredients, except dressing, on lettuce. Pour oil and vinegar dressing over all.

French Potato Salad:

4 red new potatoes, boiled
1 tablespoon white wine
1 tablespoon chicken bouillon
¼ cup oil and vinegar
  dressing

1 tablespoon chopped green
  onion tops
2 tablespoons chopped parsley
  or watercress
Salt to taste

While potatoes are warm, pare, if desired, and slice. Combine remaining ingredients and pour over potatoes. Chill.

Yield: 6 to 8 servings   Louise Hooper Tate (Mrs. William M.)

Artichoke Rice Salad

1 (6-ounce) package Uncle Ben's Rice
  for Chicken—French Style
¾ teaspoon curry powder
4 green onions, thinly sliced
½ green pepper, chopped

1 (14-ounce) can artichoke
  hearts, chopped
⅓ cup mayonnaise
12 stuffed olives, chopped

Prepare rice according to package directions, adding curry during cooking. Cool and add remaining ingredients. Chill before serving.

Yield: 4 to 6 servings   Anne Rogers Killefer (Mrs. Robert)

Fresh Rice Salad

1 cup Uncle Ben's Converted Rice
1 cup sliced celery
1 (11-ounce) can mandarin
   oranges, drained
¾ cup green pepper strips
½ cup sliced carrots
2 cups ham cubes

¾ cup mayonnaise
2 tablespoons chopped onion
½ teaspoon salt
⅛ teaspoon pepper
Lettuce leaves
Carrot curls and parsley (optional)

Prepare rice according to package directions; then chill. Combine rice, celery, oranges, green pepper, carrots, ham, mayonnaise, onion, and seasonings. Mix lightly and chill. Serve on lettuce-covered platter and garnish with carrot curls and parsley, if desired.

Yield: 6 to 8 servings   Kathy Fouche Kerr

Cold Rice Stuffed Tomatoes

Excellent as a salad or vegetable dish

½ cup rice, cooked
¼ cup olive oil
1 tablespoon wine vinegar
Salt
Freshly ground pepper
1 teaspoon minced onion

1 tablespoon minced parsley
6 medium tomatoes
Boston lettuce or Romaine
Mayonnaise (optional)
Parsley (optional)

While rice is hot, add oil and toss lightly. Add vinegar, salt, pepper, onion, and parsley. Toss lightly and let stand, covered, at room temperature 3 hours. At serving time, cut stem ends off tomatoes. Remove pulp and mix with rice. Pile mixture lightly in tomatoes and set on bed of lettuce. If desired, serve with mayonnaise and parsley on top as garnish.

Yield: 6 servings   Ena Taylor Kirkpatrick (Mrs. David M.)

Almond Fettucini Salad

4 ounces spinach noodles,
  cooked and chilled
3 cups shredded lettuce
2 (6½-ounce) cans tuna,
  drained

1 large tomato, cut in
  thin wedges
Toasted almonds, slivered
Almond Cream Dressing
  (recipe follows)
Grated Parmesan cheese

In serving dish, arrange noodles, lettuce, tuna, and tomato. Sprinkle with almonds. Just before serving, pour dressing over all; toss thoroughly. Sprinkle with grated cheese, if desired.

Almond Cream Dressing:

⅔ cup sour cream
¼ cup vegetable oil
¼ cup tarragon vinegar
¼ cup grated Parmesan cheese
½ teaspoon salt

⅛ teaspoon pepper
½ cup slivered almonds,
  toasted
2 tablespoons sliced green
  onions

Whisk together sour cream, oil, vinegar, cheese, salt, and pepper. Stir in almonds and onions.

Yield: 4 to 6 servings   Jane Blanton Gavin (Mrs. C. Edward)

Sour Cream Potato Salad

16 to 18 medium-sized new
  potatoes
4 eggs
½ cup Italian dressing
1 small onion, chopped
6 to 8 slices bacon, cooked
  and crumbled

1 (6-ounce) can pitted ripe olives
½ cup chopped sweet pickle
1 tablespoon celery seed
1 (8-ounce) carton sour cream
¾ cup mayonnaise
1 tablespoon prepared mustard
Salt and pepper to taste

In the same water, boil potatoes in their jackets and eggs in their shells until potatoes are tender (about 20 minutes). Cool potatoes only until jackets can be removed easily. Cube carefully. Dip eggs in cold water, peel, and chop. Gently toss dressing, onion, warm potatoes, and eggs. When cool, add remaining ingredients and toss gently.

Note: This salad is better the second day and should appear to have an abundance of dressing as it firms up when kept overnight.

Yield: 20 to 24 servings   Lane Schreeder Hays (Mrs. Charles, Jr.)

Stuffed Tomatoes

12 medium tomatoes
1 pound cottage cheese
1 medium green pepper,
  finely chopped
1½ tablespoons onion juice

1 tablespoon Worcestershire sauce
Salt to taste
Red pepper to taste
Mayonnaise to taste
Crabmeat Dressing (recipe follows)

Peel tomatoes. Scoop out stem end, forming cup. Salt generously and place in dish, cut side down,to drain. Chill in refrigerator. Wash and drain cottage cheese. Combine cottage cheese, green pepper, onion juice, Worcestershire, salt, red pepper, and mayonnaise. Stuff tomatoes with cottage cheese mixture and serve with crabmeat dressing.

Crabmeat Dressing:

1 (6½-ounce) can crabmeat
⅓ cup chili sauce

½ cup finely chopped celery
2 cups mayonnaise

Flake the crabmeat. Add chili sauce, celery, and crabmeat to mayonnaise just before serving.

Yield: 12 servings   Carter Jones

Lobster Salad Nantucket

2 pounds lobster meat,
  cooked and cubed
⅓ cup chopped red onion
⅓ cup chopped green pepper
⅓ cup chopped avocado
⅓ cup sliced celery

Hellman's mayonnaise (or homemade)
Fresh lemon juice to taste
Salt and pepper to taste
Worcestershire sauce to taste
Curry powder to taste

Combine lobster with vegetables. Add enough mayonnaise to bind together and season to taste. Serve on French rolls or hot dog buns.

Note: Also delicious made with shrimp or crab. If using shrimp, add sliced green olives.

Yield: 4 to 6 servings   Ann Pittman Bond (Mrs. Jackson)

Chicken Salad Pie

1 (9-inch) pastry shell
2 cups cooked chicken
¾ cup grated American cheese
¼ cup diced celery
½ cup drained crushed pineapple
½ cup chopped walnuts

½ teaspoon paprika
¼ teaspoon salt
¾ cup mayonnaise, divided
½ cup whipping cream
Grated carrots

Bake pastry and set aside. Blend chicken, cheese, celery, pineapple, walnuts, paprika, salt, and ½ cup mayonnaise. Pour into baked pastry. Whip cream and ¼ cup mayonnaise together; spread over pie. Cool in refrigerator for 2 to 3 hours or overnight. Before serving, sprinkle grated carrots around crust edge.

Yield: 6 servings

Jo Ann Catlett McCallen (Mrs. Perry)

Jean's Chinese Chicken Salad

3 chicken breasts
1 bunch green onions, chopped
1 bunch celery, chopped
1 bunch Chinese parsley, chopped
1 (16-ounce) bottle vinaigrette
  dressing
Spice Island fines herbes

2 heads iceberg lettuce,
  shredded
1 (6-ounce) jar Macadamia
  nuts, chopped
Soy sauce to taste
1 (5-ounce) can dried chow
  mein noodles

Cook and shred chicken, reserving skin. Dice chicken skin and cook crisp. Combine shredded chicken, onion, celery, and parsley. Combine dressing with fines herbes to taste. Mix half dressing with chicken mixture. (Recipe can be prepared ahead to this point.) Before serving, add lettuce, nuts, crisp chicken skin, soy sauce, and remaining dressing. Add noodles and toss lightly.

Yield: 6 to 10 servings

Judy Gardiner Martin (Mrs. James R.)

Curried Chicken Salad

8 cups coarsely cut cooked
  chicken or turkey (about 5 pounds
  of chicken breasts)
1 to 2 pounds seedless grapes,
  cut in half
2 cups toasted slivered almonds

3 cups diagonally sliced celery
1 (20-ounce) can pineapple
  chunks, drained
2 tablespoons curry powder
2 tablespoons soy sauce
3 cups mayonnaise

In a large bowl combine chicken, grapes, almonds, celery, and pineapple.
Set aside. Combine curry powder, soy sauce, and mayonnaise, and add to
chicken mixture, gently tossing to mix,

Yield: 12 to 16 servings   Peg Martin Vise (Mrs. Guy T., Sr.)
                                                    Meridian, Mississippi

Pineapple Frozen Yogurt

1 (8-ounce) package cream
  cheese, softened
¼ cup sugar
¼ cup firmly packed brown sugar

2 cups pineapple yogurt
1 (15¼-ounce) can crushed
  pineapple, drained
2 tablespoons chopped pecans

Blend cream cheese and sugars. Stir in yogurt, pineapple, and pecans. Pour
into a 9-inch square pan and freeze. To serve, cut into squares and place on
lettuce cup.

Note: Banana yogurt can be substituted for pineapple.

Yield: 8 to 10 servings   Kane Watson McAfee (Mrs. Joe M.)

Strawberry Nut Mold

1 cup boiling water
1 (6-ounce) package strawberry
  gelatin
1 envelope unflavored gelatin
1 (20-ounce) can crushed
  pineapple, drained

1 cup broken pecan pieces
2 (10-ounce) packages frozen strawberries with syrup, defrosted
3 mashed bananas
Sour cream
Fresh strawberries

Pour boiling water over strawberry gelatin and unflavored gelatin in a
large bowl. Stir until dissolved. Add remaining ingredients and mix well.
Pour into an 8-cup mold. Serve with sour cream and fresh strawberries.

Yield: 6 servings   Sheila Prial Jacobstein (Mrs. Richard)

Strawberry and Avocado Salad

1 (8-ounce) package cream
  cheese, softened
¼ cup milk
¾ teaspoon ginger
1 (6-ounce) can frozen limeade,
  thawed and divided

2 cups avocados cut into
  bite-size pieces
2 cups strawberry halves
Romaine or other lettuce
  leaves

Combine cream cheese, milk, ginger, and 3 tablespoons limeade concentrate in mixer until smooth. Set aside. In a large bowl, toss avocado and strawberries with remaining limeade concentrate. With slotted spoon, transfer avocado-strawberry mixture to lettuce-lined plates or fruit cups. Pass cream cheese mixture as dressing.

Yield: 6 servings   Kae Gilmore Lakenan (Mrs. William K.,Jr.)

Frosted Fruit Salad

1 (3-ounce) package lemon gelatin
1 (3-ounce) package lime gelatin
2 cups boiling water
1 (20-ounce) can crushed pineapple
1 (10-ounce) bottle 7-Up
2 cups miniature marshmallows
2 to 3 bananas, sliced
½ cup sugar
2 tablespoons all-purpose flour

1 egg, slightly beaten
2 tablespoons butter
1 (8-ounce) carton non-dairy
  whipped topping
1 (3-ounce) package cream cheese,
  softened
Shredded Cheddar cheese
  (optional)
Chopped pecans (optional)

In a 9- x 13-inch pan, combine both gelatins. Add 2 cups of boiling water and stir until dissolved. Cool. Drain pineapple and reserve liquid. Add pineapple, 7-Up, marshmallows, and bananas. Congeal.
  In medium saucepan combine sugar, flour, egg, and 1 cup reserved pineapple juice. Cook over medium heat until thick. Remove from heat; add butter and cream cheese. Cool. Fold in whipped topping. Spread over congealed gelatin and top with shredded cheese and/or pecans.

Yield: 12 servings   Beth Pettit Stivers (Mrs. Robert M.)

Cinnamon Applesauce Salad

1 (3-ounce) package cream
  cheese, softened
2 tablespoons half and half
  cream
1 tablespoon mayonnaise

½ cup red cinnamon candies
1 cup boiling water
1 (3-ounce) package lemon
  gelatin
2 cups applesauce

Combine cream cheese, cream, and mayonnaise and blend well. Set aside.
Dissolve candies in boiling water. Add gelatin and stir until dissolved.
Stir applesauce into above mixture. Chill until slightly thickened. Pour
gelatin mixture into 9-inch square pan or 10-cup mold. Spoon cream cheese
mixture on top of gelatin and swirl to marbleize. Chill until firm.

Yield: 8 servings   Catherine Cowell Fowler (Mrs. S. Frank)

Asparagus Mold

1 tablespoon unflavored gelatin
¼ cup cold water
2 (14½-ounce) cans asparagus,
  reserve liquid
½ cup heavy cream, whipped

½ cup mayonnaise
1 teaspoon salt
2 to 4 tablespoons lemon juice
1 cup pecans

Dissolve gelatin in cold water and let stand until partially set. Drain
asparagus and add enough water to liquid to equal 1 cup. Heat liquid and
add to gelatin mixture. Fold in whipped cream, mayonnaise, salt, and
lemon juice. Add asparagus and pecans. Pour into a 6-cup mold and
congeal.

Note: Serve with mayonnaise mixed with a small amount of lemon juice.

Yield: 8 to 10 servings   Georgia Walker Seagren

Molded Cucumber Salad

2 (3-ounce) packages cream cheese
1 (3-ounce) package lime gelatin
¾ cup hot water
¼ cup chopped onion

1 teaspoon or more prepared
 horseradish
1 cup mayonnaise
1 cucumber, peeled and
 cut in chunks

Mix cream cheese in blender. Add gelatin, hot water, onion, horseradish, and mayonnaise. Blend on and off. Add cucumber. Pour into well-oiled 1-quart mold. Chill until firm. Unmold and garnish with fresh parsley and cucumber slices.

Yield: 4 to 6 servings

Jean L. Nichols Alsentzer (Mrs. John S.)

Mustard Ring

4 eggs
½ cup cider vinegar
1 cup water
¾ cup sugar
1 tablespoon plain gelatin

1½ tablespoons dry mustard
½ teaspoon turmeric
¼ teaspoon salt
1 cup whipping cream, whipped

In top of double boiler place eggs and beat slightly. Add vinegar and water to eggs. Combine sugar, gelatin, mustard, turmeric, and salt. Mix well and add to egg mixture. Cook until slightly thickened, stirring constantly. Cool. Fold in whipped cream and place in 1½-quart ring mold.

Note: Delicious with ham!

Yield: 1 ring

Wilma Additon Bradford
Bangor, Maine

Celery Seed Dressing

½ cup plus 2 tablespoons sugar
1 teaspoon dry mustard
1 teaspoon salt
1 small onion, grated

1 cup corn oil
½ cup vinegar
¼ cup celery seeds

Mix sugar, dry mustard, salt, onion, and oil in mixing bowl and beat approximately 10 minutes on medium speed. *Slowly* add vinegar and celery seeds. Serve over fruit salad.

Note: This keeps well in refrigerator if kept in tightly closed jar. Shake well before serving.

Yield: 1 pint   Kathryn Wilson Cockrill (Mrs. William G.)

"Free" Salad Dressing

⅓ cup vinegar
½ cup corn oil
½ cup water
½ teaspoon honey
½ teaspoon pepper

¼ teaspoon garlic powder
¼ teaspoon dry mustard
¼ teaspoon dried basil
¼ teaspoon dried parsley

Combine all ingredients and store in glass jar at room temperature.

Note: You can eat all of this salad dressing that you desire without feeling guilty.

Yield: 1⅓ cups   Marti Schmitz Hobson (Mrs. Leonard)

French Roquefort Dressing

1 cup mayonnaise
¼ cup prepared French
  dressing

¼ cup grated Roquefort
  or Bleu cheese
4 cloves garlic, pressed

Mix all ingredients well. Refrigerate.

Note: Can be mixed on low speed in blender, but be careful not to blend too long or mayonnaise will separate.

Yield: 1 pint   Gail Taylor Woods (Mrs. Gene)
                                                 Memphis, Tennessee

Granny's Salad Dressing

1 cup vegetable oil
¾ cup sugar
1 small onion, diced

⅓ cup catsup
1 tablespoon Worcestershire sauce
¼ cup white vinegar

Mix all ingredients. Refrigerate. Shake well before serving. Delicious on spinach salad.

Yield: Approximately 1 pint

Jan Spitzer Frey (Mrs. David M.)

Herb Dressing

1 teaspoon capers
1 cup mayonnaise
½ tablespoon lemon juice
¼ teaspoon salt
¼ teaspoon paprika
¼ cup finely chopped parsley

1 teaspoon grated onion
1 teaspoon chopped chives
⅛ teaspoon curry powder
½ teaspoon Worcestershire sauce
1 clove garlic, minced
½ cup sour cream

Combine all ingredients except sour cream. Fold in sour cream. Chill and serve with tomato aspic or any green salad.

Suggestion: Fill half of a fresh artichoke with dressing and place in center of aspic ring to serve.

Yield: 2 cups, approximately

Ann Lovejoy Browning (Mrs. Louis A., Jr.)

Honey French Dressing

1 cup vegetable oil
½ cup honey
½ cup catsup
⅓ cup vinegar

⅓ cup chopped onion
1 tablespoon Worcestershire sauce
½ teaspoon salt

Combine in blender and serve on green salad or fruit.

Yield: 2⅔ cups

Virginia Thurston Stivers (Mrs. Robert)
Memphis, Tennessee

Poppyseed Dressing

1 cup vegetable oil
⅓ cup sugar
1 teaspoon salt
1 teaspoon dry mustard

⅓ teaspoon grated onion
½ cup vinegar
1 tablespoon poppy seeds

Combine all ingredients in jar and shake. Store in refrigerator. Serve over sliced fresh fruit.

Yield: 1½ cups   Pam Pfeiffer Fritts (Mrs. George Brownlow)

Slaw Dressing

¼ cup vinegar
¼ cup vegetable oil

3 tablespoons sugar
1 teaspoon salt

Place all ingredients in pint jar and shake.

Note: Makes enough dressing for medium head of shredded cabbage.

Yield: ⅔ cup   Letty Bartlett Taylor (Mrs. George C.)

Sweet and Sour Salad Dressing

1 cup vegetable oil
½ cup red wine vinegar
½ teaspoon salt

Pinch garlic salt
½ teaspoon paprika
2 tablespoons sugar

Combine ingredients and serve over spinach salad or tossed salad with bleu cheese.

Yield: 1½ cups   Ena Taylor Kirkpatrick (Mrs. David M.)

Breads

Italian Cheese Loaf

½ cup butter, softened
½ cup parsley, chopped
½ cup Parmesan cheese,
   freshly grated
1 clove garlic, crushed

1 tablespoon olive oil
½ teaspoon basil
½ teaspoon oregano
Salt and pepper
1 loaf Italian bread

Preheat oven to 375°. In a bowl combine butter, parsley, Parmesan, garlic, olive oil, basil, oregano, salt and pepper to taste. Cut loaf of Italian bread crosswise into 1½-inch slices without cutting through bottom crust. Spread butter mixture between slices and wrap bread in foil. Bake 20 minutes.

Yield: 1 loaf   Jeanne Holmes Hyatt (Mrs. Hugh C.)

Browning's Buttermilk Biscuits

2 packages dry yeast
¼ cup warm water
5 cups all-purpose flour
4 teaspoons baking powder
2 teaspoons salt

1 teaspoon soda
¼ cup sugar
¾ cup vegetable shortening
2 cups buttermilk

Preheat oven to 425°. Dissolve yeast in warm water. Sift dry ingredients in large mixing bowl. Cut shortening into dry ingredients. Stir in buttermilk and yeast mixture. Turn onto lightly floured board and knead several times. Roll dough to ½-inch thickness and cut with biscuit cutter. Place on cookie sheet and allow 30 minutes to rise. Bake 8 to 12 minutes or until brown.

Yield: 3 to 4 dozen   Louis A. Browning, Sr.

Brown Sugar Muffins

½ cup butter
1 cup firmly packed dark
   brown sugar
1 egg
2 cups all-purpose flour
1 teaspoon soda

1 teaspoon baking powder
Dash salt
1 cup milk
½ cup chopped pecans
   (optional)
1 teaspoon vanilla

Preheat oven to 400° and grease muffin tins. Cream butter and sugar. Add egg and mix well. Add remaining ingredients, except vanilla. Mix well; add vanilla. Bake 15 minutes.

Yield: 18 muffins   Suzanne Wallace Stowers (Mrs. Eugene)

Blueberry Muffins Deluxe

5 tablespoons vegetable shortening
½ cup sugar
1 egg, well-beaten
1½ cups all-purpose flour
1½ teaspoons baking powder
¼ teaspoon salt

¼ teaspoon nutmeg
½ cup milk
Frozen blueberries
½ cup margarine, melted
Topping (recipe follows)

Preheat oven to 350°. Cream shortening and sugar; add egg. Combine flour, baking powder, salt, and nutmeg. Add alternately with milk. Oil small muffin tins or use paper-lined muffin cups. Fill half of cups with batter and press 4 or 5 frozen blueberries into each cup. Add more dough to cover berries. Bake 12 minutes or until muffins are light brown. Cool slightly.

Dip tops of muffins in melted margarine. Gently shake muffins in a bag which contains topping.

Topping:

½ cup confectioners' sugar
2 teaspoons cinnamon

½ teaspoon nutmeg

Combine ingredients and use accordingly.

Yield: 12 to 16 servings   Lillian Astley Rayson (Mrs. Edwin)

Feather Muffins

1 package dry yeast
¼ cup lukewarm water
2 tablespoons vegetable shortening
2 tablespoons sugar
1 teaspoon salt

1 cup milk, scalded
1 egg, beaten
2½ cups sifted all-purpose
  flour, divided

Preheat oven to 400°. Grease muffin tins. Dissolve yeast in water. Combine shortening, sugar, and salt in mixing bowl. Add milk, stirring until shortening is melted. Add yeast, egg, and 1¼ cups flour; beat well. Add remaining flour and beat until smooth. Cover and let rise until doubled in bulk. Stir down and spoon into muffin tins, filling half full. Bake 15 to 20 minutes.

Note: For wheat muffins, substitute 1¼ cups whole wheat flour for half of all-purpose flour.

Yield: 30 muffins   Alice Hale Clayton (Mrs. Edward S., III)

Fresh Apple Muffins

1½ cups sifted all-purpose flour
1¾ teaspoons baking powder
⅓ teaspoon salt
½ teaspoon nutmeg
½ cup sugar

⅓ cup vegetable shortening
¼ cup milk
1 egg, beaten
½ cup grated fresh apple
Topping (recipe follows)

Preheat oven to 350°. Sift flour, baking powder, salt, nutmeg, and sugar. Set aside. Combine shortening, milk, egg, and apple. Mix apple mixture into dry ingredients and stir until blended. Spoon into greased muffin tins and bake 20 to 25 minutes or until brown. Apply topping to muffins as directed.

Topping:

⅓ cup sugar
1 teaspoon cinnamon

½ cup butter, melted

Combine sugar and cinnamon. Roll baked muffins in butter and then in sugar mixture.

Yield: 12 muffins   Sue Arnold Herrmann (Mrs. Milo)
                                                     Boggy Bayou, Florida

Sally Lunn Muffins

¼ cup margarine
⅓ cup sugar
2 eggs, beaten
2 cups all-purpose flour

4 teaspoons baking powder
½ teaspoon salt
⅔ cup milk

Preheat oven to 400° and grease muffin tins. Cream margarine and sugar, and add eggs. Combine flour, baking powder, and salt in sifter. Alternate dry ingredients and milk to sugar mixture. Spoon into tins and bake 15 to 20 minutes.

Note: Best if baked immediately before serving.

Yield: 12 muffins   Frances LaNieve Sexton (Mrs. Charles F., Jr.)

Ice Box Ginger Muffins

1 cup butter or margarine,
  softened
1 cup sugar
4 eggs
1 cup light corn syrup
1 teaspoon baking powder
1 cup sour cream

4 cups all-purpose flour
2 teaspoons soda
½ teaspoon salt
3 teaspoons ginger
⅔ cup nuts
¾ cup raisins

Preheat oven to 350°. Cream butter and sugar. Add eggs and syrup. Stir
baking powder into sour cream until it foams. Add to butter mixture. Sift dry
ingredients and add to butter mixture. Fold in nuts and raisins. Pour into
muffin tins. Bake 15 to 20 minutes.

Yield: 3 dozen muffins   Anne Miller Roberts (Mrs. Monty)

Dorothy's Popovers

3 eggs
1 cup milk

1 cup all-purpose flour
½ teaspoon salt

Grease 6 custard cups or 12-muffin tins and chill. Combine all ingredients
and mix well. Pour into prepared containers and place in cold oven. Bake 30
minutes at 450°. Don't open oven door! Serve immediately.

Yield: 6 large or 12 small   Katherine Spencer McNab (Mrs. R.B.)

Applesauce Bread

1½ cups all-purpose flour
1 teaspoon soda
1 teaspoon baking powder
1 teaspoon salt
1 teaspoon cinnamon
½ teaspoon nutmeg
1 cup quick-cooking oats

½ cup firmly packed
  light brown sugar
2 eggs
⅓ cup vegetable oil
1 cup applesauce
1 cup raisins
1 cup chopped pecans

Preheat oven to 350°. Grease 1 loaf pan. Combine flour, soda, baking
powder, salt, cinnamon, nutmeg, oats, and brown sugar. Add eggs, oil, and
applesauce; stir until well-blended. Stir in raisins and pecans. Pour into loaf
pan and bake 1 hour.

Yield: 1 loaf   Preston Pratt Gentry (Mrs. Edgar C., Jr.)

Banana Brunch Bread

½ cup butter
1 cup sugar
2 eggs
1 cup mashed bananas
½ teaspoon vanilla
½ cup sour cream

2 cups sifted all-purpose flour
1 teaspoon baking powder
¼ teaspoon salt
1 teaspoon soda
Topping (recipe follows)
Whipped cream cheese (optional)

Preheat oven to 350°. Heavily grease three 7⅜- x 3⅝-inch loafpans. Cream butter and sugar until light. Beat in eggs one at a time. Mix in bananas, vanilla, and sour cream. Sift together flour, baking powder, salt, and soda. Fold into creamed mixture, stirring only enough to moisten. Sprinkle half of topping on bottoms of prepared loafpans. Spoon in batter and sprinkle with remaining topping. Bake 45 minutes. Serve with whipped cream cheese, if desired.

Topping:

½ cup chopped nuts
½ cup sugar

½ teaspoon cinnamon

Combine all ingredients and use as directed.

Note: Topping may be doubled, if desired. Bread may be frozen after baking.

Yield: 3 loaves   Pamela Young Richardson (Mrs. Charles Franklin)

Fresh Blueberry Banana Bread

1 cup fresh blueberries
1¾ cups sifted all-purpose
   flour, divided
2 teaspoons baking powder
¼ teaspoon soda

½ teaspoon salt
⅓ cup butter or margarine
⅔ cup sugar
2 eggs
1 cup mashed ripe bananas

Preheat oven to 350°. Grease 9- x 5-inch loaf pan. Wash and thoroughly drain blueberries; toss berries with 2 tablespoons flour. Sift together remaining flour, baking powder, soda, and salt. Set aside. Cream butter. Gradually beat in sugar until light and fluffy. Beat in eggs one at a time. Add flour mixture and bananas alternately, in three parts. Fold in blueberries. Spoon into loaf pan and bake approximately 50 minutes.

Yield: 1 loaf   Rusha Kinard Sams (Mrs. Bert E.)

Carrot Walnut Bread

1 cup vegetable oil
¾ cup sugar
2 eggs
1 teaspoon vanilla
1½ cups sifted all-purpose flour
1½ teaspoons soda

1½ teaspoons ground cinnamon
½ teaspoon salt
1½ cups grated carrot
1½ cups ground walnuts
Lemon Glaze (recipe follows)

Preheat oven to 350°. Grease and flour 9- x 5-inch loaf pan. Combine oil, sugar, eggs, and vanilla. Sift flour, soda, cinnamon, and salt. Add to sugar mixture. Stir in carrots and walnuts; mix just until blended. Turn into prepared pan. Bake 1 hour or less. Cool in pan 10 minutes. Turn out on cake rack to cool completely. Top with glaze.

Lemon Glaze:

½ cup confectioners' sugar
1 teaspoon grated lemon rind

1 tablespoon lemon juice

Combine all ingredients and stir until smooth. Drizzle over top and sides of bread.

Yield: 1 loaf   Mary Frances West Fox (Mrs. Bruce, Jr.)

Lemon Bread

⅓ cup butter or margarine
1⅓ cups sugar, divided
2 eggs
1 teaspoon salt
1½ cups all-purpose flour

½ cup milk
1½ teaspoons baking powder
Rind of one lemon, grated
½ cup chopped pecans
Juice of 1 lemon

Preheat oven to 350°. Grease a 9- x 5-inch loaf pan. Combine butter, 1 cup sugar, eggs, salt, flour, milk, baking powder, grated lemon peel, and pecans. Mix well. Pour into loaf pan and bake about 45 minutes. Remove loaf from pan. Mix remaining ⅓ cup sugar and juice from 1 lemon to form topping. Pour over bread while warm.

Yield: 1 loaf   Silent Butler
                                                     Ann Bond
                                                     Alice Clayton
                                                     Di Wall

Zucchini Walnut Bread

4 eggs
1 cup vegetable oil
2 cups sugar
3½ cups unbleached flour
1½ teaspoons soda
1½ teaspoons salt

1 teaspoon cinnamon
¾ teaspoon baking powder
2 cups grated zucchini
1 cup raisins
1 cup chopped walnuts
1 teaspoon vanilla

Preheat oven to 350°. Grease and flour 2 small loaf pans. Beat eggs and add oil. Combine dry ingredients and add to eggs, alternating with squash. Stir in raisins, walnuts, and vanilla. Pour into prepared pans and bake 50 minutes.

Yield: 2 loaves   Lynn Boukard Crowell (Mrs. Michael)

Dilly Cheese Bread

3 cups Bisquick
1½ cups grated sharp
   Cheddar cheese
1 tablespoon sugar
1½ cups milk

1 tablespoon vegetable oil
1 egg, beaten
½ teaspoon dill weed
½ teaspoon dry mustard

Preheat oven to 350°. Grease 9- x 5-inch loaf pan. Combine Bisquick, cheese, and sugar. Combine remaining ingredients, and add to cheese mixture, beating until blended and smooth. Pour into prepared pan and bake 45 to 50 minutes.

Note: Great for tomato sandwiches!

Yield: 1 loaf   Melissa Cooley Gill

Pawley's Puppies

½ cup all-purpose flour
2 teaspoons baking powder
2 to 3 tablespoons sugar
½ teaspoon salt
1½ cups cornmeal

1 egg, slightly beaten
¾ cup milk
1 small onion, chopped fine
   or grated (optional)

Preheat deep fat to 360°. Combine dry ingredients. Add egg and milk, mixing lightly. Stir in onion if desired. Drop batter by teaspoonfuls into hot deep fat. Fry a few at a time until golden brown. Drain on absorbent paper.

Yield: 2 dozen   Anne Beall Hillmer (Mrs. Ralph G., Jr.)

Emma Gene's Corn Bread

¾ cup corn meal
½ cup all-purpose flour
1 teaspoon salt
1 teaspoon baking powder

½ teaspoon soda
1 cup buttermilk
2 tablespoons vegetable oil
  or bacon drippings

Preheat oven to 400° and heat greased 8-inch iron skillet. Combine all ingredients. Pour batter into heated skillet and bake 20 minutes or until done.

Note: Recipe can be doubled.

Yield: 6 to 8 servings   Carolyn Dominick Townsend (Mrs. Dalton)

Don's Genuine Corn Pone

¾ cup boiling water
1 cup corn meal
1 teaspoon salt

1½ teaspoons melted bacon
  grease

Pour boiling water over corn meal and salt in small bowl, stirring to blend well. When mixture is cool enough to handle, divide into four portions. Pat between hands to shape each portion into 2 pones. Place in hot grease in iron skillet and cook until brown crust forms. Serve hot with butter and fresh vegetables.

Yield: 4 servings   Dale Reid McCarley (Mrs. Thomas H.)

Spoon Bread

2 cups milk
½ cup corn meal
1 teaspoon salt

½ teaspoon baking powder
3 eggs, separated
2 tablespoons butter

Preheat oven to 325°. Grease 8-inch soufflé dish. Heat milk to boil; stir in cornmeal and salt. Cook until thickened. Cool slightly. Add baking powder and well-beaten egg yolks. Blend in butter. Beat egg whites until stiff and fold into cornmeal mixture. Pour into prepared dish. Bake 30 minutes. Serve immediately.

Yield: 4 to 6 servings   Joy Sanders Arnett

All Bran Rolls

2 yeast cakes
1 cup warm water
1 cup All-Bran
1 cup Crisco
¾ cup sugar
1½ teaspoons salt

1 cup boiling water
2 eggs, slightly beaten
6 to 7 cups all-purpose
  flour
Butter

Dissolve yeast in warm water. In large bowl combine All-Bran, shortening, sugar, and salt; add boiling water. Stir until shortening melts. Cool to lukewarm. Add eggs, yeast mixture, and ½ cup flour; beat with mixer until smooth. Continue adding flour and beating until dough no longer clings to side of bowl. Put in large oiled container, cover, and refrigerate 24 to 48 hours.

To make into rolls, knead until elastic on floured board, using additional flour. Roll out and form into rolls. Place in pans, brush with butter, cover with towel, and let rise until doubled in size (2 to 2½ hours). Bake 10 to 12 minutes at 425°.

Yield: 4 to 5 dozen   Suzanne Wood Fletcher

Gran'mama Shafer's Rolls

½ cup sugar
1½ cups warm water
1 package dry yeast
1½ teaspoons salt
1 egg, slightly beaten

½ cup Crisco
5½ cups all-purpose
  flour, approximately
Melted butter

Combine sugar, warm water, and yeast. Set aside 5 minutes. Add salt, egg, and Crisco. Mix well. Gradually add about 5 cups flour. At this point, dough can be refrigerated overnight. Knead dough on floured board and roll out to ⅜-inch thickness. Cut with small biscuit cutter, brush with butter, fold over, and place side by side in pans. Brush tops with butter. Let rise 1½ hours in warm place. Bake 10 to 12 minutes at 400°.

Yield: 3 to 4 dozen   Mary Gwyn Shafer (Mrs. "Bo")

Refrigerator Rolls

2 packages dry yeast
1 cup warm water
1 cup boiling water
1 cup vegetable shortening
¾ cup sugar

2 teaspoons salt
2 eggs
6 cups all-purpose flour
Melted margarine

Dissolve yeast in warm water and let stand 5 minutes. Pour boiling water over shortening, sugar, and salt in large bowl. Blend well and cool. Beat eggs into yeast water and add to cooled shortening mixture. Gradually add flour and mix well. Place in large oiled bowl, cover, and refrigerate. Three hours before serving, roll out dough and cut with biscuit cutter. Dip into melted margarine, fold over, and place in greased pans. Let rise until doubled. Bake 10 to 12 minutes at 400°.

Note: Dough will keep in refrigerator for several days. Rolls can be frozen after partially baked and cooled. To serve, thaw and complete baking at 425°.

Cinnamon Roll Variation:

⅓ recipe for Refrigerator
   Rolls
Melted margarine
Cinnamon
Sugar
Raisins (optional)

Milk
2 cups sifted confectioners'
   sugar
Dash salt
1 teaspoon vanilla

Roll dough into 10- x 18-inch rectangle. Brush with melted margarine and sprinkle with cinnamon, sugar, and raisins. Roll dough tightly, beginning with wide edge. Cut into 1-inch slices and place almost touching in greased pans or muffin tins. Cover and let rise until doubled. Bake at 350° until brown. Add enough milk to confectioners' sugar to make spreading consistency. Add salt and vanilla. Spread on cooled cinnamon rolls.

Yield: 4 to 5 dozen   Ellen Brown Adams (Mrs. Elliott D.)

Mashed Potato Rolls

1 cup mashed potatoes
½ cup sugar
2 eggs
1 teaspoon salt
⅔ cup vegetable oil
1 cup milk, scalded

1 package dry yeast
½ cup lukewarm water
5 to 6 cups all-purpose
  flour
Vegetable oil
Melted butter

Combine mashed potatoes, sugar, eggs, salt, vegetable oil, scalded milk, yeast, and water. Mix with electric mixer on low speed. Then stir in enough flour to make firm but not stiff dough. Place in greased bowl. Grease top of dough with vegetable oil and cover lightly. Refrigerate and use within 4 days. Roll into desired shape and brush with melted butter. Let rise 1½ hours in warm place. Bake 8 minutes at 400°.

Yield: Approximately 5 dozen   Sharon Kelley Thomas (Mrs. William M.)

Whole Wheat Rolls

2 cups milk
½ cup margarine
2 packages dry yeast
½ cup warm water
⅓ cup firmly packed
  brown sugar
1½ teaspoons salt

2 eggs, beaten
5 cups all-purpose flour
2 cups whole wheat flour
Additional all-purpose flour
  for kneading
½ cup melted margarine
Crisco

Scald milk; add ½ cup margarine to melt and set aside to cool. Dissolve yeast in warm water. In large mixing bowl combine sugar, salt, and eggs. Add cooled milk mixture. Add yeast and 1 cup flour. Mix well. Add remaining flour and mix well with mixer. Pour into large oiled bowl with lid and refrigerate, covered, overnight. To make rolls, knead ⅓ dough at a time (about 5 minutes per portion). Work in only enough additional flour to keep dough from sticking. Allow dough to rest after kneading. Roll out and cut with biscuit cutter. Dip each roll in melted margarine, form pocketbook shape, and place in pans that have been greased with Crisco. Cover rolls with cloth and allow to rise until doubled. Bake 10 to 12 minutes at 425°. If freezing, bake 6 to 8 minutes, cool, and freeze. Finish baking after thawing.

Note: For white rolls, delete whole wheat flour and increase all-purpose flour to 7 cups. Substitute white sugar for brown sugar.

Yield: Approximately 5 dozen rolls   Retta Finley Wood (Mrs. Van H.)

Homemade Bread

2 packages yeast
1 cup lukewarm water
1 cup vegetable shortening
½ cup sugar
1 cup water

2 eggs, beaten
6 cups all-purpose flour
1 teaspoon baking powder
½ teaspoon soda
2 teaspoons salt

Dissolve yeast in lukewarm water. Set aside. In saucepan melt shortening. Add sugar and remaining 1 cup water. Bring to boil. When cool, add eggs and dissolved yeast. Sift together flour, baking powder, soda, and salt; add to creamed mixture. Cover and refrigerate overnight or for several hours. Knead well and place in 3 greased loaf pans. Let rise until double in size (about 2 hours). Bake 30 to 40 minutes at 400°.

Yield: 3 loaves   Caroline Siler Hill (Mrs. Robert E.)

Rye Bread

2 packages dry yeast
1½ cups warm water
3 tablespoons sugar, divided
½ cup molasses
¼ cup honey
2 tablespoons vegetable shortening

1 tablespoon salt
Rind of ½ orange,
 finely grated
2½ cups rye flour
2 to 3 cups unbleached
 all-purpose flour
Corn meal

Dissolve yeast in warm water with 1 tablespoon sugar. Blend in molasses, honey, remaining sugar, shortening, salt, and orange rind. Stir in rye flour and mix until smooth. Add enough unbleached flour to handle easily. Place on floured board and knead until smooth and elastic. Place in oiled bowl, turning to oil all sides. Cover with cloth and put in warm place to rise until doubled. Return to board and shape into 2 round loaves. Place on greased cookie sheet and sprinkle with corn meal. Cover with damp cloth and let rise 1 hour. Bake 30 to 40 minutes at 375° or until brown.

Yield: 2 loaves   R. Stuart Schmitz
                                                                   Gulf Shores, Alabama

Processor French Bread

1½ packages dry yeast
2 teaspoons sugar, divided
1½ cups warm water, divided

3½ cups all-purpose flour
2 teaspoons salt

Put yeast and 1 teaspoon sugar into ½ cup warm water. Let stand 5 minutes or until foamy. Combine flour, salt, remaining sugar, and yeast mixture in food processor, fitted with knife blade. Pour 1 cup warm water slowly through feeder tube. Let machine run 15 to 20 seconds. Add more flour if dough is too soft to form ball on blade. Place dough ball on lightly floured board. Divide in half and shape into cylinders 8 to 10 inches long. Cover and let rise in warm place until doubled (about 45 minutes). Place in preheated 450° oven on middle rack with pan of boiling water on lower rack. Bake 10 minutes, reduce oven heat to 400°, and bake 15 minutes longer. Turn out on rack to cool.

Yield: 2 loaves

Silent Butler
Ann Bond
Alice Clayton
Di Wall

Honey Wheat Bread

1½ cups water
1 cup cottage cheese
½ cup honey
¼ cup margarine
5½ to 6 cups all-purpose
    flour, divided

2 tablespoons sugar
3 teaspoons salt
2 packages dry yeast
1 egg
1 cup whole wheat flour

Heat water, cottage cheese, honey, and margarine until warm. Combine with 2 cups all-purpose flour, sugar, salt, yeast, and egg. Beat 2 minutes at medium speed. Stir in remaining all-purpose and wheat flours. Knead 10 minutes. Let rise 1 to 1½ hours. Punch down and put in two 8½- x 4½-inch loafpans. Let rise again. Bake 45 minutes at 350°.

Yield: 2 loaves

Conni Hanson Collins (Mrs. Townsend S.)

Portuguese Sweet Bread

2 packages dry yeast
½ cup warm water
1 cup milk
½ cup margarine
2 teaspoons salt

6 eggs
1½ cups sugar
8 to 9 cups all-purpose
   flour, divided
Melted butter

In a large bowl, sprinkle yeast into warm water. Scald milk. Add margarine and salt, and cool to lukewarm. Combine eggs and sugar, beating until light. Add milk mixture and yeast. Gradually beat in 3 cups flour with a wooden spoon. Stir in enough additional flour to make a soft dough that leaves side of bowl. Turn dough onto floured surface. Knead, adding additional flour as necessary until smooth and elastic. Place in an oiled bowl, turning to oil top. Cover with plastic wrap and let rise in a warm place 1½ to 2 hours. Punch down. Let rest 10 minutes. Divide dough into thirds and shape each into a smooth ball. Flatten each ball into 9-inch rounds. Press into 3 greased 9-inch round cake pans. Cover and let rise in a warm place 1 hour or until doubled in bulk. Bake 30 minutes at 350° or until well browned. Brush with melted butter while still hot. Cool before slicing.

Yield: 3 loaves   Preston Pratt Gentry (Mrs. Edgar C., Jr.)

Whole Wheat Bread

2 packages dry yeast
2¾ cups warm water, divided
½ cup firmly packed
   brown sugar

1 tablespoon salt
¼ cup vegetable shortening
6 to 7 cups whole wheat flour

Dissolve yeast in ½ cup warm water. Combine remaining water, brown sugar, salt, and shortening with yeast mixture. Gradually add flour until mixture forms a manageable dough. Knead 10 minutes. Let rise 1½ hours in warm place. Punch down, divide dough, and place in two 8½- x 4½- x 2⅝-inch loafpans. Let rise until doubled. Bake 45 minutes in preheated 350° oven.

Yield: 2 loaves   Conni Hanson Collins (Mrs. Townsend S.)

Monkey Bread

1 cup milk
1 cup butter, divided
1 package dry yeast
½ cup warm water
½ cup sugar

½ teaspoon salt
2 eggs
3 cups all-purpose flour,
   divided

Scald milk and ½ cup butter; cool. Dissolve yeast in water and combine with sugar, salt, eggs, and 1½ cups flour. Beat with mixer. Add remaining flour and beat. Cover with damp towel and put in refrigerator overnight. Melt remaining butter and pour in two small loaf pans. Spoon dough on top of butter. Let rise 2 hours or until dough reaches top of pan. Bake 40 minutes at 375° or until top is golden brown.

Note: If baked ahead, warm at 300° before serving.

Yield: 2 small loaves   Wanda Schmitz
                                                  Cincinnati, Ohio

Entrée Crêpes

1 cup water
1 cup milk
4 eggs
2 cups all-purpose flour

½ teaspoon salt
4 tablespoons butter, melted
Addional butter for cooking

Put water, milk, eggs, flour, salt, and 4 tablespoons butter in blender and blend 1 minute. Refrigerate 2 hours. Cook in crêpe pan, using clarified butter to season pan. Pour about ¼ cup batter into pan at a time. Quickly tilt pan to coat evenly and pour off excess immediately. When crêpe is light brown on first side, loosen and turn. Brown for about 30 seconds on other side. Stack crêpes onto plate. Crêpes can be stacked and frozen.

Yield: 30 crêpes

Breads 97

Almond Coffee Cake

¾ cup butter, melted
1½ cups sugar
2 eggs
1½ cups sifted all-purpose flour

Pinch salt
1 teaspoon almond extract
⅓ cup slivered almonds
1½ teaspoons sugar

Preheat oven to 350°. Line 10-inch iron skillet with aluminum foil. Combine butter and 1½ cups sugar. Add eggs one at a time. Add flour, salt, and almond extract. Mix well and pour into prepared skillet. Sprinkle with almonds and 1½ teaspoons sugar. Bake 30 to 40 minutes or until golden brown. Let cool 1 hour before cutting.

Yield: 8 to 10 servings   Judith Stephens Frost (Mrs. Robert B.)

Almond Danish

Pastry:
½ cup margarine
1 cup all-purpose flour

2 tablespoons water

Filling:
½ cup margarine
1 cup water
1 teaspoon almond extract

1 cup all-purpose flour
3 eggs, well beaten

Frosting:
1½ cups confectioners' sugar
2 tablespoons butter, softened
1½ teaspoons almond extract

1½ tablespoons warm water
1 (2½-ounce) package sliced
  almonds

Preheat oven to 350°.

For pastry, combine margarine, flour, and water in food processor until well blended. Divide mixture in half and pat onto cookie sheet in two 12- x 3-inch rectangles. Set aside.

For filling, melt margarine, add water, and bring to rolling boil. Remove and add almond extract and flour. Stir over low heat until mixture forms ball (about 1 minute). Remove from heat and add eggs. Stir until smooth. Divide mixture in half and spread over pastry rectangles. Bake 1 hour or until top is crisp and brown. Cool.

For frosting, mix all ingredients except almonds and drizzle over top of each cooled pastry rectangle. Sprinkle with almonds.

Yield: 12 to 16 servings   Suzanne Wood Fletcher

Cream Cheese Braid

1 cup sour cream
½ cup sugar
1 teaspoon salt
½ cup butter, melted
2 packages dry yeast
½ cup warm water

2 eggs, beaten
4 cups all-purpose flour
Cream Cheese Filling
  (recipe follows)
Glaze (recipe follows)

Heat sour cream over low heat. Stir in sugar, salt, and butter; cool to lukewarm. In a large bowl, sprinkle yeast over warm water and stir until yeast dissolves. Add sour cream mixture, eggs, and flour; mix well. Cover tightly and refrigerate overnight. The next day divide dough into 4 parts and roll out each part on a floured board into a 12- x 8-inch rectangle. Spread ¼ of Cream Cheese Filling on each. Roll up jelly roll fashion beginning with long sides. Pinch edges together and fold ends under slightly. Place rolls seam side down on greased baking sheets. Make V-shaped slits at 1-inch intervals two-thirds of the way through the dough. Cover and let rise in a warm place for 1 hour. Bake at 375° for 12 to 15 minutes. Spread with glaze while warm.

Cream Cheese Filling:

2 (8-ounce) packages cream
  cheese, softened
¾ cup sugar

1 egg, beaten
⅛ teaspoon salt
2 teaspoons vanilla

Thoroughly combine all ingredients and use as directed.

Glaze:

2 cups confectioners' sugar
4 tablespoons milk

2 teaspoons vanilla

Combine ingredients and use as directed.

Yield: 4 braids   Ann Calhoun McMurray (Mrs. R. F.)

Christmas Gift Coffee Cake Pie

1 cup margarine
1 cup sugar
2 eggs
1 teaspoon vanilla
2 cups all-purpose flour

1 teaspoon soda
½ teaspoon salt
1 teaspoon baking powder
1 cup sour cream
Topping (recipe follows)

Preheat oven to 350°. Grease and flour two 8- or 9-inch disposable pie pans. Cream margarine and sugar. Add eggs and vanilla, and mix well. Sift together flour, soda, salt, and baking powder. Add dry ingredients to creamed mixture alternating with sour cream. Place half of batter mixture in each pie pan. Sprinkle half of topping on each pie and cut into batter with knife. Bake 25 minutes.

Topping:

¼ cup firmly packed brown sugar
¼ cup granulated sugar

½ cup chopped pecans
1 tablespoon cinnamon

Combine topping ingredients and use as directed.

Yield: 8 servings   Margie Cooley Jones (Mrs. Wm. W.)

Funnel Cakes

Jean Nelson is known regionally for her Funnel Cakes and is a popular food vendor each year on Market Square Mall during Knoxville's Dogwood Arts Festival.

3 eggs
2 cups milk
¼ cup sugar
3 to 4 cups all-purpose flour

½ teaspoon salt
2 teaspoons baking powder
Vegetable oil
Confectioners' sugar

Beat eggs; add milk and sugar. Sift together 2 cups flour, salt, and baking powder. Combine dry ingredients with milk mixture in blender or food processor until smooth. Add 1 to 2 cups remaining flour to thicken batter. (Batter should be a consistency to pass slowly through funnel.) Pour oil to ¾-inch depth in 8-inch skillet and heat to 375°. Pour ¼ cup batter into funnel, holding finger over end until batter can be released into hot oil. Release batter in lacy pattern into oil. Brown on both sides. Drain and sprinkle with confectioners' sugar.

Yield: 12 servings   Jean Nelson (Mrs. James J.)

English Scones

2 cups self rising flour
¼ teaspoon salt
¼ teaspoon soda
Pinch ground cardamon
1 cup sugar
¼ cup butter, unsalted

2 eggs, beaten
⅓ cup sour cream
½ cup raisins
Strawberry Butter
　(recipe follows)

Combine flour, salt, soda, cardamon, sugar, and sift.With hands, work butter into flour mixture until blended. Combine eggs (reserving 1 tablespoon), sour cream, and raisins, and add to flour mixture, stirring to moisten. Turn out onto floured surface and knead 6 to 10 times. Shape into 2 balls and flatten each to 1-inch thickness on greased cookie sheet. Score dough all the way through in wedges with floured knife. Brush with reserved egg and bake 10 to 15 minutes at 450°. Serve with Strawberry Butter and jam.

Strawberry Butter:

½ cup unsalted butter
7 to 10 fresh strawberries

2 tablespoons confectioners'
　sugar

Combine all ingredients in food processor and use as directed.

Yield: 16 servings   Bobbie Underwood (Mrs. Al)

French Pancakes

¾ cup all-purpose flour
½ teaspoon salt
6 tablespoons sugar
1 cup milk

4 eggs
6 tablespoons butter, melted
Jam
Confectioners' sugar

Mix flour, salt, and sugar. Add milk and blend well. Beat in eggs, one at a time. Add butter and mix well. Set aside 20 minutes. Heat small amount of oil in 8- or 10-inch skillet. Pour ⅓ cup batter in crêpe-like fashion into hot skillet. Brown lightly on one side and turn. Remove to plate and spread thinly with jam. Roll up and sprinkle with confectioners' sugar. Repeat process with remaining batter.

Note: Sweet crêpe-like pancakes delicious for breakfast or even dessert.

Yield: 12 pancakes   Nancy Bramblett Schreeder (Mrs. Charles)

Moravian Sugar Cake

2 packages dry yeast
½ cup lukewarm potato water
½ cup sugar
¼ teaspoon salt
¾ cup melted butter
1 egg plus 1 egg yolk,
   well beaten

½ to ¾ cup hot
   mashed potatoes
2¾ cups sifted
   all-purpose flour
Topping
   (recipe follows)

In a large bowl, sprinkle yeast over potato water. Stir until dissolved. Add sugar, salt, butter, eggs, and mashed potatoes. Blend thoroughly. Add half of flour and work with hands until smooth. Add remaining flour and mix well. Cover bowl with foil and refrigerate at least 14 hours. Turn dough into 15- x 10-inch greased jelly-roll pan. Spread evenly with floured fingers. Let rise in warm place about 2 hours or until doubled. (Cake should not be over 1½ inches thick when ready to bake.) Preheat oven to 350-375°. Punch impressions in dough using knuckles and fingers. Spoon topping into impressions.Bake 20 to 25 minutes. Serve hot or cold.

Topping:

1½ cups firmly packed brown sugar
1 cup melted butter

1 teaspoon cinnamon

Combine and use as directed.

Note: Topping ingredients may be increased to taste.

Yield: 12 servings

Melissa Cooley Gill

Big Orange Country Waffles

2 eggs, separated
½ cup orange juice
½ cup milk
2 tablespoons grated orange peel
1½ cups cake flour
2 tablespoons sugar

2½ teaspoons baking powder
½ teaspoon salt
½ cup chopped pecans
6 tablespoons butter,
   melted and cooled

Preheat waffle iron. In large bowl, beat egg yolks until thick and lemon-colored. Add orange juice, milk, and grated orange peel. Sift together flour, sugar, baking powder, and salt. Beat flour mixture into yolk mixture at medium speed until well-blended. Stir in pecans and melted butter. Beat egg whites until stiff and fold into batter. Pour into waffle iron and cook.

Yield: 3 waffles

Pat Campen Medley (Mrs. Mark A.)

Sausage Wheel with Syrup

1 (14-ounce) jar spiced apple
   rings
1 (8-ounce) package link sausage
1 tablespoon plus ½ cup
   vegetable oil, divided
1 egg, beaten
½ cup firmly packed light
   brown sugar

1 cup buttermilk
1 cup quick-cooking oats
1 cup all-purpose flour
1 teaspoon baking powder
½ teaspoon salt
½ teaspoon soda
Syrup (recipe follows)

Preheat oven to 400°. Drain apple rings. (Reserve liquid for syrup.) Brown
sausage in 1 tablespoon oil. Arrange sausage in spokes in greased 10-inch
iron skillet. Put 1 apple ring in center. Combine ½ cup oil and remaining
ingredients except apples. Stir until moist. Drop half of batter by
tablespoons between sausages. Spread. Place apple rings on top. Spread
remaining batter over apples. Bake 20 to 25 minutes. Turn out onto serving
platter like upside-down cake. Serve in wedges with hot syrup.

*Note: If making ahead, turn out onto foil. Cool and wrap well. Reheat,
wrapped, on cookie sheet for ease in handling.*

Syrup:

Reserved apple ring liquid plus
   water to make 1 cup

1 cup sugar
2 tablespoons butter

Combine liquid and sugar. Boil. Remove from heat and add butter. Use as
directed. Syrup may be refrigerated and reheated.

Yield: 6 to 8 servings   Betsy Boden McGehee (Mrs. Larry)

Eggs·Cheeses·Grains

Shrimp-Crab Stuffed Eggs

18 hard-cooked eggs
1 (6½-ounce) package frozen
   shrimp, thawed and drained
1 (6-ounce) package frozen
   crabmeat, thawed and drained
⅔ cup mayonnaise

1 tablespoon chili sauce
1 tablespoon grated onion
1 tablespoon finely chopped
   green pepper
1 teaspoon chopped pimiento
Parsley (optional)

Halve eggs, remove yolks, and place in small mixing bowl. Mash egg yolks
and blend with remaining ingredients except parsley. Stuff egg whites with
yolk mixture and garnish with parsley.

Yield: 3 dozen   Mimi McCammon Bury (Mrs. Fred)

Brunch Dish

Canadian bacon slices
Swiss cheese slices
Eggs

Light cream
Parmesan cheese

Preheat oven to 450°. Line 8- or 9-inch oven-proof dish with Canadian
bacon. Place layer of Swiss cheese over each bacon slice. Break one egg over
each slice; then drizzle cream over eggs until eggs peek through. Put into
oven for 10 minutes. Take out and sprinkle with Parmesan cheese. Return to
oven 3 to 5 minutes. Cut into squares and serve immediately.

Yield: 4 to 6 servings   Mimi McCammon Bury (Mrs. Fred)

Curried Eggs

5 tablespoons butter
5 tablespoons all-purpose flour
2½ cups milk
1 teaspoon curry powder
Salt and pepper to taste
1 pound fresh mushrooms,
   sliced and sautéed

1 (8-ounce) can water chestnuts,
   drained and sliced
¾ cup grated Parmesan or Romano
   cheese or combination of both
8 hard-cooked eggs, sliced
Pepperidge Farm Dressing or
   buttered bread crumbs

Preheat oven to 325°. Make cream sauce using butter, flour, and milk. When
thick add curry powder, salt, and pepper. Stir in sautéed mushrooms, water
chestnuts, and cheese; combine well. Make layers of eggs and cream sauce
in 2-quart oven-proof dish. Top with dressing or bread crumbs. Bake 30
minutes or until bubbly and bread crumbs are brown.

Yield: 8 servings   Virginia Black Snoddy (Mrs. E. C.)

Egg-Spinach Brunch Dish

6 hard-cooked eggs,
 sliced lengthwise
½ (12-ounce) package Stouffer's
 Spinach Soufflé

½ small onion, grated
1 (10-ounce) package Stouffer's
 Welsh Rarebit or
 homemade cheese sauce

Remove egg yolks and mash. Cook spinach soufflé with added grated onion according to package directions and mix with egg yolks. Stuff egg whites with mixture. Place eggs in greased baking dish and cover with Welsh Rarebit or homemade cheese sauce. Bake 15 minutes at 350°.

Yield: 6 servings

Lois Jourolmon

Eggs Florentine

¼ cup butter
¼ cup all-purpose flour
1 cup milk
1 cup whipping cream
Salt and pepper to taste

2 (10-ounce) packages frozen spinach,
 cooked and drained, or 1½ pounds
 fresh spinach, cooked and drained
¼ teaspoon nutmeg
12 eggs, poached
Grated Parmesan cheese

In small saucepan, melt butter, add flour, and stir until blended. Meanwhile, bring milk and cream to boil and add all at once to roux, stirring vigorously until thickened. Season with salt and pepper. Combine spinach with ½ cup prepared sauce and add nutmeg. Spread spinach mixture into 9- x 13-inch oven-proof dish and arrange eggs on top. Spoon remaining sauce over eggs, sprinkle with Parmesan cheese, and brown lightly under broiler or bake at 400° until brown.

Yield: 6 servings

Jeanne Holmes Hyatt (Mrs. Hugh C.)

Kentucky Derby Eggs

½ cup chopped onion
2 tablespoons butter
2 tablespoons all-purpose flour
1¼ cups milk

1 cup shredded cheese
6 hard-cooked eggs, sliced
1½ cups crushed potato chips
10 slices bacon, fried and crumbled

Preheat oven to 350°. Cook onion in butter until tender. Blend in flour and add milk. Cook until thick. Add cheese and stir until melted. In a 10- x 6-inch baking dish, layer half of the eggs, cheese sauce, potato chips, and bacon. Repeat layers. Bake 30 minutes.

Yield: 8 servings

Conni Hanson Collins (Mrs. Townsend S.)

Mountain Breakfast

6 slices bacon
6 eggs
Salt and pepper to taste
1 tablespoon butter or
  margarine, divided

¼ cup half and half cream,
  divided
3 English muffins, halved

Preheat oven to 350°. Partially cook bacon; drain on paper towel until slightly cool. Place 1-inch bacon strips in bottom of muffin tin cups. Wrap remaining bacon strip around side of muffin tin. Break egg in center of each. Top each with salt and pepper, then with ½ teaspoon butter and 2 teaspoons cream. Bake 15 to 25 minutes. Loosen edges with knife before removing. Serve on buttered, toasted English muffins.

Yield: 6 servings   Priscilla Brandau Siler (Mrs. Tom A.)

Saucy Mushrooms and Eggs

1 pound fresh mushrooms, sliced
½ cup finely chopped onion
¼ cup butter or margarine
1 (10¾-ounce) can cream of
  mushroom soup, undiluted
¼ cup chopped fresh parsley

¼ teaspoon white pepper
6 hard-cooked eggs, chopped
2 (10-ounce) packages frozen
  patty shells, baked
Paprika

Sauté mushrooms and onions in butter in large skillet about 5 minutes. Stir in soup, parsley, and pepper. Cook until bubbly, stirring constantly. Reduce heat and stir in eggs. Cook until mixture is heated thoroughly. Spoon filling into patty shells. Sprinkle with paprika.

Yield: 12 servings   Barbara Brook Eldridge (Mrs. Robert C., Jr.)

Sausage Apple Ring

2 pounds bulk sausage
1½ cups cracker crumbs
2 eggs, slightly beaten
½ cup milk

¼ cup minced onion
1 cup finely chopped apple
Scrambled eggs

Preheat oven to 350°. Combine all ingredients except scrambled eggs. Mix thoroughly and press into slightly greased ring mold, then turn out onto shallow pan. Bake 1 hour. (May be partially baked 30 minutes, then finished later.) Fill center with scrambled eggs and sprinkle with paprika.

Yield: 6 to 8 servings   Preston Pratt Gentry (Mrs. Edgar C., Jr.)

Allen's Eggs

8 slices bread, buttered and
  crust removed
2 cups grated sharp Cheddar cheese
1 teaspoon prepared mustard

1 tablespoon Worcestershire sauce
¼ teaspoon Tabasco sauce
2 cups milk
4 eggs, beaten

Grease a 9½- x 11-inch oven-proof dish. Cube bread and place in dish. Combine remaining ingredients and pour over bread. Refrigerate overnight. Bake in pan of water 1 hour at 350°.

Yield: 8 servings   Jane Newman Bankston

Make-Ahead Breakfast

1 pound sausage
2 slices bread, cubed
1 cup grated Cheddar cheese
6 eggs

2 cups milk
½ teaspoon salt
1 teaspoon dry mustard

Fry sausage, drain, and crumble. Layer cubed bread, cheese, and sausage in 9- x 13-inch oven-proof dish. Combine remaining ingredients. Pour over layers and refrigerate overnight. Bake 45 minutes at 350° or until set, puffy, and brown on top.

Yield: 8 to 10 servings   Anne Keller Walters (Mrs. Charles M.)

Swiss Eggs

4 tablespoons butter or margarine
1 cup grated Swiss cheese, divided
4 to 6 eggs

Cayenne pepper
Salt
¼ cup whipping cream

Preheat oven to 350°. Spread bottom of round 10-inch oven-proof dish with butter. Cover with ¾ cup cheese. Break eggs over cheese without breaking yolks. Season with cayenne and salt. Drizzle cream over surface and sprinkle with remaining cheese. Bake approximately 15 minutes.

Yield: 4 to 6 servings   Aelise Houston Keever (Mrs. John A.)

Bleu Cheese Soufflé

2 tablespoons butter
2½ tablespoons all-purpose flour
¾ cup milk, scalded
3 egg yolks, slightly beaten
1 (4-ounce) package Bleu cheese

½ teaspoon salt
4 egg whites
¼ teaspoon cream of tartar
¼ cup chopped pecans

Preheat oven to 400°. Butter and flour 1-quart casserole. Melt butter, add flour, and cook 3 to 5 minutes. Add milk, egg yolks, cheese, and salt. Beat egg whites with cream of tartar until stiff and shiny, but not dry. Fold egg whites and pecans into cheese mixture. Pour into prepared casserole and bake 15 to 18 minutes.

Note: Can cook either very done or soft—excellent both ways! If prepared in individual ramkins, cook 10 minutes.

Yield: 4 servings   Wanda H. Schmitz
                                                           Cincinnati, Ohio

Spinach Puff

Grated Parmesan cheese
¼ cup butter
2 cups shredded fresh spinach
1 green onion, thinly sliced
¼ cup all-purpose flour

½ teaspoon salt
Dash Tabasco sauce
1 cup milk
1 cup grated Swiss cheese
4 eggs, separated

Preheat oven to 350°. Generously butter a 1½-quart soufflé dish and sprinkle with Parmesan cheese. Melt butter in a skillet or saucepan. Add spinach and green onion. Cook until spinach is wilted (about 2 minutes). Blend in flour, salt, and Tabasco. Gradually add milk and cook, stirring constantly, until sauce comes to a boil and thickens. Remove from heat and stir in cheese until melted. Set aside to cool slightly. Beat egg yolks and add a small amount of creamed spinach to yolks, beating constantly. Add egg yolks to spinach. In a separate bowl, beat egg whites until stiff. Fold ⅓ of egg whites into spinach mixture. Fold in remaining egg whites just until blended. Carefully spoon mixture into prepared soufflé dish. Bake 30 to 40 minutes or until lightly browned. Serve at once.

Yield: 4 to 6 servings   Jo Ann Cattlett McCallen (Mrs. Perry)

Broccoli Soufflé

1½ cups cooked chopped broccoli
½ cup whipping cream
½ cup bouillon
⅓ cup butter
¼ cup all-purpose flour

3 eggs, separated
1 teaspoon finely minced parsley
1 teaspoon finely minced onion
Salt and pepper to taste
⅓ cup grated Cheddar cheese

Preheat oven to 425°. Butter a 2-quart soufflé dish. Purée cooked broccoli in food processor. Scald cream with bouillon. Melt butter, blend in flour, and gradually stir into cream and bouillon until thickened. Remove from heat, add yolks, parsley, onions, salt, and pepper. Stir in broccoli purée and grated cheese. Beat egg whites until stiff and fold into broccoli mixture. Turn into prepared dish and bake 25 to 30 minutes. Serve immediately.

Yield: 8 servings

Cheryl Sherling Magli (Mrs. Boyce)
Spring Hill, Tennessee

Beef-Sausage Quiche

2 (9-inch) unbaked pie shells
¼ pound ground beef
¼ pound sausage
½ cup mayonnaise
½ cup milk
2 to 3 eggs
1 tablespoon cornstarch
½ pound Monterey Jack
  cheese, grated

½ pound medium sharp
  cheese, grated
1 (4-ounce) can mushrooms
½ cup chopped green onions
Salt
Pepper
Oregano
Rosemary
Basil

Preheat oven to 400°. Prick bottom of pie shells with fork and bake 8 minutes. Remove pie shells and reduce heat to 350°. Brown ground beef and sausage; drain well. Mix mayonnaise, milk, eggs, cornstarch, grated cheeses, mushrooms, and onions. Add seasonings to taste. Add meat. Place in pie shells. Bake 40 to 45 minutes or until centers are firm.

Yield: 10 to 12 servings

Courtney Carmichael Jackson (Mrs. J. Presley)

Mexican Quiche

10-inch unbaked pie shell
2 tablespoons melted butter
1 (8-ounce) package cream cheese,
  diced
2 (4-ounce) cans chopped
  green chilies

1 cup grated Swiss, Cheddar,
  or Jack cheese
5 eggs
1½ cups whipping cream
½ teaspoon salt
Dash pepper

Preheat oven to 425°. Brush pie shell with butter and arrange cream cheese over bottom. Refrigerate until butter is set. Drain chilies on paper towels. Sprinkle chilies over cream cheese and top with grated cheese. Combine eggs, cream, and seasonings, beating until well blended. Evenly pour egg mixture over all. Bake 15 minutes. Reduce heat to 350° and bake 30 minutes or until inserted knife comes out clean. Cool 5 to 10 minutes before cutting.

Yield: 6 to 8 servings   Swann Brown McMillan (Mrs. William Albert)

Onion Pie

3 cups chopped onion
¼ cup butter
1 (9- to 10-inch) deep dish
  pie crust, baked
2 cups grated Swiss cheese

3 eggs, well beaten
1 cup milk, scalded
⅛ teaspoon cayenne pepper
1 tablespoon all-purpose flour
1 teaspoon salt

Preheat oven to 350°. Sauté onion in butter. Pour onion into baked pie shell. Combine remaining ingredients and pour over onion. Bake 40 minutes.

Note: Vidalia onions are best, if available.

Yield: 6 servings   Julia Bedinger Huster (Mrs. Edwin C., Jr.)

Spinach Pie

1 (10½-ounce) package frozen
  chopped spinach
4 tablespoons butter, melted
1 cup cottage cheese
3 eggs, slightly beaten
½ cup grated Parmesan cheese

½ cup whipping cream
1 teaspoon nutmeg
1 teaspoon salt
½ teaspoon pepper
1 (9-inch) unbaked pastry shell

Preheat oven to 350°. Cook, drain, and cool spinach. Combine butter, cottage cheese, eggs, Parmesan cheese, cream, and seasonings. Add to spinach and pour into pastry. Bake 30 minutes.

Yield: 6 servings   Letty Bartlett Taylor (Mrs. George C.)

Zucchini Quiche

2 cups zucchini, thinly sliced
1 cup sliced onion
1 clove garlic, minced
3 tablespoons olive oil
1½ teaspoons salt

1 (10-inch) unbaked pie shell
4 eggs, beaten
1 cup milk
1 cup whipping cream
½ cup grated Mozzarella cheese

Preheat oven to 375°. Sauté zucchini, onions, and garlic in olive oil. Spread over bottom of pie shell. Combine remaining ingredients and pour into pie shell. Bake 30 to 35 minutes until crust is set. Serve hot or cold. (If using 9-inch frozen pie shell, alter milk and cream to ¾ cup each.)

Yield: 6 servings   Catherine Baer Ambrose (Mrs. WIlliam L.)

South Carolina Okra Pilaf

4 slices bacon, diced
1 onion, chopped
1 tablespoon minced
   green pepper
2 cups stewed tomatoes

2 cups thinly sliced okra
Salt and pepper to taste
2 cups rice
2 quarts water
1 teaspoon salt

Cook bacon in deep frying pan until golden brown. Remove bacon. Fry onion and green pepper in bacon fat until brown. Add tomatoes and okra and cook until reduced, stirring occasionally. Season with salt and pepper. Cook rice 12 minutes in water to which salt has been added. Drain. Mix rice with tomato mixture and pour into top of double boiler. Let steam 15 to 20 minutes or until rice is tender and thoroughly flavored with tomato. Add bacon and serve.

Note: Tomato mixture can be prepared ahead and reheated before adding to rice. Recrisp bacon in warm oven.

Yield: 6 to 8 servings   Mary E. Heatherington Lutz (Mrs. John E.)

Sour Cream Rice

1 cup rice
Salt
Sugar

12 ounces Cheddar cheese, grated
Crushed red pepper
1 pint sour cream

Cook rice. Place layer of cooked rice in bottom of 1-quart oven-proof dish. Sprinkle with salt and sugar, and add layer of cheese. Sprinkle with red pepper. Repeat layers. Spread top with sour cream and sprinkle with remaining cheese. Bake 25 to 30 minutes at 350°.

Yield: 4 to 6 servings   Retta Finley Wood (Mrs. Van H.)

Charleston Red Rice

2 onions, finely chopped
4 tablespoons margarine, divided
1 (8-ounce) can tomato paste
2 cups water

3 teaspoon salt
2 teaspoons sugar
1 cup uncooked rice
4 strips bacon, cooked crisp

Sauté onions in 2 tablespoons margarine until tender. Add tomato paste, water, salt, and sugar. Cook slowly, uncovered, for 10 minutes until reduced to 2 cups. Add rice and remaining margarine. Cook slowly 30 to 45 minutes. Add bacon and serve.

Yield: 6 to 8 servings   Charlsie James Proffitt (Mrs. Douglas W.)
Tampa, Florida

Pilaf á la Valenciennes

¼ cup chopped onion
¼ cup chopped green pepper
¼ cup sliced mushrooms
1 small zucchini, thinly sliced
¾ cup peeled and diced
  eggplant
1 tomato, peeled and chopped
1 garlic clove, crushed

½ cup butter
1 teaspoon salt
½ teaspoon monosodium glutamate
½ teaspoon paprika
1 cup rice
⅓ cup frozen peas
⅓ cup pimiento strips
1¾ cups chicken stock

Sauté in butter onion, green pepper, mushrooms, zucchini, eggplant, tomato, and garlic approximately 10 minutes. Add remaining ingredients and simmer approximately 30 minutes.

Yield: 6 to 8 servings   Reprinted from *Culinary Classics*,
by Gloria Preston Olson,
Charter House Publishers, Inc.

Rice Supreme

6 tablespoons margarine
1 medium onion, chopped
1¼ cups uncooked rice
1 (10½-ounce) can beef
  consommé
1 (10½-ounce) can water

1 teaspoon salt
½ teaspoon pepper
½ cup slivered almonds
1 (2-ounce) can chopped
  mushrooms, drained

Preheat oven to 350°. Melt margarine and sauté onions. Add remaining ingredients and mix well. Pour into 1½-quart oven-proof dish. Cover and bake 1 hour, stirring once.

Yield: 4 to 6 servings   Judith Stephens Frost (Mrs. Robert B.)

Wild Rice with Mushrooms

½ pound wild rice
¾ pound fresh mushrooms, sliced
½ cup margarine
2 tablespoons all-purpose flour

1 cup whipping cream
½ cup sherry
Salt to taste
1 cup buttered bread crumbs

Preheat oven to 350°. Generously grease 2-quart oven-proof dish. Cook and steam rice and set aside. Sauté mushrooms in butter. Add flour and cream, stirring constantly, until thickened. Remove from heat and stir in rice, sherry, and salt. Place mixture in prepared dish and top with buttered crumbs. Bake 20 to 30 minutes or until heated through.

Note: If this is to be reheated, add more cream.

Yield: 8 servings   Rose "Posey" Stewart Congleton (Mrs. Joseph)

Garlic Grits Soufflé

2 cups grits
8 cups water
½ cup butter
1 teaspoon salt
1 tube Kraft garlic cheese
4 egg yolks, beaten well

4 egg whites, beaten stiff
Cracker or bread crumbs
½ to 1 cup grated sharp
  Cheddar cheese
Paprika

Preheat oven to 350°. Grease 3-quart oven-proof dish. Cook grits in water with butter and salt until done. Add cheese and cook until melted. Add egg yolks and stir well. Fold in egg whites and pour in prepared dish. Sprinkle crumbs, cheese, and paprika on top. Bake 40 minutes.

Yield: 8 servings   Cassandra (Candy) Johnson Brownlow (Mrs. William G.)

Jalapeño Grits

6 ounces processed Jalapeño
  cheese
1 (6-ounce) tube garlic cheese
4 cups water

1 teaspoon salt
1 cup uncooked grits
¼ cup butter

Preheat oven to 350°. Tear cheese into small pieces. Combine water and salt; bring to boil. Slowly add grits and bring to second boil; reduce heat and cook over medium heat 4 or 5 minutes, stirring often. Add cheese and butter to grits, stirring until thoroughly combined. Pour into ungreased 1½-quart casserole and bake uncovered 30 minutes.

Yield: 6 servings   Jeanne Holmes Hyatt (Mrs. Hugh C.)

Fine Spaghetti with Green Sauce

2 tablespoons basil
2 tablespoons parsley flakes
¼ cup butter, softened
1 (8-ounce) package cream cheese,
   softened
⅓ cup grated Parmesan cheese

¼ cup olive oil
1 clove garlic, crushed
½ teaspoon pepper
⅔ cup boiling water
1 (10-ounce) package spaghetti,
   cooked

Combine basil, parsley, and butter. Blend in cream cheese, Parmesan cheese, olive oil, garlic, and pepper. Add water, stirring until smooth. Place hot spaghetti on warm platter and cover with sauce. If desired, pass additional Parmesan cheese.

Yield: 6 servings   Betty DuPree (Mrs. William)

Cold Pasta - New Orleans Style

1 (3-pound) chicken
½ pound vermicelli or spaghetti
1 cup Salad Dressing with
   Garlic (recipe follows)
1 cup mayonnaise (recipe follows)
1 (14-ounce) can artichoke hearts
1 avocado, cut in wedges

12 cherry tomatoes or
   tomato slices
Mushrooms á la Greque
   (recipe follows)
Chopped scallion
Parsley

Cook chicken, debone, cut into bite-size pieces, and set aside. Reserve 2 tablespoons broth for Mushrooms á la Greque. Cook pasta according to package directions and drain well. Place warm pasta in bowl and add ⅓ cup Salad Dressing with Garlic and toss. Cool. Cover and refrigerate overnight. Add chicken and mayonnaise to pasta, tossing to blend. Set aside. Place artichokes, avocado slices, and tomatoes in separate bowls; add equal parts of remaining Salad Dressing with Garlic to each. Stir to coat vegetables with dressing.

To serve, mound pasta mixture on round serving platter. Garnish with Mushrooms á la Greque; arrange artichoke hearts, avocado slices, and cherry tomatoes around pasta. Sprinkle with scallion and parsley.

Salad Dressing with Garlic:

¼ cup wine vinegar
2 teaspoons Dijon mustard
2 teaspoons finely chopped garlic

1 teaspoon paprika
Salt and pepper to taste
1 cup olive or vegetable oil

In mixing bowl combine all ingredients except oil. Gradually add oil, beating rapidly with wire whisk. Stir dressing prior to each use.

Mayonnaise:

1 egg yolk
1 tablespoon lemon juice
1 tablespoon Dijon mustard
Salt and pepper to taste

½ cup olive oil
½ cup vegetable oil
Dash Tabasco sauce

In mixing bowl combine egg yolk, lemon juice, mustard, salt, and pepper. Gradually add oil, beating rapidly with wire whisk (as mixture thickens oil can be added more rapidly). Add Tabasco and adjust seasonings.

Mushrooms á la Greque:

½ pound small fresh mushrooms
1½ tablespoons lemon juice
4½ tablespoons olive oil
½ teaspoon coriander seeds

1 small garlic clove, crushed
Salt and pepper
2 tablespoons reserved
  chicken broth

Place mushrooms in saucepan with lemon juice and stir to coat. Add remaining ingredients. Cover and cook 7 to 8 minutes, stirring occasionally. Uncover and cook over high heat about 5 minutes, stirring occasionally. Let cool.

Note: Everything except mushrooms can be prepared one day ahead and assembled just before serving.

Yield: 6 to 8 servings   Lucy J. Giesler

Pasta Con Pesto

2 cloves garlic
2 tablespoons basil
1 teaspoon salt
1 cup parsley
Ground pepper to taste
1 cup olive oil

2 tablespoons pine nuts
  or walnuts (optional)
8 ounces thin spaghetti,
  cooked and drained
2 tablespoons butter, melted
½ cup freshly grated
  Parmesan cheese

In blender or food processor, combine garlic, basil, salt, parsley, pepper, oil, and nuts. Pour mixture into saucepan and keep warm on range. Put drained spaghetti in 2-quart serving dish and stir in melted butter. Add cheese to heated sauce and combine with spaghetti. Mix well and serve immediately.

Yield: 6 servings   Ena Taylor Kirkpatrick (Mrs. David M.)

Stuffed Shell Macaroni

2 tablespoons vegetable oil
¼ cup minced onion
1 clove garlic, crushed
2 (8-ounce) cans tomato sauce
1 teaspoon salt, divided
Pepper to taste
1 teaspoon sugar
½ teaspoon basil
½ teaspoon oregano

2 (8-ounce) packages cream
  cheese
2 eggs
1 (8-ounce) package shredded
  Mozzarella cheese
2 tablespoons parsley
1 (12-ounce) package jumbo
  shell macaroni
Parmesan cheese

Preheat oven to 350°. Sauté onion and garlic in oil 2 to 3 minutes. Add tomato sauce, ½ teaspoon salt, pepper, sugar, basil, and oregano; simmer 10 minutes. Beat together cream cheese and eggs until smooth. Add Mozzarella cheese and mix well. Add parsley, ½ teaspoon salt, and pepper to creamed mixture. Cook shell macaroni according to package directions and drain well. Stuff shells with creamed mixture. Place half sauce on bottom of 9- x 13-inch baking dish; top with stuffed shells. Pour remaining sauce over shells and sprinkle Parmesan cheese over all. Bake 20 minutes.

Yield: 6 to 8 servings

Carol Pfeiffer Wachowski
North Huntington, Pennsylvania

Canneloni with Meat Filling

2 tablespoons olive oil
½ cup chopped onion
1 clove garlic, minced
1 carrot, grated
1 pound ground beef
¼ pound pork sausage
1½ teaspoons salt
½ teaspoon black pepper
½ cup dry red wine
1 cup beef broth

1 tablespoon tomato paste
2 egg yolks, beaten
¾ cup grated Parmesan
  cheese, separated
8 manicotti shells, cooked
2 cups medium white sauce
1 (6-ounce) package
  mozzarella cheese
2 tablespoons butter

Sauté onion, garlic, and carrot in hot olive oil 3 minutes. Add beef and sausage. Cook and stir over high heat until brown. Add salt, pepper, wine, broth, and tomato paste. Cover and cook over low heat 1 hour, stirring often. Drain meat and reserve gravy. Cool meat; then mix with egg yolks and half Parmesan cheese. Stuff shells and arrange in shallow casserole in single layer. Cover with gravy. Prepare medium white sauce; add mozzarella cheese and pour over stuffed shells. Sprinkle with remaining Parmesan cheese, dot with butter, and bake 20 minutes at 350° or until sauce bubbles.

Yield: 8 servings

Bette Rayson (Mrs. Ed)

Baked Manicotti

2 cups Italian Style meat sauce
8 stuffed Manicotti noodles
   (recipe follows)
8 tablespoons Creamy Swiss
   Cheese Sauce (recipe follows)

4 ounces sliced Mozzarella
   cheese
Grated Romano cheese

Preheat oven to 350°. Grease 9- x 13-inch oven-proof dish. Cover bottom of dish with meat sauce. Arrange Stuffed Manicotti Noodles over meat sauce and pour 1 tablespoon Creamy Swiss Cheese Sauce over each noodle. Cover with Mozzarella cheese. Sprinkle with Romano cheese and bake 20 minutes or until bubbly.

Stuffed Manicotti Noodles:

2 pounds ground beef
¼ pound pork sausge
1 small onion, finely chopped
1 clove garlic, minced
3 teaspoons monosodium glutamate
¼ teaspoon oregano
½ teaspoon salt

¼ teaspoon pepper
1 cup cooked spinach
2 eggs
¼ cup grated Romano cheese
1 cup dried bread crumbs
14 to 16 manicotti noodles,
   cooked

In heavy skillet, cook beef, sausage, onion, garlic, monosodium glutamate, oregano, salt, and pepper until browned. Add spinach. In blender liquefy eggs and cheese; add to meat mixture. Reduce heat and add bread crumbs, stirring until blended. Remove from heat and cool. Stuff noodles compactly with meat filling. Refrigerate or freeze.

Creamy Swiss Cheese Sauce:

2 tablespoons butter
1 tablespoon cornstarch
2 cups milk
1 teaspoon salt

Pinch white pepper
4 ounces American Swiss
   cheese, shredded

Melt butter over medium heat; blend in cornstarch. Add milk slowly, stirring constantly. Add salt, pepper, and cheese. Continue stirring until smooth. Chill and use as directed. Makes 1¼ cups.

Yield: 4 servings   Judy Hobson Maschmeyer (Mrs. William Michael)

Alberto's Pasta

From Ristorante Alberto, Messina, Sicily, Italy

2 cloves garlic, thinly sliced
2 tablespoons olive oil
4 tablespoons butter
1 cup broccoli florets
1 tablespoon fresh chopped basil
  or 1 teaspoon dried basil
⅓ cup dry white wine

⅔ cup tomato sauce or purée
¼ cup grated Parmesan cheese
1 (16-ounce) box Delmonico jumbo
  pasta shells, cooked
½ pint whipping cream
Salt and pepper

Sauté garlic slices in olive oil over medium heat until brown. Lower heat and remove garlic. Add butter, then broccoli, and toss in butter-oil mixture. Add basil; cover skillet, and steam 4 to 5 minutes, stirring once or twice. Add wine and cook uncovered until almost dry. Stir in tomato sauce and cheese. Cook and stir 2 to 3 minutes. Add cooked pasta and blend. Just before serving, add cream and cook over low heat until thick. Salt and pepper to taste. Serve immediately.

Yield: 4 to 6 servings   Donna Dukes Trimble (Mrs. William Scott, Jr.)

Lasagna

1 (3½-ounce) package sliced
  pepperoni
1 pound or more ground chuck
1 clove garlic, minced (optional)
1 (16-ounce) can tomatoes, drained
2 (6-ounce) cans tomato paste
1 tablespoon basil
3 (1-pint) cartons cottage cheese

½ cup grated Parmesan cheese
2 tablespoons parsley flakes
2 eggs, beaten
½ teaspoon salt
7 lasagna noodles
2 (8-ounce) packages sliced
  mozzarella cheese

Brown pepperoni in large skillet; remove and drain. Brown meat in same skillet. Return pepperoni to pan. Add garlic, tomatoes, tomato paste, and basil. Simmer uncovered 30 minutes, stirring occasionally. If mixture looks very dry, add dash of water or liquid from tomatoes. Combine cottage cheese, Parmesan cheese, parsley, eggs, and salt in large bowl and set aside. Cook noodles until tender; drain and rinse in cold water. Place 3½ noodles on bottom of 13- x 9-inch baking dish. Spread with half cottage cheese mixture, then half sliced mozzarella, and half meat sauce. Repeat layers. Bake 30 minutes at 375°. Let stand 10 minutes before serving.

Note: If made ahead and refrigerated, let dish come to room temperature before baking. This may require longer baking time.

Yield: 8 servings   Diana Carter Samples (Mrs. Robert F.)

Microwaved Lasagna

1 pound ground beef
1 medium onion, chopped
1 (32-ounce) jar spaghetti sauce
½ cup water
1½ pounds Ricotta cheese
2 teaspoons basil
1 egg

½ teaspoon pepper
6 to 8 lasagna noodles,
   uncooked
12 ounces sliced Mozzarella
   cheese
½ cup Parmesan cheese

In large bowl, crumble ground beef and add onion. Microwave 3 to 4 minutes at full power until beef is browned. Drain well. Stir in spaghetti sauce and water. Combine Ricotta cheese, basil, egg, and pepper. Spoon ½ cup spaghetti sauce in bottom of 2-quart oven-proof dish. Add noodles, egg-Ricotta mixture, Mozzarella cheese, and sauce in layers (2 layers each). Cover and microwave 8 minutes at full power. Then microwave 30 to 32 minutes at 50% power. Top with Parmesan cheese. Cover and let set 15 minutes.

Yield: 8 servings

Ann Muse

Fettucine with Ham

3 ounces shelled fresh peas,
   frozen peas, or canned
   petits-pois
1 clove garlic, pressed
4 ounces sliced mushrooms
3 ounces julienne ham
6 tablespoons butter, divided

¾ cup whipping cream
Fresh basil
12 ounces fettucine or
   vermicelli
1 cup Parmesan and/or
   Mozzarella cheese
Salt and pepper to taste

Cook and drain peas. Sauté garlic, mushrooms, and ham in 4 tablespoons butter. Add peas, cream, and basil. Mix well. Cook pasta according to package directions. Drain and turn into warm serving dish. Toss pasta with remaining butter and cheese. Pour warm cream sauce over pasta and toss. Season to taste. Serve with extra Parmesan cheese.

Yield: 6 servings

Helen Powell McNabb (Mrs. William R.)

Fettucine á la Continental

1 pound ½-inch wide noodles
1 cup butter
1 egg, coddled
½ cup whipping cream

½ cup Ricotta cheese
1½ cups grated Parmesan
  cheese
Freshly ground pepper

Cook noodles according to package directions and drain. Melt butter in double boiler over hot water. Add cooked noodles to melted butter and toss gently. Transfer to sauté pan. Over low heat, add egg and toss until blended. Add cream, Ricotta cheese, and Parmesan cheese. Toss until mixture congeals. Add pepper and more Parmesan cheese to taste. Serve immediately.

Yield: 8 servings   Joyce Zirkle Tapscott (Mrs. Jack L.)

Clam Sauce

½ cup butter
1 cup all-purpose flour
1 (28-ounce) bottle clam juice
1 teaspoon crushed garlic
1 teaspoon basil
1 teaspoon oregano

Juice of 1 lemon
8 ounces fresh or canned clams,
   reserve liquid and chop
2 tablespoons chopped fresh parsley
Cooked linguini noodles
Freshly grated Parmesan cheese

In 3½-quart saucepan, melt butter; add flour to form roux. Cook 5 minutes
over low heat. Add clam juice slowly to avoid lumping, while beating with
wire whisk. Stir in garlic, basil, oregano, and lemon juice. Add clams with
liquid. Simmer over low heat 15 minutes. Before serving, add parsley for
color. Serve over linguini noodles with Parmesan cheese.

Yield: 8 to 10 servings   Cappucino's Restaurant
                                                      Knoxville, Tennessee

Microwaved Herb Sauced Fish

¼ cup sliced celery
¼ cup chopped onion
3 tablespoons margarine
3 tablespoons all-purpose flour
¼ teaspoon salt
¼ teaspoon crushed tarragon leaves

Dash pepper
1¼ cups milk
1 cup shredded natural
   Monterey Jack cheese
1 pound fish fillets

Microwave vegetables and margarine in 2-quart glass dish on full power 4
to 5 minutes, or until vegetables are tender, stirring after 2 minutes. Blend in
flour and seasonings. Gradually add milk, stirring constantly. Cover and
microwave 4 to 5 minutes or until sauce boils and thickens, stirring once
each minute. Add cheese and stir until melted.
   Arrange fillets in 11¾- x 7¼-inch glass baking dish. Top with cheese sauce
and cover. Microwave on full power 4½ minutes or until fish flakes easily
with a fork, turning after 2 minutes. Let stand covered 2 to 3 minutes before
serving.

Yield: 4 servings   Betty Schmitz (Mrs. R. S.)
                                                     Gulf Shores, Alabama

Sauce for Sole Oscar

1 pound butter
2 cups all-purpose flour
2 teaspoons chicken stock
2 quarts whipping cream
½ pound Jarlsberg cheese
½ bottle mustard sauce (Nance's)

½ cup chopped parsley
⅛ teaspoon nutmeg
⅛ teaspoon thyme
Few drops lemon juice
Salt
White pepper

Melt butter in medium size stock pot. Add flour to make roux. Slowly add chicken stock and cream, stirring constantly until sauce becomes thick and smooth. Add remaining ingredients. Heat through until cheese melts. Serve over poached sole or flounder.

Yield: 12 servings   Jean L. Nichols Alsentzer (Mrs. John S.)

Grilled Salmon Steaks

2 tablespoons lemon juice
1 tablespoon chopped fresh parsley
½ teaspoon dried tarragon

½ to 1 teaspoon Accent
⅓ cup butter
4 (¾-inch thick) salmon steaks

Blend lemon juice, parsley, tarragon, and Accent. Melt butter in skillet, add lemon juice mixture, and blend. Coat salmon steak with mixture.
   Preheat grill 15 minutes. Put each steak in aluminum foil and drizzle with remaining sauce. Close foil. Place on grill, cover, and reduce heat to low. Bake 10 minutes, turn, and bake 10 minutes longer or until flaky.

Yield: 4 servings   Louise Gabbard (Mrs. Charles)

Top of the World

6 (8- or 10-ounce) filets of
   red snapper or mackerel
Juice of 2 lemons
4 teaspoons Worcestershire sauce
1 cup butter, melted

2 cups dried bread crumbs
12 Ritz crackers, crumbled
Salt and pepper to taste
½ pound mushrooms, sliced

Marinate filets 2 hours in mixture of lemon juice, Worcestershire sauce, salt, and pepper.
   Preheat oven to 400°. Dip filets in melted butter. Mix together bread crumbs, crackers, salt, and pepper, and sprinkle over filets. Cover all with mushrooms. Bake 15 minutes, reduce heat to 300°, and bake additional 10 minutes.

Yield: 6 servings   Suzanne L. McMillen

Heavenly Sole

6 fish filets (any white fish)   ¼ cup butter
2 tablespoons lemon juice   Dash Tabasco sauce
3 tablespoons mayonnaise   Dash Worcestershire sauce
3 tablespoons chopped green onion   Dash salt
½ cup grated Parmesan cheese

Place filets in greased pan and brush with lemon juice. Set aside. Make
sauce by combining remaining ingredients. Broil fish 6 to 8 minutes. Top
with sauce and broil an additional 2 to 3 minutes or until bubbling.

Yield: 6 servings   Mailande Vise Turner (Mrs. Francis M., III)
                                                             Pensacola, Florida

Jacksonville Shrimp Scampi

½ cup butter   2 tablespoons chopped parsley
2 tablespoons olive oil   2 tablespoons dry white wine
24 jumbo shrimp, peeled   1 tablespoon lemon juice
  and deveined   Salt and pepper to taste
3 cloves garlic, crushed   Hot cooked rice

Heat butter and oil in large skillet, add shrimp, and sauté on both sides
about 5 minutes. Pour pan drippings into small saucepan and add
remaining ingredients. Cook over high heat 1 minute. Pour sauce over
shrimp. Serve over rice.

Yield: 4 servings   Pamela Young Richardson (Mrs. Charles Franklin)

Paradise Shrimp

Vegetable oil   Salt
6 to 8 cloves garlic   Pepper
5 pounds green unpeeled shrimp   4 to 6 lemons, cut in half
1 (⅘-quart) bottle dry vermouth

Pour oil to ¼-inch depth in 12-inch skillet. Sauté garlic cloves over medium
high heat until light brown. Remove cloves from oil. Add shrimp, vermouth,
salt, and pepper. Squeeze lemon juice into mixture and add lemon rinds.
Cook until shrimp are pink.

Note: Everyone peels his own. Leftover shrimps are delicious in salads.

Yield: 10 to 12 servings   Ross Hanna, III

Herbed Shrimp

¾ cup olive oil
2 tablespoons lemon juice
1 tablespoon minced parsley
2 garlic cloves, crushed
1 teaspoon salt

½ teaspoon oregano
Pepper to taste
2 pounds shrimp
Parsley and lemon slices
   for garnish

In long, shallow baking dish, combine olive oil, lemon juice, parsley, garlic, salt, oregano, and pepper. Rinse shrimp. With scissors, slit through shells of shrimp on underside and devein. (Do not remove shells.) Using 10- to 12-inch flat skewers, first thread each shrimp at wide end, then curl shrimp into round and secure through at tail end. Arrange skewers in dish and marinate shrimp, turning every 30 minutes for 2 hours. Grill shrimp over hot coals 3 minutes on each side, or until just cooked. Remove from skewers, arrange in bowl, and garnish with parsley and lemon slices.

Yield: 6 servings   Jeanne Holmes Hyatt (Mrs. Hugh C.)

Shrimp in Beer Creole

½ cup sliced, blanched almonds
7 tablespoons butter, divided
1 tablespoon vegetable oil
Salt to taste
2 pounds shrimp, shelled and
   deveined
¼ cup minced scallions
1 green pepper, cut in strips

½ pound small mushrooms
1 tablespoon paprika
Pepper to taste
1 teaspoon tomato paste
1 cup light beer
¾ cup whipping cream
¼ cup sour cream
Hot cooked rice

Sauté almonds in 1 tablespoon butter and oil, tossing until golden. Place almonds on paper towels to drain and sprinkle with salt. Cook shrimp in 4 tablespoons butter over moderate heat until pink. Transfer shrimp and pan drippings to bowl, cover with buttered round of wax paper, and set aside. Sauté scallions and green pepper in 2 tablespoons butter. Add mushrooms, paprika, salt, and pepper to taste. Cook, tossing until mushrooms are tender. Stir in tomato paste, beer, and reserved pan drippings. Reduce volume over high heat to ½ cup. Turn heat to low. Add cream combined with sour cream and shrimp. Simmer until mixture is hot. Arrange shrimp mixture on heated platter with rice, and garnish with almonds.

Yield: 6 to 8 servings   Nancy Davis Gill (Mrs. Hoyle)

Shrimp Crabmeat Casserole

2 tablespoons butter
2 tablespoons all-purpose flour
1 cup whipping cream
1 cup milk
1 egg yolk
1 small onion
½ cup grated sharp Cheddar
  cheese
½ teaspoon salt
¼ teaspoon dry mustard

¼ teaspoon nutmeg
⅛ teaspoon curry
⅛ teaspoon cayenne pepper
½ cup buttered bread crumbs
2 cups shrimp, cooked and
  split lengthwise
7 ounces fresh crabmeat, if
  available, or 1 (7-ounce)
  can crabmeat
¼ cup dry white wine

Preheat oven to 350°. Melt butter in top of double boiler, then add flour. Cook until frothy. Add warmed cream and milk. Stir constantly until thick. Beat egg yolk, add small amount of hot sauce, and mix well. Return to double boiler. Add whole onion to cook with sauce. Add cheese and seasonings. Stir until cheese melts. Remove from heat; remove onion, and add seafood and wine. Pour into 2-quart greased casserole. Top with buttered crumbs. Bake 20 to 25 minutes. (Be careful not to leave in oven too long or sauce will separate.) Serve with rice.

Note: Sauce can be prepared ahead and rewarmed carefully in double boiler before combining with fish and wine.

Yield: 4 servings   Suzanne Wood Fletcher

Shrimp and Wild Rice Casserole

2 (6-ounce) boxes long grain and wild
  rice mix with seasonings
1 large onion, chopped
½ cup margarine
3 (10¾-ounce) cans mushroom soup
1½ (10¾-ounce) cans water

1½ to 2½ pounds cooked shrimp
1 large green pepper, chopped
1 (2½-ounce) can sliced
  mushrooms, drained
1 (8-ounce) can water chestnuts,
  sliced

Preheat oven to 325°. Sauté rice and onion in margarine. Add soup, water, and rice seasonings. Place in 3-quart casserole and bake 1 hour. Add water if dry. (Up to this point, dish can be prepared ahead.) Combine shrimp, green pepper, mushrooms, and water chestnuts. Add to rice dish. Return to oven and bake 30 minutes uncovered.

Yield: 10 servings   Brenda "Bee" Bomar McCallie (Mrs. Robert C.)

Shrimp-Mushroom-Artichoke Casserole

1 pound mushrooms, sliced
9½ tablespoons butter, divided
1 (14-ounce) can artichoke hearts
2 pounds shrimp, cooked and shelled
4½ tablespoons all-purpose flour
¾ cup milk

¾ cup whipping cream
½ cup dry cream sherry
1 tablespoon Worcestershire sauce
Salt and pepper to taste
½ cup grated Parmesan cheese
Paprika

Sauté mushrooms in 5 tablespoons butter. Quarter artichoke hearts. Layer shrimp, mushrooms, and artichokes in 2-quart casserole. Melt remaining 4½ tablespoons butter; add flour, milk, and cream. Cook until thick, and add sherry, Worcestershire, salt, and pepper. Pour over casserole and refrigerate 24 hours. Top with Parmesan and sprinkle with paprika. Bake 30 minutes at 375°.

Yield: 6 to 8 servings   Ann Calhoun McMurray (Mrs. R. Fred)

Coquilles St. Jacques

7 tablespoons butter, divided
3 tablespoons all-purpose flour
  + additional all-purpose flour
½ cup bottled clam juice
½ cup white wine
Pinch tarragon
Pinch thyme
2 egg yolks, slightly beaten
½ cup half and half cream

Salt and pepper to taste
2 pounds scallops
1 teaspoon olive oil
2 cloves garlic, minced
½ cup minced shallots
  (or onion)
12 seafood baking shells
½ cup grated Swiss cheese

Melt 3 tablespoons butter and stir in 3 tablespoons flour. Cook until smooth and add clam juice and wine. Add tarragon and thyme. Cook 2 to 3 minutes or until sauce becomes smooth and thick. Combine egg yolks with cream. Slowly beat sauce into egg mixture. Season with salt and pepper and cook slowly, stirring occasionally. Cut scallops into bite-size pieces. Dust with flour and sauté in remaining 3 tablespoons butter and oil until lightly browned. Remove scallops and sauté garlic and shallots in same skillet, adding additional butter if needed. Combine sauce, scallops, and garlic mixture. Refrigerate until ready to serve. Spoon mixture into individual shells and sprinkle with cheese. Brown under broiler. Serve at once.

Yield: 12 servings   Vandy Cifers Leake (Mrs. Donelson)

Baked Crab Salad

1 large green pepper, chopped
1 small onion, chopped
1 cup diced celery
1 (6½-ounce) can crabmeat
½ cup shrimp pieces
1 cup mayonnaise
1 teaspoon Worcestershire sauce
½ teaspoon salt
Dash pepper
1 (6-ounce) can mushrooms,
  drained
Bread crumbs
Butter
Paprika
Lemon wedges

Preheat oven to 350°. Combine green pepper, onion, celery, crabmeat, shrimp, mayonnaise, Worcestershire sauce, salt, pepper, and mushrooms in a bowl and toss lightly. Put into 1½-quart oven-proof dish. Top with bread crumbs and dot with butter. Bake 45 minutes. Sprinkle with paprika and garnish with lemon wedges.

Yield: 4 servings

Patricia Gilham Groves (Mrs. David M., Jr.)

King Crab Au Gratin

3 tablespoons butter
3 tablespoons all-purpose flour
1 cup milk
½ cup half and half cream
½ cup chicken broth
¾ cup grated sharp Cheddar
  cheese
1 (4-ounce) can sliced mushrooms,
  drained
2 tablespoons grated onion
1 teaspoon salt
¼ teaspoon paprika
2 tablespoons white wine
2 (6-ounce) packages frozen king
  crab, thawed and drained
¼ cup fine dry bread crumbs
Hot cooked rice

Preheat oven to 400°. Grease 1½-quart oven-proof dish. Melt butter and stir in flour until smooth. Gradually stir in milk, cream, and broth. Cook, stirring constantly, over low heat until sauce is smooth and thick. Add cheese, mushrooms, onion, salt, paprika, and wine. Stir until cheese is melted. Stir in crab meat. Pour mixture into prepared dish. Sprinkle bread crumbs over top. Bake 10 to 15 minutes or until top is golden brown. Serve over rice.

Yield: 6 servings

Beth Pettit Stivers (Mrs. Robert M.)

Eggplant with Crabmeat

1 eggplant, peeled
Salt
⅓ cup minced parsley
2 cloves garlic, crushed
1 teaspoon salt
Pepper to taste
¾ cup tahini
3 tablespoons water
Juice of 2 lemons plus 1
   tablespoon lemon juice,
   divided

2 cups flaked and picked
   crabmeat
1 teaspoon basil
2 eggs, beaten
½ cup milk
1 cup all-purpose flour
¼ cup olive oil
¼ cup butter, melted
Sautéed mushrooms
Lemon wedges (garnish)
Sprigs of parsley (garnish)

Cut eggplant into eight ¾-inch slices. Sprinkle with salt and place between paper towels on rack; weight down for 30 minutes. In large bowl, combine parsley, garlic, 1 teaspoon salt, and pepper to taste. Mash together with back of spoon. In another bowl, stir together tahini, water, and 1 tablespoon lemon juice. Combine tahini mixture with parsley mixture. Stir in juice of 2 lemons and let mixture stand 5 minutes. Add crabmeat and basil, and toss mixture to coat crabmeat. Pat eggplant slices dry with paper towels, dip into beaten eggs combined with milk, and dredge in 1 cup flour seasoned with salt and pepper to taste, shaking off excess. In skillet, sauté half the slices in olive oil until golden on both sides. Drain on paper towels. Repeat with remaining slices. Pour melted butter into baking dish just large enough to hold eggplant slices in 1 layer. Arrange eggplant and top each slice with ¼ cup crabmeat mixture. Bake in preheated 400° oven 5 minutes, or until heated through. Serve with sautéed mushrooms and garnish each serving with lemon wedge and sprigs of parsley.

Yield: 4 servings

Bahou Restaurant
Knoxville, Tennessee

Annapolis Crab Cakes

2 slices bread soaked in milk
2 eggs, slightly beaten
1 tablespoon mayonnaise
1 teaspoon dry mustard
⅛ teaspoon cayenne pepper

1 tablespoon cider vinegar
1 teaspoon salt
¼ cup butter
1 pound backfin or
   lump crabmeat

Squeeze out bread and discard milk. Mash bread with hands. Add all ingredients except crab and mix well. Add crab carefully. Refrigerate for at least 2 hours. Shape into cakes and refrigerate again several hours before cooking. Fry in butter until brown.

Yield: 4 servings

Jeanne Holmes Hyatt (Mrs. Hugh C.)

Seafood Lasagna

1 cup chopped onion
2 tablespoons butter
1 (8-ounce) package cream cheese
1½ cups cottage cheese
1 egg
2 teaspoons basil
½ teaspoon salt
⅛ teaspoon freshly ground pepper
2 (10¾-ounce) cans cream
  of mushroom soup

⅓ cup milk
⅓ cup white wine
1 to 1½ pounds shrimp,
  cooked
8 ounces crabmeat
8 lasagna noodles, cooked
¼ cup grated Parmesan cheese
½ cup grated sharp
  Cheddar cheese

Preheat oven to 350° and grease 13- x 9-inch oven-proof dish. Sauté onion in butter until brown; blend in cream cheese. Add cottage cheese, egg, basil, salt, and pepper. Set aside. Combine soup, milk, and wine; stir in shrimp and crabmeat. Place 4 lasagna noodles in bottom of oven-proof dish. Spread half cheese mixture on top of noodles. Spread half shrimp mixture on top of cheese mixture. Repeat layers. Sprinkle Parmesan cheese over top and bake uncovered 45 minutes. Top with Cheddar cheese and bake 2 to 3 minutes. Let stand 15 minutes before serving.

Note: Can be frozen.

Yield: 12 servings   Marti Schmitz Hobson (Mrs. Leonard)

Spicy Hot Oysters

½ cup butter
1 quart oysters, drained
1 rib celery, chopped
6 tablespoons Worcestershire sauce

20 drops hot sauce
Salt and pepper
¼ pound saltine crackers
Paprika

Preheat oven to 250°. Heat butter in 9- x 13-inch pan until very hot. Drop layer of oysters into hot butter. Top with layers of celery, Worcestershire, hot sauce, salt, pepper, and crackers which have been broken into ¼- to ½-inch pieces. Repeat layers. Sprinkle generously with paprika. Bake 1 hour. Serve in same pan as these should not be stirred at any time.

Yield: 6 to 10 servings   Martha Spencer Fowler (Mrs. Michael F.)

Crab or Tuna Stuffed Rolls

5 to 6 hard rolls
1 (7-ounce) can crab or tuna,
  drained
4 hard-cooked eggs, chopped
Grated onion to taste

2 cups grated American cheese
½ cup chopped Spanish olives
Salt and pepper
1 to 2 tablespoons mayonnaise

Preheat oven to 300°. Hollow out rolls. Combine ingredients and fill rolls.
Heat 30 minutes.

Yield: 5 to 6 rolls

Sue Arnold Herrmann (Mrs. Milo)
Boggy Bayou, Florida

Ruby's Shrimp Sandwiches

Whole wheat bread, homemade
Mayonnaise
Fresh lemon juice to taste
Paprika

Pepper
Fresh boiled shrimp
Swiss cheese, sliced

Preheat oven to 350°. Cut thick slices of bread. Combine mayonnaise,
lemon juice, paprika, and pepper. Generously spread mixture on each
slice of bread. Completely cover with shrimp. Top with sliced cheese.
Bake 10 to 15 minutes; then broil to bubble cheese. Serve open faced.

Ruby Tuesday Restaurant
Knoxville, Tennessee

Filet of Beef Roll

This is an easy, haute cuisine recipe which leaves the hostess relatively free to enjoy her guests. Be prepared for applause.

1 (4½- to 5-pound) filet of beef
Salt
Pepper
1 cup chopped fresh mushrooms
½ cup chopped onion
¼ cup snipped parsley

4 tablespoons butter
1 cup (6-ounces) chicken livers,
   thinly sliced
Watercress
Wine sauce (recipe follows)

Cut thin end from filet. Cut a horizontal pocket not quite through meat. Spread meat open and pound with wooden mallet to an even thickness of about ¾ inch. Sprinkle well with salt and pepper. In covered saucepan, cook mushrooms, onions, and parsley in butter until tender. Add chicken livers. Cook uncovered 1 to 2 minutes more or until livers are lightly browned. Drain. Arrange mixture over meat. Roll up from long side; tie with string at 3-inch intervals. Wrap in foil and chill.

In preheated 425° oven, approximately 45 to 50 minutes before serving time, place unwrapped filet in shallow roasting pan and roast 20 to 30 minutes for rare or 45 to 50 minutes for well done. Check for doneness by making a small slit in thickest part of meat. Untie; slice. Place on serving platter and garnish with watercress. Serve with wine sauce.

Wine Sauce:

1 tablespoon butter or margarine
4 teaspoons cornstarch
⅛ teaspoon salt
Freshly ground black pepper
1 (10½-ounce) can condensed
   beef broth

3 sprigs parsley
1 bay leaf
¼ teaspoon dried thyme,
   crushed
½ cup dry red wine
Watercress

Melt butter; blend in cornstarch, salt, and pepper. Add broth. Cook, stirring constantly over medium heat until thick and bubbly. Reduce heat. Add parsley, bay leaf, and thyme. Cover and simmer 10 minutes. Remove parsley and bay leaf. Prepare to this point and set aside. Just before serving time, add wine; heat just until bubbly over low heat. Serve in gravy boat.

Yield: 12 servings   Marion Arwood Brown

Beef Tender

1½ cups vegetable oil
¾ cup soy sauce
¼ cup Worcestershire sauce
2 tablespoons dry mustard
2½ teaspoons salt
1 tablespoon pepper

½ cup wine vinegar
1½ teaspoons parsley
1 clove garlic
⅓ cup fresh lemon juice
Beef tender

Combine all ingredients except tender. Add beef to mixture and marinate overnight. Place on grill and charcoal until tender is charred on all sides, about 30 minutes. Finish cooking in 250° oven 1 hour.

Yield: 3½ cups marinade   Mary Culver Spengler (Mrs. Joseph)

Beef Tyrolean

1 carrot, chopped
1 medium onion, chopped
1 rib celery, chopped
2 tablespoons olive oil
2 tablespoons butter
2 teaspoons basil
1 teaspoon thyme

Salt and pepper
½ pound bacon, fried crisp
Whole beef tenderloin
  (5 pounds or larger)
4 slices Swiss or Gruyère
  cheese

Preheat oven to 375°. Sauté carrot, onion, and celery in oil and butter until crunchy but tender. Drain. Add seasonings and crumbled bacon to cooked vegetables. Split tenderloin lengthwise ⅔ way through for pocket and fill with mixture. Roast 40 minutes. Top with cheese and broil 1½ minutes. Slice and serve.

Note: Raw bacon slices can be placed over tenderloin as it roasts to flavor and moisten meat. Remove bacon before topping with cheese.

Yield: 8 servings   Suzanne Wood Fletcher

Gurth's Easy Rump Roast

4-pound rump roast   Salt and pepper

Preheat oven to 325°. Place two pieces of heavy aluminum foil crossing in iron skillet. Salt and pepper generously. Place roast fat side up on foil. Salt and pepper again. Seal foil. Bake 4 hours. Let stand 20 minutes before slicing.

Yield: 6 to 8 servings   Mildred Wright Robinson (Mrs. Gurth)

Beef Bordelaise

5- to 6-pound rolled rib, rib
  eye, or rump of beef
2 large onions, sliced
½ cup chopped green onions
2 cloves garlic, crushed
1 bay leaf
½ teaspoon leaf thyme, crumbled
1 teaspoon peppercorns

4 to 5 sprigs parsley
1 teaspoon salt
2 cups dry red wine
5 tablespoons butter, melted
  and divided
2 (10½-ounce) cans beef broth
1 tablespoon all-purpose flour

Put meat in enamel or stainless steel pan just large enough to hold meat and vegetables. Combine vegetables, herbs, salt, and wine; pour over meat. Cover. Refrigerate 8 to 12 hours, turning occasionally.

Heat oven to 475°. Remove meat from marinade; pat dry. Strain marinade; reserve liquid and vegetables. Place meat on rack in shallow roasting pan. Roast 30 minutes, basting once or twice with marinade or 4 tablespoons butter. Reduce heat to 400°. Add reserved vegetables to pan. Cook about 12 minutes per pound for rare roast. Baste occasionally. Remove meat to platter; let stand 15 to 20 minutes before carving. Boil pan drippings 1 minute. Discard fat; add marinade. Bring to boiling; reduce liquid to a few tablespoons. Add broth. Blend 1 tablespoon butter and flour. Add to pan. Cook, stirring constantly, until sauce is thick and smooth. Correct seasonings. Strain before serving with meat.

Yield: 8 to 10 servings   Sherri Parker Lee

Lendenbraten

3-pound sirloin roast
1 slice bacon, diced
Salt and pepper
1 onion, sliced
1 tomato, sliced
4 tablespoons butter

½ cup water
2 tablespoons all-purpose flour
1 cup sour cream
Red wine
Paprika

Preheat oven to 400°. Lard meat with fine sliver of bacon. Season with salt and pepper. Brown roast, onion, and tomato in butter over high heat. Add water and transfer pan to hot oven. Bake 30 to 40 minutes, basting frequently. Remove roast. Add remaining ingredients to pan drippings and cook briskly. Serve sauce with roast.

Yield: 4 to 6 servings   Pat Campen Medley (Mrs. Mark A.)

Beef Barbecue

3-pound chuck roast
½ cup water
3 tablespoons margarine
1½ cups chopped onion
3 teaspoons paprika
¾ teaspoon pepper

3 tablespoons sugar
1½ teaspoons dry mustard
3 tablespoons cider vinegar
3 tablespoons Worcestershire sauce
1 cup tomato paste

Cook chuck roast with ½ cup water in pressure cooker 30 minutes. Let cool and shred or chop meat as for barbecue. Combine remaining ingredients and cook 10 minutes, adding water if sauce is too thick. Add meat. Serve on buns.

Yield: 8 servings

Kathryn Kizer Schwarzenberg (Mrs. O. C., Jr.)
Belle Glade, Florida

Roast with Chili Sauce

5-pound chuck or shoulder
  roast
Vegetable oil

Very strong tea (4 or 5
  tea bags)
Chili sauce (recipe follows)

Brown roast in small amount of oil. Cover with strong tea and simmer roast 5 to 6 hours or until tender. Remove meat from Dutch oven and pull apart with fork. Put roast into 3-quart oven-proof dish and cover with sauce. Bake 30 minutes at 350°.

Chili Sauce:

1 (12-ounce) bottle chili sauce
3 tablespoons brown sugar
1 tablespoon Worcestershire sauce
2 tablespoons vegetable oil
½ cup chopped onion

1 cup water
4 tablespoons lemon juice
1 teaspoon paprika
1 teaspoon salt

Combine all ingredients and simmer 20 minutes. Pour over meat as directed.

Yield: 8 servings

Shirley Ponto Rechenbach (Mrs. Thomas R.)

Sherried Chuck Roast

3-pound boneless chuck roast
1 (1-ounce) package dry onion
  soup mix

2 (10¾-ounce) cans cream of
  mushroom soup
¾ cup dry sherry
1 (4-ounce) can whole mushrooms

Trim fat from roast, cut into 1-inch cubes, and place in 3-quart oven-proof dish. Combine remaining ingredients and pour over roast. Cover and bake 3 hours at 325°.

Yield: 6 servings   Gail Cifers Pettit (Mrs. Michael)

Beef with Oyster Sauce

1 teaspoon cornstarch
Dash of salt and pepper
⅓ cup water
1 pound flank steak, cut into
  ¼-inch x 1½-inch strips
½ cup water chestnuts, sliced
4 tablespoons vegetable oil,
  divided

2 teaspoons wine
1 scallion cut diagonally
  into 1-inch pieces
2 slices fresh ginger root
1 clove garlic, crushed
2 cups snow peas
Oyster Sauce (recipe follows)

Combine cornstarch, salt, and pepper; mix well with water. Add to beef in mixing bowl and marinate at least 30 minutes. Turn and stir often to coat all meat surfaces. Preheat wok or large skillet with 2 tablespoons oil and, when hot, add beef. Stir vigorously for 1 minute over high heat. When meat begins to brown, add wine. Continue to stir for 1 minute. Remove meat and set aside. Beef should be partially done. Add remaining oil to heated wok and, when hot, add scallion, ginger, and garlic. Stir briskly over medium heat for 2 minutes or until brown. Add snow peas and water chestnuts. Continue to stir vigorously for 1 minute. Add beef, stirring once or twice. Add Oyster Sauce and stir-fry until thick, about 2 minutes.

Oyster Sauce:

1 tablespoon cornstarch
⅓ cup cold water
3 tablespoons commercially
  prepared oyster sauce
1 teaspoon sugar

1 teaspoon salt
1 teaspoon monosodium glutamate
Dash of salt and pepper
Dash of sesame seed oil

Mix cornstarch with water and add remaining ingredients.

Yield: 2 to 3 servings   Jeanne Holmes Hyatt (Mrs. Hugh C.)

Oriental Beef and Green Peppers

½ pound round steak,
  cut in thin strips
Marinade (recipe follows)
6 tablespoons vegetable oil,
  divided
1 cup sliced water chestnuts
1 cup sliced green pepper strips

¼ teaspoon salt
¼ teaspoon Accent
1 teaspoon cornstarch
2 teaspoons soy sauce
⅓ cup water
Hot cooked rice

Marinate beef strips in marinade. Heat 3 tablespoons vegetable oil in electric skillet or wok. Sauté water chestnuts and green pepper. Add salt and Accent. Fry 2 minutes. Remove to platter. Heat remaining vegetable oil in skillet or wok, and fry beef 2 to 3 minutes. Combine cornstarch, soy sauce, and water. Return water chestnuts and green pepper to skillet with beef and add cornstarch mixture. Cook briefly and serve over rice.

Marinade:

1½ tablespoons soy sauce
2 teaspoons cornstarch
1 tablespoon red or white wine
1 tablespoon sesame seed oil

2 tablespoons water
Pepper to taste
1 clove garlic, minced
¼ teaspoon ginger

Combine ingredients and use as directed.

Yield: 4 servings

Nancy Stivers Rowland (Mrs. Lloyd)
Sumter, South Carolina

Stir-Fried Beef

¼ cup vegetable oil
2 large stalks broccoli, trimmed
  and sliced diagonally
1 pound top round beef, sliced
  in strips across grain
1 (20-ounce) can pineapple chunks,
  reserve syrup
¼ cup soy sauce

2 tablespoons vinegar
½ teaspoon crushed red pepper
2 tablespoons cornstarch
1 cup bean sprouts
2 tablespoons sesame seeds,
  toasted
Hot cooked rice or noodles

Heat oil in wok until very hot. Stir-fry broccoli 2 to 3 minutes until barely tender. Add beef strips and cook just until brown. Combine pineapple syrup with soy sauce, vinegar, pepper, and cornstarch. Add pineapple, sprouts, and syrup mixture to beef. Heat and stir until thickened. Sprinkle with sesame seeds and serve over rice or noodles.

Yield: 4 servings

Scott Davis Wilson (Mrs. Don)

The Best Beef Stroganoff

2 pounds lean boneless beef
3 to 4 tablespoons all-purpose flour
Salt and pepper to taste
½ cup margarine
2 large onions, sliced
2 cups fresh mushrooms, sliced

1 (10½-ounce) can beef bouillon
¾ cup dry sherry
½ teaspoon thyme
Grated rind and juice of 1 lemon
1 cup sour cream
Cooked noodles

Cut beef into narrow strips and dust with flour seasoned with salt and pepper. Set aside. Melt margarine in heavy iron skillet. Add sliced onions and sauté until golden brown. Remove and set aside. In same margarine, sauté sliced mushrooms until tender and lightly browned. Remove and set aside. Add more margarine as necessary and quickly brown the floured meat. Return browned onions and mushrooms to skillet with bouillon, sherry, thyme, lemon rind, and juice. Cover and simmer 1 hour. Just before serving, stir in sour cream. Serve over cooked noodles.

Yield: 8 servings   Sheila Prial Jacobstein (Mrs. Richard)

Sour Cream Goulash

½ pound mushrooms
1½ tablespoons butter
2 pounds stew beef
2 large onions, sliced
1 tablespoon curry powder
1 cup consommé
1 cup dry red wine

1½ tablespoons all-purpose flour
Water
1 tablespoon prepared horseradish
2 cups sour cream
Salt to taste
Cooked rice

Preheat oven to 325°. In large oven-proof skillet, sauté mushrooms in butter. Add beef, onions, curry powder, consommé, and wine. Bring to boil. Cover and bake 1½ hours or until meat is tender. Return to range surface. Combine flour and small amount of water to form paste. Stir into hot mixture. (Can be prepared ahead to this point.) Add horseradish, sour cream, and salt. Reheat, but do not boil. Serve over cooked rice.

Yield: 4 servings   Pat Minskey Allen (Mrs. Robert H., III)

Flank Steak Pinwheels

1 package Good Seasons
   Italian Dressing Mix

1 flank steak
3 slices bacon

Prepare dressing according to directions. Score steak on both sides. Lay bacon strips lengthwise on steak, roll up starting at small end and secure with toothpicks. Slice into 6 pinwheels and marinate in salad dressing several hours, turning once. Grill 6 to 7 minutes on each side.

Yield: 3 servings
          Geri Carmichael Muse (Mrs. William Scott, Jr.)

Flank Steak Marinade

Flank steak
Meat tenderizer
2 tablespoons vegetable oil
2 tablespoons lemon juice

1 teaspoon salt
½ teaspoon pepper
4 teaspoons parsley
2 cloves garlic, minced

Score steak on both sides and sprinkle with meat tenderizer on each side. Combine remaining ingredients. Marinate steak for at least 30 minutes. Broil 4 minutes on each side, 6 inches from broiler. Slice thin on diagonal.

Yield: Allow 5-7 ounces per serving
      Sandy Mourfield Goode (Mrs. Gerald)
                  Canyon Lake, Texas

Lemon-Marinated Steak

4 pounds chuck steak,
   cut 1½ inches thick
1 teaspoon grated lemon peel
½ cup lemon juice
⅓ cup vegetable oil
2 tablespoons sliced green
   onion with tops

4 teaspoons sugar
1½ teaspoons salt
1 teaspoon Worcestershire
   sauce
1 teaspoon prepared mustard
⅛ teaspoon pepper

Score fat edges and place meat in shallow dish. Combine remaining ingredients and pour over steak. Let stand 3 hours at room temperature or overnight in refrigerator, turning steak several times. Remove steak and reserve marinade. Pat steak dry with paper towel. Cook, covered, over medium-hot coals 17 to 20 minutes on each side for rare to medium-rare. Heat marinade and spoon over sliced steak.

Yield: 6 servings
          Suzanne L. McMillen

Marinade for London Broil

1 teaspoon salt
½ teaspoon freshly ground pepper
¼ teaspoon basil
¼ teaspoon rosemary, crushed
1 clove garlic, crushed

1 small onion, chopped
1 tablespoon wine vinegar
2 tablespoons vegetable oil
1¾ pounds flank steak

Mix all ingredients except steak in shallow glass dish. Add steak and marinate at least 2 hours. Broil over charcoal about 15 minutes. Slice diagonally across grain into very thin pieces. Pour any remaining marinade over sliced meat.

Yield: 4 servings   Suellen Brown Roehl (Mrs. Jay)

Tangy Marinade

1 cup pineapple juice
⅓ cup soy sauce
1 teaspoon ground ginger

1 teaspoon sugar
1 clove garlic, crushed
⅓ cup salad oil

Combine all ingredients. Use to marinate steak or pork chops before grilling. Also use marinade to baste meat during grilling.

Yield: 1⅔ cups   Kaye McIntyre Littlejohn

Meat Loaf in Sauce

1 green pepper, chopped
1 onion, chopped
1½ pounds ground beef
1 teaspoon salt
¼ teaspoon pepper
2 cups tomato sauce, divided
1 egg

2 slices white bread,
  torn into pieces
2 tablespoons prepared mustard
3 tablespoons vinegar
¼ cup water
3 tablespoons brown sugar
2 teaspoons Worcestershire sauce

Preheat oven to 350°. Combine green pepper, onion, beef, salt, and pepper. Combine ½ cup tomato sauce, egg, and bread in food processor. Add to meat mixture and combine thoroughly (hands are best for this). Shape into two loaves and place in shallow 2-quart oven-proof dish. Combine remaining ingredients in food processor to form sauce and pour over loaves. Bake 1 hour and 15 minutes, basting four times during baking.

Note: Sauce is wonderful over whipped potatoes. Meat loaf sliced cold makes delicious sandwiches with plenty of mustard and mayonnaise.

Yield: 6 to 8 servings   Suellen Brown Roehl (Mrs. Jay)

Nancy's Apple Meat Loaf

2 cups soft bread crumbs
1 cup applesauce
1/3 cup tomato sauce
1 tablespoon instant onion
  or 2 tablespoons minced
  fresh onion

1/4 cup chopped green pepper
1/8 teaspoon pepper
1 egg, beaten
1 pound ground beef
1 pound ground veal
Apple Glaze (recipe follows)

Preheat oven to 350°. Measure crumbs into large mixing bowl. Combine applesauce, tomato sauce, onion, green pepper, and pepper; heat. Pour over crumbs and mix well. Add eggs, ground meat; mix well. Shape into loaf and place in 2-quart baking dish. Bake 1½ hours. After 35 minutes cooking time, begin basting with Apple Glaze every 15 minutes. To serve, slice and pass remaining Apple Glaze as sauce.

Apple Glaze:

1 cup canned applesauce
1 teaspoon prepared
  hot mustard

2 tablespoons vinegar
2 tablespoons brown sugar

Combine and stir over moderate heat until well-blended.

Note: 2 pounds ground chuck can be used instead of 1 pound ground beef and 1 pound ground veal.

Yield: 6 servings

Nancy Word Woodcock
Pensacola, Florida

Cheddar Beef Pie

1 pound ground chuck
1 egg
1/3 cup chopped onion
3/4 cup cracker crumbs
2 tablespoons barbecue sauce
1 teaspoon salt
Dash pepper

½ cup sliced celery
2 tablespoons margarine
1½ cups grated sharp
  Cheddar cheese
1 (4-ounce) can mushrooms,
  drained

Preheat oven to 400°. Combine meat, egg, onion, crumbs, barbecue sauce, salt, and pepper. Mix well and press mixture into bottom and sides of 9-inch pie plate. Bake 15 minutes. Remove from oven and drain off fat. Reduce oven temperature to 350°. Sauté celery in margarine. Combine celery, cheese, and mushrooms; toss lightly. Spoon into hot meat shell. Bake 10 minutes.

Yield: 4 to 6 servings

Judith Stephens Frost (Mrs. Robert B.)

Tomato Meat Sauce San Ruffillo

1 cup diced onion
1 clove garlic, chopped
2 tablespoons olive oil
1½ cups grated carrots
1 pound lean ground beef
1 (28-ounce) can tomato purée
1 (18-ounce) jar meatless
   marinara sauce
1 (6-ounce) can tomato paste
½ pound mushrooms,
   thinly sliced

½ cup diced green pepper
1 tablespoon chopped parsley
1 teaspoon salt
1 teaspoon dried basil
1 teaspoon oregano
1 bay leaf
½ teaspoon pepper
½ teaspoon allspice
⅛ teaspoon crushed
   red pepper
½ cup dry red wine

Brown onion and garlic in olive oil. Add carrots, stirring until carrots are soft. Add meat and brown until all liquid evaporates. Reduce heat to low and add remaining ingredients except wine. Simmer uncovered 1½ hours, stirring occasionally. Add wine and simmer 30 minutes longer.

Yield: 8 servings

Vicki Vorder Bruegge Keller

Creole Stuffed Peppers

6 medium green peppers
1¼ pounds ground beef
¼ small onion, chopped
⅓ cup finely chopped celery

1 cup cooked rice
1¼ teaspoons salt
¼ teaspoon pepper
Creole Sauce (recipe follows)

Preheat oven to 375°. Remove tops and seed from peppers. Turn upside down to drain. Brown beef, stirring slightly to keep meat in small particles. Add onion and celery and cook 5 minutes or until vegetables are tender. Stir in rice, salt, pepper, and 1 cup Creole Sauce. Fill peppers with mixture and place in shallow baking dish. Add water to barely cover bottom of dish. Cover tightly with foil. Bake 25 to 30 minutes. Spoon remaining Creole Sauce over peppers before serving.

Creole Sauce:

3 tablespoons vegetable oil
½ cup finely chopped green
   pepper
½ cup chopped onion
1 (28-ounce) can tomatoes,
   coarsely chopped

1 tablespoon sugar
⅛ teaspoon ground cloves
1 teaspoon salt
¼ teaspoon pepper

Combine all ingredients and simmer 20 to 25 minutes. Use as directed.

Yield: 4 to 6 servings

Priscilla Brandau Siler (Mrs. Tom A.)

Moussaka

10 tablespoons butter, divided
1 cup chopped onion
1½ pounds ground chuck or lamb
1 clove garlic, crushed
½ teaspoon dried oregano
1 teaspoon dried basil
½ teaspoon cinnamon
1 teaspoon salt
Dash of pepper

2 (8-ounce) cans tomato sauce
2 eggplants
Salt to taste
Cream Sauce (recipe follows)
½ cup grated Parmesan
  cheese, divided
½ cup grated Cheddar
  cheese, divided
2 tablespoons dry bread crumbs

In a 3½-quart Dutch oven, sauté onion, chuck, and garlic in 2 tablespoons butter until brown. Add oregano, basil, cinnamon, 1 teaspoon salt, pepper, and tomato sauce; bring to boil while stirring. Reduce heat and simmer uncovered ½ hour. Halve unpared eggplant lengthwise; slice crosswise in ½-inch thick slices. Place slices in bottom of broiler pan; salt to taste and brush lightly with remaining half-cup butter, melted. Broil 4 inches from heat, 4 minutes per side or until golden. Make Cream Sauce and set aside.

Preheat oven to 350°. To assemble casserole, layer half of eggplant overlapping slightly in shallow 2-quart oven-proof dish; sprinkle with 2 tablespoons Parmesan cheese and 2 tablespoons Cheddar cheese. Stir bread crumbs into meat sauce and spoon evenly over eggplant. Sprinkle again with 2 tablespoons each of Parmesan and Cheddar cheese. Layer remainder of eggplant. Pour Cream Sauce over all. Sprinkle top with remaining cheese. Bake 35 to 40 minutes or until golden brown and top is set. If browner top is desired, broil 1 minute. Cool slightly. Cut into squares.

Cream Sauce:

2 tablespoons butter
2 tablespoons flour
½ teaspoon salt

Dash of pepper
2 cups milk
2 eggs

In medium saucepan, melt butter. Remove from heat; stir in flour, salt, and pepper. Add milk gradually. Bring to boil, stirring until mixture is thickened. Remove from heat. In small bowl, beat eggs. Beat in some hot cream sauce mixture; return mixture to saucepan and mix well. Set aside. Use as directed in Moussaka.

Yield: 12 servings   Lucie Carlson Polk (Mrs. Robert H.)

Sour Cream Enchilada Casserole

1 pound ground beef
½ cup water
1 (1¼-ounce) envelope taco
  seasoning mix
Vegetable oil
12 to 16 corn tortillas

1 pint sour cream
1 (10-ounce) can mild or hot
  enchilada sauce
1 (3-ounce) can chopped green chilies,
  drained (optional)
1 cup grated Monterey Jack cheese

Preheat oven to 325°. Fry beef and drain. Add water and seasoning mix; simmer 15 minutes. In small amount of oil, fry tortillas one at a time to soften. Drain well. Fill each tortilla with 2 tablespoons beef mixture. Roll and place in 9- x 13-inch baking dish. Heat sour cream and sauce, but do not let mixture boil or sour cream will curdle. Add green chilies, if desired. Pour sauce over tortillas and sprinkle with cheese. Cover with foil and bake 15 minutes. Remove foil and bake 3 to 5 minutes longer.

Yield: 6 servings   Helen Dean Bruner (Mrs. Joseph)

Wine Sauce with Mushrooms

2 tablespoons butter, divided
1 tablespoon chopped parsley
1 clove garlic, crushed
1 small onion, chopped
1 tablespoon all-purpose flour

1 cup chicken broth
⅛ teaspoon nutmeg
¾ pound fresh mushrooms,
  sliced thin
¼ cup dry sherry

In a saucepan heat 1 tablespoon butter; add parsley, garlic, and onion. Cook over medium heat about 3 minutes. Stir in flour and gradually add chicken broth, stirring constantly. Add nutmeg. In a skillet heat remaining butter. Add mushrooms and sauté 5 to 7 minutes. Add mushrooms to sauce and simmer 15 minutes. Add sherry, bring to boil, and then reduce heat. Leave on warm until ready to serve.

Note: Serve with beef tenderloin, rib eye roast, or large open-face hamburger patties over English muffins.

Yield: 6 to 8 servings   Ena Taylor Kirkpatrick (Mrs. David M.)

Meats

Veal Epicurean

1 tablespoon vegetable oil
1 tablespoon butter
2 pounds veal round steak,
  cut into thin strips
3 tablespoons all-purpose flour
¾ teaspoon salt
⅛ teaspoon pepper
1½ cups water

1 chicken bouillon cube
½ pound small onions, cut
  in eighths (about 2 cups)
½ cup dry white wine
2 tablespoons snipped parsley
1 bay leaf
Hot cooked rice

In a large skillet, heat together oil and butter. Add veal, a small amount at a time, and brown lightly. Push meat to one side; blend flour, salt, and pepper into skillet drippings. Add water and bouillon cube; cook and stir in onions, wine, parsley, and bay leaf. Cover and simmer 25 minutes or until tender, stirring occasionally. Remove bay leaf. Serve veal over hot cooked rice.

Yield: 6 servings   Geri Carmichael Muse (Mrs. William Scott, Jr.)

Veal Parmigiana

1 cup chopped onion
1 large clove garlic, crushed
4 tablespoons olive oil,
  divided
1 (16-ounce) can Italian
  style tomatoes
2 (8-ounce) cans tomato sauce
1½ teaspoons basil
½ teaspoon thyme
1 teaspoon salt

½ teaspoon pepper
1 cup fine bread crumbs
¾ cup grated Parmesan
  cheese, divided
3 thin veal round steaks
  or veal cutlets
2 eggs, slightly beaten
2 tablespoons butter
1 (6-ounce) package sliced
  mozzarella cheese

In a saucepan, sauté onion and garlic in 2 tablespoons olive oil until tender. Add tomatoes, tomato sauce, basil, thyme, salt, and pepper. Cover and simmer 15 minutes. Preheat oven to 350°. Mix crumbs and ¼ cup Parmesan cheese in shallow plate. Salt and pepper each side of veal, dip in eggs, and then in crumb mixture. Heat remaining olive oil and butter in skillet. Sauté veal on both sides until browned. Spoon half of the tomato mixture in an oven-proof dish and arrange veal on sauce. Cover veal with slices of mozzarella. Cover with remaining tomato mixture and sprinkle with ½ cup Parmesan cheese. Bake 15 to 20 minutes or until bubbly.

Note: If using veal steaks, cut in serving-size pieces before breading.

Yield: 4 to 6 servings   Pat Campen Medley (Mrs. Mark A.)

Veal Scallopine

2 to 3 pounds veal
All-purpose flour
2 tablespoons olive oil
6 tablespoons butter
4 medium green onions, chopped
1 pound fresh mushrooms, sliced

2 cloves garlic, minced
Pinch of rosemary
Salt
Freshly ground pepper
1 cup Marsala wine
Pinch of chopped parsley

Cut veal in 2-inch squares and pound to about ¼-inch thickness. Dip in flour and brown in hot olive oil and butter. Add onions, mushrooms, garlic, and rosemary. Add salt and pepper to taste. Let all brown gently. Add wine and parsley. Simmer 15 to 20 minutes or until veal is tender.

Note: Can be prepared a few hours ahead and gently reheated before serving.

Yield: 4 servings   Carole Cody Reeves (Mrs. W. P., III)

Barbecued Leg of Lamb

1 leg of lamb, boned and
  cut to lie flat
1 clove garlic
1 cup French or Italian
  dressing

⅔ cup chopped onion
2 teaspoons barbecue spice
1 teaspoon salt
½ teaspoon oregano
1 bay leaf, crushed

Place leg of lamb in large bowl. Make marinade with remaining ingredients and pour over lamb. Marinate 24 hours, turning several times. When ready to cook, place lamb inside wire grill rack and lock securely. Cook over charcoal 45 minutes to 1 hour, turning frequently and basting with marinade.

Note: Lamb can be cooked in oven also. Brush with marinade and broil on both sides until fat takes on golden brown color (about 10 minutes on each side). Then bake 35 to 40 minutes at 450°. Cook longer if well-done meat is desired.

Yield: 6 to 8 servings   Mary Beth Cranwell Montgomery (Mrs. George)

Rack of Lamb

4- to 5-pound rack of lamb
  (about 12 rib chops)
1 cup fresh bread crumbs
¼ cup chopped parsley
1 clove garlic, crushed

1 teaspoon salt
¼ teaspoon pepper
2 tablespoons Dijon mustard
¼ cup butter, melted

Preheat oven to 375°. Wipe lamb and trim off all fat. Place lamb on ribs in shallow roaster. Roast 15 minutes per pound. Let cool 15 minutes. Combine bread crumbs, parsley, garlic, salt, and pepper. Spread mustard over lamb. Pat crumb mixture into mustard, pressing firmly. Drizzle with butter. Insert meat thermometer into center of middle chop. Roast 20 minutes or until thermometer registers 175°, or less if you like meat pink.

Yield: 4 to 6 servings   Rosemary Morris Trimble (Mrs. H. B., Jr.)

Lamb á la Turque

(Turkish Lamb)

¼ cup butter
2 pounds boned lamb shoulder,
  cubed
3 medium onions, sliced
¼ teaspoon cinnamon
¼ teaspoon pepper
2 cups water
1 teaspoon salt

½ cup raisins
Boiling water
¾ cup chopped pitted prunes
2 cups cooked rice
1½ tablespoons butter, melted
3 tablespoons lemon juice
1 tablespoon minced fresh parsley
½ cup chopped toasted almonds

Melt ¼ cup butter in heavy skillet. Add lamb and brown. Add onions, cinnamon, pepper, and water. Cover and simmer 2½ hours. Stir in salt and cool. Cover raisins with boiling water. Let stand until plump and drain. Drain lamb. Toss raisins and prunes with lamb. Place in large casserole and top with rice. Cover and bake 35 minutes in preheated 350° oven. Combine 1½ tablespoons butter and lemon juice and spoon over rice. Sprinkle with parsley and almonds before serving.

Yield: 6 to 8 servings   The Lord Lindsay Restaurant
                                      William Johnson, Chef
                                      Knoxville, Tennessee

Lamb in a Bag

6 large loin lamb chops
Salt, pepper, and oregano,
  to taste
2 cloves garlic, slivered
2 onions, cut in thirds
3 carrots, halved

3 small zucchini, halved
¼ pound Feta cheese, cut
  in 6 squares
Juice of 1 lemon
¼ cup butter, melted

Preheat oven to 350°. Grease baking pan. Season each chop with salt, pepper, and oregano. Insert garlic slivers in meat. Place each chop on large piece of aluminum foil. On each chop add 1 piece onion, carrot, zucchini, and cheese. Sprinkle with lemon juice and butter. Fold foil in double fold on top and sides; secure sides with paper clips. Place in baking pan and bake 1 hour.

Yield: 6 servings   Helen Powell McNabb (Mrs. William R.)

Roast Pork á l'Orange

2 tablespoons salt
½ teaspoon thyme
¼ teaspoon pepper
1 clove garlic, crushed
3½-pound loin of pork with
  bone cracked, or boneless
  and rolled
5 oranges, divided

2 tablespoons oil
1 onion, chopped
1 carrot, diced
1 stalk celery, chopped
Bouquet garni of 4 sprigs
  parsley, 3 sprigs thyme,
  and 1 bay leaf

Combine salt, thyme, pepper, and garlic and rub all over pork. Let pork marinate, covered, 4 hours or overnight in refrigerator..
Preheat oven to 350°. Remove rind from 2 oranges and cut into julienne strips. Blanch strips in boiling water 2 minutes. Drain and pat dry with paper towel. Set aside. Cut remaining oranges in half, squeeze juice, and remove pith, reserving shells in halves. Scrape some seasoning from pork and brown roast all over in oil. Pour off all but 2 tablespoons rendered fat after removing pork from pan. Sauté onion, carrot, and celery in fat over medium heat until tender. Put pork and sauce in roasting pan and cook covered 2 hours with bouquet garni. Remove fat from juices. Put pork on platter. Garnish with orange rind strips. Add orange juice to pan juices and heat. Thicken sauce with flour if necessary.

Note: Serve hot cooked rice in orange shells as an accompaniment.

Yield: 6 servings   Pat Campen Medley (Mrs. Mark A.)

Laura's Pork Chops

Pork chops
Salt and pepper to taste
Garlic powder

Vegetable oil
Cooking sherry
Rosemary

Salt and pepper pork chops. Sprinkle generously with garlic powder. Brown chops slowly in small amount of vegetable oil. Remove from heat; add cooking sherry to about ¼ depth of chops. Add crushed rosemary. Return to *very* low heat. Cover and simmer 30 to 40 minutes.

Marie Humphreys O'Neill

Pork Chops Normandy

6 lean pork chops
Salt
Pepper
¼ teaspoon mace
2 tablespoons grated orange peel
1 tablespoon margarine

4 apples (Jonathan or Grovenstein), peeled and cored
⅓ cup dry white wine or apple juice
¾ cup whipping cream

Preheat oven to 350°. Salt and pepper chops. Rub in mace and peel. Brown in margarine. Cut peeled-cored apples into eighths. Place apples in baking dish and top with chops and wine or apple juice. Bake 35 minutes, basting occasionally. Pour cream over all and bake 30 more minutes.

Yield: 4 to 6 servings

Conni Hanson Collins (Mrs. Townsend S.)

Stuffed Pork Chops

4 (1-inch thick) pork chops
4 slices Swiss cheese, diced
¼ cup snipped parsley
½ cup chopped mushrooms
½ teaspoon salt

1 egg, slightly beaten
½ cup bread crumbs
3 tablespoons vegetable oil
½ cup Chablis wine

Have butcher make pocket in each chop by cutting through bone and meat almost to fat. Pocket opening should be on bone side of chop. Combine cheese, parsley, mushrooms, and salt. Stuff pockets. Dip chops in beaten egg and then in bread crumbs. Brown on both sides in hot oil. Add wine and simmer covered 1 hour or until tender. Add more wine if skillet becomes dry.

Yield: 4 servings

Cheryl Sherling Magli (Mrs. Boyce)
Spring Hill, Tennessee

Marinated Pork Chops

6 (1-inch thick) pork chops
¾ cup honey
1½ teaspoons ginger
¼ teaspoon crushed thyme
1 clove garlic

Marinate pork chops in mixture of honey, ginger, thyme, and garlic overnight. Remove chops from marinade and partially cook 30 minutes at 350°. Cook on grill, turning frequently and basting with marinade, 30 minutes or until done.

Yield: 6 servings   Carla Bonham Livingston (Mrs. Jay H.)

Pork Barbecue

1 (10½-ounce) can beef consommé
1⅓ cups water
¾ cup Worcestershire sauce
⅓ cup vinegar
⅓ cup vegetable oil
1½ teaspoons monosodium glutamate
   (optional)
1½ teaspoons dry mustard
1 teaspoon minced garlic
1 teaspoon cayenne pepper
1 bay leaf
½ teaspoon paprika
6 to 8 pounds pork roast
   (Boston butt or shoulder)
Heinz 57 Sauce

Bring above ingredients except roast and Heinz 57 sauce to boil. Pour over roast. Bake overnight at 275°. Shred when cooled. Mix leftover sauce with Heinz 57 for thicker consistency. Heat and serve sauce with barbecue sandwiches.

Yield: 16 to 20 servings   Jennifer Logan Brown (Mrs. L. Daniel)

Barbecue Sauce

½ pound margarine
1 pint catsup
1½ cups vinegar
½ cup wine
1 tablespoon Tabasco sauce
2 tablespoons salt
1 tablespoon firmly packed
   brown sugar
1 tablespoon onion juice
Dash garlic powder
Dash red pepper
Dash black pepper
½ cup Worcestershire sauce

Bring all ingredients to boil. Store in refrigerator. Delicious on pork.

Note: This sauce is very hot.

Yield: 2 quarts   Rhys Jones Swan

Sausage-Zucchini Casserole

6 medium zucchini,
  about 2 pounds
½ pound pork sausage
¼ cup chopped onion
½ cup crushed saltine
  crackers

½ cup Parmesan cheese
2 eggs, slightly beaten
1 teaspoon salt
Dash pepper
⅛ teaspoon thyme
Dash garlic powder

Preheat oven to 350° and grease a 1½-quart casserole. Cook zucchini until just tender. Drain, but reserve ½ cup liquid. Coarsely chop squash. Cook sausage and onion together. Drain fat. Add zucchini and reserved liquid. Blend in remaining ingredients and turn into prepared casserole. Bake 45 minutes or until firm and bubbly.

Yield: 8 servings   Anne Keller Walters (Mrs. Charles M.)

Ham Baked in a Pastry Crust

4 (10-ounce) packages pie crust mix
1 teaspoon orange flower water
1 (8-pound) canned, boneless ham

1 egg white
½ cup Madeira

Preheat oven to 350°. Make pie crust according to package directions, add orange flower water. Roll out and cover sides and top of ham with pie crust. (Crust should be quite thick, almost ¼-inch on top.) Place ham in shallow baking pan. Brush crust with egg white. Bake 1 hour or longer according to directions on can. Ten minutes before serving, pour Madeira through slits in pastry.

Yield: 16 to 20 servings   Betty Rankin Graves

Mom's Baked Country Ham

One whole country ham
3 tablespoons sherry

2 tablespoons brown sugar

Cover ham with water and soak overnight. Change water and simmer over low heat 4 to 5 hours, until tender. Cool in liquid. When cold, drain and remove skin. Put ham in roasting pan. Make crisscross cuts in fat. Sprinkle with sherry and brown sugar. Bake in 425° preheated oven 25 minutes. Cool and slice paper thin.

Note: For half a ham, simmer 2 hours and follow all other directions.

Yield: 40 servings   Martha Spencer Fowler (Mrs. Michael F.)

Grilled Ham with Fruit Kabobs

1 (15¼-ounce) can pineapple
  chunks
2 apples, cut in wedges
1 medium green pepper,
  cut in 1-inch pieces
2 tablespoons minced onion

1 cup apricot preserves
¼ cup bottled Russian
  Salad Dressing
2 (¾-inch thick) fully
  cooked, center-cut
  smoked ham slices

Drain pineapple chunks, reserving ¼ cup juice. On metal skewers, alternately thread pieces of apple, pineapple chunks, and green pepper. Set aside. Combine ¼ cup reserved pineapple juice with minced onions and let stand 5 minutes. Add apricot preserves and Russian dressing, stirring well. Place ham slices and fruit kabobs on charcoal grill 3 to 5 inches from fire set at low to moderate heat. Cook 10 to 15 minutes, brushing ham and fruit with apricot sauce and turning occasionally.

Yield: 4 generous servings   Carla Bonham Livingston (Mrs. Jay H.)

Crêpes Ensenada

12 thin slices ham
12 tortillas
1 pound Monterey Jack cheese,
  cut in ½-inch sticks
1 (3-ounce) can green chilies,
  cut in ¼-inch strips
Wood picks
½ cup butter

½ cup all-purpose flour
4 cups milk
1 teaspoon prepared mustard
½ teaspoon salt
Dash pepper
½ teaspoon monosodium glutamate
  (optional)
¾ pound grated Cheddar cheese
Paprika

Preheat oven to 350°. Place one slice ham on each tortilla. Put one stick of cheese in center of ham and top with one green chili strip. Roll tortilla and secure with wood pick. Place rolled tortillas, slightly separated, in greased 13- x 9-inch oven-proof dish and set aside. Melt butter in saucepan and blend in flour. Add milk, mustard, salt, pepper, monosodium glutamate, and cheese. Cook and stir until smooth. Pour cheese sauce over crêpes to cover all. Sprinkle with paprika and bake 45 minutes.

Yield: 6 servings   Judy Gardiner Martin (Mrs. James R.)

Crêpes Specialty

½ cup chopped celery
½ cup chopped onion
¼ cup margarine
½ cup all-purpose flour
2 cups half and half cream
¾ teaspoon salt
2 cups sliced pitted ripe olives
1 teaspoon prepared mustard

1 cup cooked diced ham
2 tablespoons chopped parsley
¾ cup grated Swiss cheese
12 crêpes
Thin tomato slices (optional)
Whole ripe olives (optional)
Parsley sprigs (optional)

Preheat oven to 350°. Sauté celery and onion in margarine. Blend in flour. Gradually add half and half cream, stirring constantly. When smooth and very thick, add salt, sliced olives, mustard, ham, chopped parsley, and cheese. Stir until cheese melts. Fill crêpes and place in 3-quart oven-proof dish. Garnish with tomatoes and bake 10 minutes. Garnish with olives and parsley before serving.

Yield: 6 servings   Conni Hanson Collins (Mrs. Townsend S.)

Baked Ham Sauce

1 (17-ounce) can unpeeled
  apricot halves, drained
¼ cup corn syrup

¼ cup vinegar
1 teaspoon curry powder
¼ teaspoon dry mustard

Combine all ingredients in blender. Baste sauce over ham while it bakes. This is also good served with ham.

Yield: 2½ cups, approximately   Letty Bartlett Taylor (Mrs. George C.)

Creamy Mustard Sauce

3 tablespoons butter
¼ cup all-purpose flour
1 teaspoon salt
⅛ teaspoon pepper

2 cups half and half cream
1 cup sour cream
¼ cup prepared mustard

Melt butter. Blend in flour, salt, and pepper. Add cream and cook, stirring constantly until thick and smooth. Remove from heat. Fold in sour cream and mustard.

Note: Serve with corned beef, ham, or tongue.

Yield: 3½ cups   Margaret Thomas Frincke (Mrs. Harold C.)

Grandmother's Cream Gravy

3 tablespoons bacon or sausage
   drippings
3 tablespoons all-purpose flour

3 cups milk
Salt and pepper to taste

Combine drippings and flour in skillet. Heat on medium heat and stir 1 to 2 minutes. Add milk. Cook until slightly thickened, stirring constantly. Season with salt and pepper. Serve over hot biscuits.

Note: If gravy lumps, put all ingredients in jar or blender, blend thoroughly, and then cook.

Yield: 3 cups   Martha Spencer Fowler (Mrs. Michael F.)

Chicken in Mustard Sauce

2½ pounds boned chicken
   breasts
Salt and pepper
3 tablespoons clarified butter

½ cup dry white wine
½ cup whipping cream
3 tablespoons Dijon mustard

Pat and dry chicken breasts. Sprinkle with salt and pepper. Sauté chicken in clarified butter 15 to 20 minutes, turning until brown and cooked through. Keep chicken warm while making sauce. Pour wine into skillet over high heat and reduce liquid to a glaze. Add cream. Stir and bring to boil. Boil 3 minutes or until thickened. Reduce heat and whisk in mustard. Return chicken to skillet; spoon sauce over chicken and simmer 5 minutes.

Yield: 4 servings   Marie Humphreys O'Neill

Chicken in Wine

4 chicken breasts, skinned
3 tablespoons vegetable oil
1 (10¾-ounce) can cream
   of mushroom soup
½ cup cooking sherry
¼ cup grated sharp Cheddar cheese

3 tablespoons chopped
   onions
2 tablespoons Worcestershire
   sauce
Salt and pepper to taste

Preheat oven to 350°. Brown chicken breasts in oil. Place in 9-inch square baking pan. Combine soup, wine, cheese, onions, Worcestershire sauce, salt, and pepper. Pour over chicken. Cover and bake 1 hour and 15 minutes.

Yield: 4 servings   Lynne Greek Fain (Mrs. Walter D.)

Sweet and Sour Chicken

1 (20-ounce) can pineapple chunks
1 (8-ounce) bottle Russian dressing
1 (1.3-ounce) package onion soup mix

1 (10-ounce) jar apricot preserves
4 to 6 chicken breasts

Preheat oven to 350°. Drain pineapple and reserve liquid. Combine pineapple, Russian dressing, soup mix, half of reserved liquid, and apricot preserves. Arrange chicken breasts in 8-inch oven-proof dish and top with mixture. Bake 1 hour.

Yield: 4 servings

Nancy Willson Walker

Mexican Chicken

5 chicken breasts
2 pounds Velveeta cheese
1 (10¾-ounce) can tomato soup

Jalapeño peppers to taste
5 tablespoons diced onion
2 (8-ounce) bags regular Doritos

Preheat oven to 325° and bake chicken 1 hour. While chicken is cooling, melt cheese in double boiler. When completely melted, add soup, peppers, and onions. (For mild hot sauce add 1½ peppers, diced and seeded, and 3 tablespoons pepper juice from jar.) Debone chicken and tear into larger-than-bite-size pieces. In 9- x 13-inch oven-proof dish, alternate Doritos, chicken, and sauce. Repeat and top with crushed Doritos. Bake 30 minutes at 350°.

Yield: 6 servings

Debbie Brown Ledbetter (Mrs. Paul E.)

Chicken Maharani

4 whole chicken breasts
2 teaspoons Accent
1 teaspoon salt
¼ teaspoon pepper

8 ounces Cheddar cheese, grated
1 (8-ounce) package cream cheese
¼ cup corn oil
1 (10-ounce) jar chutney, mashed

Preheat oven to 350°. Skin, halve, debone, and flatten chicken breasts. Sprinkle each with Accent, salt, and pepper. Combine cheeses and beat until light and fluffy. Spoon cheese mixture onto each chicken piece, leaving ½ inch all around. Roll up each breast and secure with toothpicks. Place on 9- x 13-inch baking pan; brush all sides with corn oil. Bake uncovered 40 minutes. Spoon chutney over chicken and continue cooking about 10 minutes or until sauce is warm and fork can be inserted with ease. Serve on rice and garnish with parsley.

Yield: 8 servings

Susan Additon Farris (Mrs. R. Kent)

Chicken Saltimbocca

3 large whole chicken
  breasts, skinned, boned,
  and halved lengthwise
6 thin slices boiled ham
3 slices Mozzarella cheese,
  halved
1 medium tomato, chopped
½ teaspoon sage, crushed

⅓ cup fine dry bread
  crumbs
2 tablespoons grated Parmesan
  cheese
4 tablespoons snipped
  parsley
4 tablespoons melted
  margarine

Preheat oven to 350°. Flatten chicken breasts. Place one ham slice and one-half slice of cheese on each cutlet, cutting to fit. Top with some tomato and dash of sage. Tuck in sides and roll up jelly-roll style. Secure with toothpicks, pressing to seal well. Combine bread crumbs, Parmesan cheese, and parsley. Dip chicken in margarine and roll in crumbs. Place in shallow 2-quart oven-proof dish and bake 40 to 45 minutes.

Yield: 6 servings   Virginia Pert Rainwater (Mrs. J. Earl)

Chicken á l'Orange

3 whole chicken breasts, boned
  and cut in half
Salt and pepper
All-purpose flour
½ cup butter
2 cups chicken stock

1 cup port wine
1 cup orange juice
1 tablespoon currant jelly
Pinch of ginger
2 tablespoons cornstarch
4 tablespoons sherry

Preheat oven to 350°. Season chicken with salt and pepper and roll in flour. Melt butter in large iron skillet and sauté chicken until golden brown. Add chicken stock, cover, and bake 20 minutes. Remove chicken. Add wine, orange juice, jelly, and ginger to stock and cook over low heat 15 minutes. Adjust seasonings. Combine cornstarch and sherry to make paste and add to stock. Cook until thickened and strain if necessary. Return chicken to sauce, cover, and bake 15 to 20 minutes or until heated thoroughly.

Yield: 4 to 6 servings   Aileen Vise Pettit (Mrs. Cliff)

Chicken Normandy

2 to 3 whole chicken breasts,
  boned and halved
Salt and pepper to taste
½ teaspoon thyme
½ cup margarine, divided
½ cup chopped chicken livers
2 tablespoons chopped onion

1 teaspoon salt
1 (4-ounce) can mushrooms
1 cup grated Swiss cheese
1 egg, beaten
Fine, dry bread crumbs
Sauce Supreme
  (recipe follows)

Flatten chicken breasts. Sprinkle with salt, pepper, and thyme; set aside. Heat ¼ cup margarine. Add livers, onion, and salt, and cook slowly 5 minutes. Remove from heat; add mushrooms and cheese. Stuff chicken breasts. Roll in beaten egg and then in bread crumbs. Chill at least 2 hours. Brown breasts in remaining margarine. Bake 45 minutes at 350°. Serve with Sauce Supreme.

Sauce Supreme:

¼ cup margarine
¼ cup all-purpose flour
2 cups chicken stock
  or canned broth

1 tablespoon lemon juice
½ cup half and half cream

Melt margarine and blend in flour. Add stock. Cook, stirring constantly until mixture thickens. Boil gently 3 minutes longer. Add lemon juice; stir in cream. Heat, but do not boil. Makes approximately 3 cups.

Yield: 4 to 6 servings

Margaret Thomas Frincke (Mrs. Harold)

Chicken with Walnuts en Brochette

1½ cups chopped walnuts
½ cup lime juice
⅓ cup chopped scallions
2 tablespoons chicken broth
2 garlic cloves

Salt and pepper to taste
2 (8-ounce) chicken breasts, boned
  and cut in ¾-inch cubes
¾ cup plain yogurt

Place nuts, juice, scallions, broth, garlic cloves, salt, and pepper in blender and blend until nuts are finely ground. Reserve ½ cup of mixture. Place chicken cubes in bowl and marinate in nut mixture 3 hours, turning occasionally. Divide chicken among six 7-inch skewers. Broil and turn 5 inches from heat for 5 minutes. Add yogurt to reserved marinade and serve as sauce for chicken.

Yield: 6 skewers

Nancy Davis Gill (Mrs. Hoyle)

Party Chicken

4 chicken breasts, boned
¼ cup all-purpose flour
1 teaspoon salt, divided
¼ teaspoon paprika
2 dashes pepper
2 cups dry bread crumbs

1 tablespoon chopped onion
¼ teaspoon poultry seasoning
10 tablespoons butter
¼ cup hot water
Chopped parsley
Mushroom sauce (recipe follows)

Preheat oven to 325°. Split chicken breasts enough to fold. Combine flour, ½ teaspoon salt, paprika, and 1 dash pepper in paper bag. Add chicken and shake to coat. For stuffing, combine bread crumbs, onion, ½ teaspoon salt, poultry seasoning, and 1 dash pepper. Add 2 tablespoons butter and hot water; toss gently to moisten. Fill cavity of each chicken piece with stuffing and skewer opening shut with toothpicks. Dip chicken in remaining melted butter and place in baking dish, drizzling any remaining butter over top. Bake 45 minutes; turn and bake an additional 45 minutes or until tender. Sprinkle with chopped parsley. Serve with mushroom sauce.

Mushroom Sauce:

½ pound fresh mushrooms
½ cup chopped onion
2 tablespoons butter or margarine
1 to 2 tablespoons all-purpose flour

½ cup whipping cream
½ cup sour cream
½ teaspoon salt
½ teaspoon pepper

Cook mushrooms and onion lightly in butter until tender but not brown. Cover and cook 10 minutes over low heat. Push mushrooms to one side and stir flour into butter. Add cream, sour cream, salt, and pepper. Heat slowly, stirring constantly almost to boiling point.

Yield: 1½ cups Mushroom Sauce
    4 servings of Party Chicken

Margie Parker Young (Mrs. L. R.)
Marshall, Texas

Country Style Chicken Kiev

½ cup bread crumbs
2 tablespoons Parmesan cheese
1 teaspoon basil
1 teaspoon oregano
½ teaspoon garlic salt
¼ teaspoon salt

4 to 6 boned chicken breasts
½ cup margarine, melted
¼ cup dry white wine
  or apple juice
¼ cup chopped green onions
¼ cup chopped fresh parsley

Preheat oven to 375°. Grease 8-inch oven-proof dish. Combine bread crumbs, cheese, basil, oregano, garlic salt, and salt. Dip chicken breasts in melted margarine, then roll in crumb mixture to coat. Place in prepared dish and bake 45 to 50 minutes. Combine remaining margarine with wine and pour over chicken. Mix remaining bread crumb mixture with onions and parsley and sprinkle over chicken. Bake 15 minutes longer.

Yield: 4 servings

Nancy Willson Walker

Stir Fry Chicken with Walnuts

2 whole chicken breasts, boned
1 teaspoon salt
1 teaspoon sugar
3 tablespoons sherry
1 tablespoon soy sauce
3 tablespoons cornstarch
1 egg, beaten

½ cup vegetable oil
1 cup blanched walnuts
2 teaspoons minced ginger
2 garlic cloves, minced
½ cup boilng water
1 teaspoon Accent
1 cup sliced bamboo shoots

Cut chicken into 1-inch cubes. Combine salt, sugar, sherry, and soy sauce. Place chicken in mixture and toss to coat. Let stand 30 minutes. Drain, reserving marinade. Roll chicken in cornstarch and dip in egg. Heat oil in deep skillet; brown walnuts and remove. Pour off all but 2 tablespoons oil. Brown chicken, ginger, and garlic; add water, Accent, bamboo shoots, and reserved marinade. Cover and simmer 15 minutes. Return walnuts to mixture and cook 1 minute longer.

Yield: 4 to 6 servings

Mitty Chang

Microwaved Taco Chicken

2 tablespoons butter
1 (5-ounce) jar cheese spread
½ onion, chopped
1 teaspoon salt
2 teaspoons green chilies, chopped
8 chicken breasts, deboned and flattened

1 cup crushed cheddar cheese crackers
1½ tablespoons taco seasoning mix
¼ cup butter, melted
Shredded lettuce
Diced tomatoes
Olives

Combine butter and cheese spread. Add onion, salt, and green chilies. Divide mixture evenly over each chicken breast, placing at one end. Roll chicken up, tuck ends, and secure with toothpick. Combine crackers and taco seasoning mix. Dip chicken in melted butter and roll in cracker mixture. Place in 12- x 8- x 2-inch dish. Cover and microwave at full power 10 to 12 minutes. Serve on bed of shredded lettuce, surround with diced tomatoes, and top with olives.

Yield: 8 servings   Geri Carmichael Muse (Mrs. William Scott, Jr.)

Sauté of Lemon Chicken

1 (3- to 4-pound) chicken
Juice of 1 lemon
3 tablespoons butter
¼ cup vegetable oil
½ cup dry white wine

1 cup chicken stock
1 teaspoon dried thyme
½ cup whipping cream
1 teaspoon salt
¼ teaspoon white pepper

Cut chicken into serving portions. Rub lemon juice thoroughly on all pieces. Melt butter with oil in large frying pan. Add chicken; fry over medium heat 10 to 15 minutes or until golden. Drain chicken grease, add wine, and simmer. Add chicken stock and thyme. Simmer about 20 minutes or until chicken is tender. Transfer chicken to heated serving dish and keep warm. Add cream to liquid in frying pan; boil until mixture thickens to heavy consistency (about 5 to 8 minutes). Salt and pepper to taste. Pour over chicken and serve.

Yield: 4 to 6 servings   William Johnson
The Lord Lindsay Restaurant
Knoxville, Tennessee

Chicken Renoir

Chicken pieces (2 to 3 per person)
Olive oil
1 tablespoon butter
1 clove garlic, minced
2 medium onions, finely chopped
2 medium tomatoes, chopped
2 parsley sprigs, chopped and
    divided

1 bay leaf
1 tablespoon thyme
1 teaspoon salt
½ teaspoon pepper
¾ cup hot water
12 small fresh mushrooms
12 pitted black olives, sliced
¼ cup brandy, flaming

Brown chicken in hot oil and place on warm platter. Discard oil from pan. Return chicken to pan with butter, garlic, onions, tomatoes, half parsley, bay leaf, thyme, salt, pepper, and water. Cover and simmer about 15 minutes, stirring occasionally. Add mushrooms and olives, and simmer 15 minutes. When serving, heat brandy, ignite, and pour over all. Sprinkle with remaining chopped parsley.

Yield: 4 servings

Marie Humphreys O'Neill

Quick Chicken Chasseur

1 pound chicken breasts,
    boned and skinned
⅓ cup cornstarch
¼ cup vegetable oil
½ teaspoon tarragon
½ teaspoon ground thyme
¼ teaspoon pepper

1 cup sliced scallions
2 cups chicken broth
¾ cup cooking sherry
1 cup sliced mushrooms
3 tomatoes, cut in eighths
3 to 4 cups hot cooked rice

Cut chicken into strips and dredge in cornstarch. In a large skillet, brown chicken in oil. Stir in seasonings and scallions. Cook 2 minutes. Add broth and sherry. Cover and simmer 10 minutes. Gently stir in mushrooms and tomatoes. Cover and simmer 5 minutes. Serve over rice. Sauce may be served separately.

Yield: 4 to 6 servings

Nancy Helton O'Callaghan

Chicken with White Wine Barbecue Sauce

8 green onions, chopped
2 pounds butter
6 lemons, squeezed (reserve rinds)
½ cup corn oil
5 tablespoons soy sauce
2 tablespoons Worcestershire sauce

1 teaspoon garlic powder
1 teaspoon salt
2 tablespoons Tabasco sauce
½ cup Sauterne
Dash pepper
4 to 6 chickens, split

In saucepan, sauté onions in butter over low heat. Add all remaining ingredients, except chicken, and cook over low heat 30 minutes. Grill chicken halves 1 hour, basting often. Turn chicken with tongs to prevent piercing skin.

Yield: 8 to 12 servings   Anne Walters Pittenger (Mrs. Gaines Sherman)

Honey Barbecued Broilers

¾ cup melted margarine
⅓ cup vinegar
¼ cup honey
2 cloves garlic, minced
2 teaspoons salt

½ teaspoon dry mustard
½ teaspoon marjoram leaves
Freshly ground pepper
2 to 3 pounds chicken pieces

Mix together all ingredients except chicken. Grill chicken over charcoal fire until done, basting with marinade during last 15 minutes.

Note: Be careful not to let chicken burn after marinade is applied.

Yield: 4 servings   Carolyn Dominick Townsend (Mrs. Dalton)

Chicken Cutlets

4 whole chicken breasts, boned
 and halved
All-purpose flour
3 eggs, beaten

Fresh white bread crumbs
½ cup unsalted butter
Thin lemon slices

Pound chicken breasts with rolling pin between sheets of waxed paper. Place flour, eggs, and bread crumbs in 3 separate bowls. Dip each chicken breast in flour, eggs, and crumbs, in that order. Chill at least 1 hour. Sauté over medium low heat in melted butter until brown on both sides. Garnish with lemon slices.

Note: These can be prepared few minutes ahead and kept warm.

Yield: 6 to 8 servings   Betsy Guinn Foster (Mrs. Bruce, Jr.)

Gourmet Fried Chicken

1 cup plus 2 tablespoons
  all-purpose flour
1 teaspoon baking powder
¼ teaspoon salt
2 eggs
⅔ cup milk
1 teaspoon vegetable oil

1 teaspoon sugar
2 teaspoons brandy
2 teaspoons lemon juice
Butter and vegetable oil
  for frying
1 fryer, cut up, or 8
  chicken breasts

Sift together flour, baking powder, and salt. Beat eggs until fluffy and add milk, 1 teaspoon vegetable oil, sugar, brandy, and lemon juice. Add flour mixture and blend. Melt butter and oil to depth of 1½ to 2 inches in electric skillet. Dip chicken in batter and fry.

Note: For a crisp crust, cover and cook for half the required time; remove cover for the last half of cooking time.

Yield: 8 servings   Margie Cooley Jones (Mrs. William W.)

Chicken Breasts with Wild Rice

6 chicken breast halves,
  boned and skinned
Salt
Pepper
½ cup butter
4 to 6 servings cooked wild rice

1 pound fresh mushrooms, sliced
1 tablespoon minced onion
¼ cup brandy
¼ cup sherry
2 cups whipping cream
Minced parsley

Flatten chicken breasts between sheets of waxed paper. Season with salt and pepper. Melt butter in large skillet. Cook chicken, covered with buttered round of waxed paper and skillet lid, over low heat 10 minutes, or until cooked through. Remove chicken and arrange on platter of wild rice. Keep chicken and rice warm. Sauté mushrooms and onions until golden, adding more butter if necessary. Remove skillet from heat; add brandy and sherry. Cook over moderately high heat until liquid is reduced by half. Stir in cream, ½ cup at a time, letting each addition reduce 1 minute before adding next. Season sauce with salt and pepper and pour over chicken and rice. Garnish with parsley.

Yield: 4 to 6 servings   Sandy Turner Fiser (Mrs. John R.)

Spaghetti with Chicken and Mushrooms

1 (3-pound) chicken, cut up
½ cup butter, divided
1 teaspoon salt
½ cup chopped celery leaves
1 small onion, chopped
3 cups water
1 pound fresh mushrooms

3 tablespoons all-purpose flour
1½ cups whipping cream
⅔ cup grated Romano cheese
2 cloves garlic, crushed
¼ cup dry sherry (optional)
Cooked spaghetti

Brown chicken in 3 tablespoons butter. Add salt, celery, onion, and water. Cover and simmer until chicken is tender, about 30 minutes. Cool, bone chicken, and cut into cubes. Strain and reserve 1½ cups broth. Sauté mushrooms in 2 tablespoons butter until tender. Add chicken. Melt remaining 3 tablespoons butter in heavy saucepan. Add flour and blend with whisk. Meanwhile, combine 1½ cups chicken broth and whipping cream; bring to boil and add at once to flour and butter mixture, stirring vigorously with whisk. Stir in grated cheese, chicken, garlic, mushrooms, and sherry, if desired. Serve over hot spaghetti.

Yield: 6 servings   Ena Taylor Kirkpatrick (Mrs. David M.)

Microwaved Chicken Spectacular

3½ cups cooked and diced
   chicken
1 (6-ounce) package wild and white
   rice mixed with herbs,
   prepared as directed
1 (10-ounce) package frozen French
   style green beans, blanched
1 onion, chopped

1 (10¾-ounce) can cream of
   celery soup
1 (2-ounce) jar chopped pimiento
½ cup mayonnaise
1 (8-ounce) can water
   chestnuts, diced
Salt and pepper to taste

Combine all ingredients. Pour in 2-quart oven-proof dish. Cover and microwave at medium power 5 minutes.

Yield: 6 servings   Betty Newbill Threadgill

Scalloped Chicken

1 (5-pound) hen
1 onion, sliced
1 carrot
2 teaspoons salt

2 quarts water
Stuffing (recipe follows)
Sauce (recipe follows)
Topping (recipe follows)

Grease 9- x 13-inch oven-proof dish. Cook hen 2½ hours with onion, carrot, salt, and water. Cool hen in liquid. When cool, debone and cut meat into bite-size pieces. Reserve broth and chicken skin. Place Stuffing in prepared dish; cover with half of Sauce. Top with chicken and cover with remaining Sauce. Sprinkle with Topping and bake 20 minutes at 375° or until golden brown.

Stuffing:

1½ loaves two-day-old bread
½ cup butter
6 sprigs parsley, chopped
6 scallions with tops, chopped
2 ribs celery with leaves,
   chopped

Cooked giblets
1 teaspoon salt
Dash white pepper
1 teaspoon poultry seasoning
6 tablespoons reserved chicken
   broth

Trim crust from bread and crumble bread. Melt butter; add parsley, scallions, and celery. Cook 5 minutes. Lightly mix with crumbs. Grind giblets and add to crumb mixture. Add remaining ingredients and use as directed.

Sauce:

1 cup chicken fat skimmed
   from broth
1 cup all-purpose flour
1 cup milk

4 cups reserved chicken broth
2 teaspoons salt
4 eggs, lightly beaten
Reserved chicken skin, ground

Heat fat in large pan. (If necessary, add butter to make 1 cup fat.) Add flour and blend until smooth. Stir in milk, broth, and salt. Cook until thick. Gradually add eggs. Cook 3 to 4 minutes and add ground chicken skin. Use as directed.

Topping:

1 cup bread crumbs

4 tablespoons butter, melted

Toss crumbs with butter and use as directed.

Yield: 12 servings

Donna Peters Clark (Mrs. Steven A.)

Party Chicken Casserole

6 pounds chicken breasts
1 onion, quartered
2 bay leaves
2 ribs celery
Salt
Water

4 (14-ounce) cans artichoke hearts,
　rinsed and quartered
5 (6- or 8-ounce) jars whole
　mushrooms
Cream Sauce (recipe follows)
Cheese Sauce (recipe follows)

Place chicken, onion, bay leaves, celery, and salt in large pot; cover with water and simmer until tender. Strain stock and reserve for cream sauce. Skin, bone, and cube chicken. Divide chicken between two 9- x 13-inch oven-proof dishes. Cover with artichoke hearts, mushrooms, and combined sauces. Bake 1 hour at 350°.

Cream Sauce:

1 pound butter (or use half
　butter and half margarine)
1¼ cups all-purpose flour
8 cups chicken stock
　(reserved from above)

1 tablespoon salt
2 tablespoons Accent
1 teaspoon cayenne pepper
⅛ teaspoon garlic salt

In a saucepan, melt butter; remove from heat and stir in flour until it forms smooth paste. Return to heat and let mixture bubble, then add stock all at once, and remaining ingredients. Whisk and cook over medium heat until thickened. Use as directed.

Cheese Sauce:

¼ pound sharp Cheddar
　cheese, grated

1 (8-ounce) round Munster
　cheese, cubed
1 (8-ounce) can tomato sauce

Melt cheeses in warmed tomato sauce. Use as directed.

Yield: 24 servings　　　　　　　　　　　　　　　　　　Nancy Reynolds

Chicken Rotel

2 frying chickens
2 bell peppers, chopped
2 onions, chopped
½ cup butter
½ teaspoon Worcestershire sauce

1 (16-ounce) package vermicelli
1 pound Velveeta, cut in small
    pieces or grated
1(10-ounce) can Rotel tomatoes
1 (3-ounce) can mushrooms

Boil chickens until tender. Cut chicken meat into bite-size pieces. Reserve 2 quarts broth. Preheat oven to 300°. Sauté peppers and onions in butter.Add Worcestershire sauce. Cook vermicelli in broth and drain. Add cheese to hot vermicelli and allow to melt. Blend in remaining ingredients. Place in two 3-quart oven-proof dishes and bake 20 to 30 minutes.

Note: If halving recipe, 4 chicken breasts can be substituted for chicken.

Yield: 12 servings   Linda Jetton Livaudais (Mrs. Denny)

Company Casserole

¾ pound spaghetti
½ cup all-purpose flour
½ cup butter
1½ cups milk
2 cups cream or evaporated milk
1 (10¾-ounce) can cream of
    mushroom soup
½ cup chicken broth
1 cup grated Cheddar cheese,
    divided
1 tablespoon lemon juice

1½ tablespoons grated onion
1 tablespoon dry mustard
1 tablespoon chopped parsley
2½ teaspoons salt
½ teaspoon pepper
1 cup mayonnaise
6 cups cooked chicken, cubed
2 tomatoes, sliced
½ cup French dressing
Cracker crumbs

Cook spaghetti and set aside. Make sauce in pan with flour, butter, milk, cream, soup, and chicken broth. Add ¾ cup cheese and lemon juice. Season with onion, dry mustard, parsley, salt, and pepper. Remove from heat and add mayonnaise. Mix sauce with drained spaghetti and chicken. Place in two 2-quart casseroles. Add rest of grated cheese and tomatoes. Dribble dressing on top. Sprinkle with cracker crumbs. Bake 35 to 45 minutes at 350°.

Yield: 12 servings   Letty Bartlett Taylor (Mrs. George C.)

Old-Fashioned Chicken and Dumplings

1 (3-pound) broiler-fryer, cut up
1 medium onion, halved
1 tablespoon salt
¼ teaspoon pepper

Approximately 6 cups water
2 cups self-rising flour
¼ teaspoon thyme
½ cup ice water

Combine chicken, onion, salt, pepper, and about 6 cups water in Dutch oven. Bring to boil; cover and simmer 2 hours or until chicken is tender. Remove chicken from broth and cool. Bone chicken. If necessary, add additional water to broth to make 6 cups. Return chicken to broth and bring to boil. Combine flour and thyme. Add about ½ cup ice water to make soft dough and stir well. Turn dough onto lightly floured surface. Knead gently 30 seconds. Roll dough to ⅛-inch thickness and cut into ½- x 4-inch strips. Drop strips into boiling broth. Cover and reduce heat; simmer 30 to 40 minutes.

Yield: 6 to 8 servings   Nancy Helton O'Callaghan

Chicken Pot Pie

¼ cup butter
1 cup chopped onion
½ cup chopped celery
6 to 7 tablespoons all-purpose flour
1 cup milk
1 cup chicken broth
1 cup sour cream
1 cup white wine
3 cups chopped, cooked chicken

¼ teaspoon rosemary
¼ teaspoon savory
1 tablespoon parsley
1 teaspoon salt
¼ teaspoon pepper
2 cups cooked carrots
2 cups peas
Pastry for 9-inch pie crust

Melt butter in large saucepan over moderate heat. Sauté onion and celery; blend in flour. Add milk, broth, and sour cream. Stir over low heat until thickened. Add wine, chicken, rosemary, savory, parsley, salt, and pepper. Cover and simmer 10 to 15 minutes, stirring occasionally. Cool to room temperature. Mix in carrots and peas. Spoon into ungreased 2½-quart casserole. Prepare pastry and roll into circle 3 inches larger than casserole. Make steam slits near center of pastry and place over casserole. Roll edges under, even with rim. Bake 30 to 40 minutes at 350° until brown and bubbly.

Yield: 6 to 8 servings   Sandy Turner Fiser (Mrs. John R.)

Chicken with Curry Sauce

3½ pounds chicken
1 large carrot, chopped
1 medium onion, chopped
1 clove garlic or 4 shallots,
  chopped
6 sprigs parsley, chopped
1 stalk celery with leaves, chopped
1 bay leaf

¼ teaspoon thyme
¼ teaspoon peppercorns
1½ teaspoons salt
6 cups water
2 cups Chablis
Sauce (recipe follows)
Steamed rice

Place chicken, ready to cook and trussed, breast side down in large pot. Add remaining ingredients, except sauce. Bring liquid to boil, cover, and poach chicken 55 minutes. Remove chicken from stock and cut into quarters. Reserve stock for sauce. Arrange parts on warm platter and pour sauce over. Serve with steamed rice.

Sauce:

½ large apple, peeled and minced
2 small onions, minced
3 tablespoons butter
1 tablespoon curry powder
3 tablespoons all-purpose flour

2 cups hot chicken stock
½ cup whipping cream
Salt to taste
1 teaspoon lemon juice

Sauté apples and onions in butter. Cook over moderate heat 3 minutes, stirring occasionally. Stir in curry and cook, stirring 2 minutes. Blend in flour. Gradually stir in stock and cook over low heat 25 minutes, stirring occasionally. Strain sauce through fine sieve; return to heat. Stir in remaining ingredients. Pour sauce over chicken.

Yield: 4 servings

Margie Parker Young (Mrs. L. R.)
Marshall, Texas

Chicken Curry

¼ cup minced onion
¼ cup pared and chopped apple
¼ cup butter
¼ cup all-purpose flour
1 cup half and half cream
1 cup chicken broth

1 to 2 teaspoons curry powder
Salt and pepper to taste
3 tablespoons white raisins
3 cups cooked and diced chicken
Hot cooked yellow rice

Sauté onion and apple in butter until tender. Stir in flour and blend. Gradually add cream and broth, stirring until thickened. Season with curry powder, salt, and pepper. Add raisins and chicken. Serve over yellow rice and with condiments, if desired.

Yield: 6 servings

Donna McNab Cobble (Mrs. Bill. L.)

Curry Chicken Casserole

2 (10-ounce) packages frozen broccoli
2 cups cooked chicken or turkey
    or 3 whole chicken breasts,
    cooked and boned
2 (10¾-ounce) cans cream of
    mushroom soup
¾ cup mayonnaise

1 tablespoon curry powder
1 teaspoon lemon juice
½ cup grated sharp
    Cheddar cheese
½ cup soft bread crumbs
1 tablespoon butter, melted

Preheat oven to 350°. Cook broccoli and arrange half in greased 9- x 13-inch oven-proof dish. Arrange half cut-up chicken pieces on top of broccoli. Combine soup, mayonnaise, curry, and lemon juice. Pour half soup mixture over chicken. Repeat layers. Sprinkle with cheese. Combine bread crumbs with butter and spread on top. Bake 25 to 30 minutes.

Yield: 8 servings   Mary Frances West Fox (Mrs. Bruce, Jr.)

Chicken and Wild Rice Casserole

6 pounds chicken
1 cup water
1 cup dry sherry
1½ teaspoons salt
½ teaspoon curry powder
1 medium onion, sliced
½ cup diced celery
1 pound fresh mushrooms

¼ cup butter
2 (6-ounce) packages long grain
    quick-cooking wild rice,
    cooked
1 cup sour cream
1 (10¾-ounce) can cream of
    mushroom soup
Fresh mushrooms, sliced

Place chicken in deep kettle and add water, sherry, salt, curry, onion, and celery. Bring to boil. Cover tightly and simmer 1 hour. Strain broth. Remove chicken from bones in bite-size pieces. Refrigerate chicken and broth at once. Wash mushrooms and pat dry. Sauté in butter. Measure broth and use as part of liquid for cooking rice. Combine chicken, cooked rice, and mushrooms. Blend sour cream and mushroom soup and toss with chicken mixture. Arrange fresh mushrooms on top. Cover and bake 1 hour at 350°.

Yield: 8 to 10 servings   Sherri Parker Lee

Poultry and Game

171

Chicken Crêpes

6 tablespoons butter, divided
1 cup sliced fresh mushrooms
1 cup diced chicken
3 hard-cooked egg yolks, mashed
½ cup sour cream
1 tablespoon minced fresh parsley
1 teaspoon salt

¼ teaspoon pepper
½ (10-ounce) package frozen spinach, cooked and well drained
12 to 18 crêpes
3 tablespoons grated Parmesan cheese
Velouté Sauce (recipe follows)

Preheat oven to 425°. Melt 3 tablespoons butter and sauté mushrooms. Remove from heat. Mix in chicken, egg yolks, sour cream, parsley, salt, pepper, and spinach. Fill crêpes and roll tightly. Arrange in oven-proof dish. Sprinkle with cheese. Dot with remaining butter. Bake 15 minutes. Serve with Velouté Sauce.

Velouté Sauce:

2 tablespoons butter
2 tablespoons all-purpose flour
2 cups chicken stock

¼ cup chopped mushrooms
Pinch of nutmeg
Salt and white pepper to taste

Melt butter in top of double boiler and stir in flour. When blended, add stock and cook, stirring until thickened. Add mushrooms and simmer about 1 hour. Add nutmeg and seasonings to taste.

Yield: 1½ cups

Donna McNab Cobble (Mrs. Bill L.)

Tetrazzini Crêpes

2 whole chicken breasts
½ cup chicken broth
6 tablespoons butter, divided
5 ounces fresh mushrooms, sliced
⅛ cup all-purpose flour
¾ cup whipping cream, warmed

⅓ cup dry sherry
1 cup grated sharp Cheddar cheese
2 tablespoons chopped ripe olives
14 crêpes
2 tablespoons grated Parmesan cheese

Cook chicken in broth and enough water to cover for 20 minutes or until tender. Reserve 1¼ cups broth. Remove skin and dice chicken. Melt 3 tablespoons butter in skillet and brown mushrooms. Set aside. Melt remaining butter in saucepan; stir in flour and cook until frothy. Add broth and warmed cream. Cook sauce until thickened, stirring constantly. Add sherry and Cheddar cheese and stir until melted. Combine chicken, mushrooms, olives, and 1 cup sauce. Spoon 3 tablespoons filling onto each crêpe, roll up, and place in buttered 11- x 7-inch oven-proof dish. Pour remaining sauce over crêpes. Sprinkle with Parmesan cheese. Bake 20 minutes at 375°.

Yield: 7 servings

Suzanne Wood Fletcher

Baked Chicken Sandwich

2 cups chopped cooked chicken
1 cup grated Cheddar cheese
½ cup mayonnaise
12 slices trimmed white bread
6 eggs

1 pint half and half cream
1 cup milk
¾ teaspoon salt
Sliced almonds

Mix chicken, cheese, and mayonnaise, and spread between slices of bread. Place in greased 9- x 13-inch oven-proof dish. Beat eggs, cream, milk, and salt. Pour over bread and let stand overnight, refrigerated. Bake covered 35 minutes at 350°. Remove cover, sprinkle with almonds, and bake an additional 15 minutes. Do not freeze.

Yield: 6 servings   Betsy Guinn Foster (Mrs. E. Bruce, Jr.)

Hot Chicken and Cheese Sandwich

6 English muffins, split and
   toasted
3 tomatoes, sliced

4 chicken breasts, cooked,
   boned, and sliced
12 slices bacon, cooked
Cheese Sauce (recipe follows)

Preheat oven to 350°. Place muffins on pan, place tomato slice on each muffin, and top with slice of chicken. Break each slice of bacon in half and crisscross on top of chicken. Cover with Cheese Sauce and heat until just warmed through.

Cheese Sauce:

½ cup butter
½ cup all-purpose flour
½ teaspoon salt

4 cups milk
3 cups grated cheese

In saucepan melt butter, remove from heat and add flour and salt, stirring until smooth. Return to heat and cook until bubbly; add milk all at once. Cook, stirring frequently, until thickened. Remove from heat and add cheese, stirring until melted.

Note: This is also an excellent way to use leftover turkey.

Yield: 6 servings   Connie Bell Taylor (Mrs. Alexander M.)

Oriental Turkey Breast

1 (4- to 6-pound) turkey breast
1 tablespoon curry powder
1 tablespoon basil
½ teaspoon salt
1 teaspoon paprika
1 onion, quartered

1 carrot, quartered
1 stalk celery, quartered
1 orange, quartered
1 cup gin
1 cup water

Preheat oven to 350°. Wash and dry turkey breast. Combine curry, basil, salt, and paprika. Rub turkey with herb mixture. Place in roasting pan with vegetables and orange. Combine gin and water, and pour over turkey breast. Bake uncovered 3 hours, basting with water mixture. When done, spoon fat from pan juices and strain. Serve turkey thinly sliced with unthickened pan juices.

Yield: 8 servings   Carol Smith Hudgens (Mrs. James F.)

Broccoli-Stuffed Cornish Hens

1 (10-ounce) package frozen chopped
   broccoli, cooked and drained
1 cup cooked long-grain rice
½ cup grated Swiss cheese

2 tablespoons butter, melted
¼ teaspoon salt
Dash pepper
4 Cornish game hens

Combine broccoli, rice, cheese, butter, salt, and pepper. Rinse birds; pat dry with paper towel. Lightly salt cavities. Stuff with broccoli mixture. Tie legs to tail. Secure neck skin to back with small skewers. Mount birds crosswise on spit, alternating front-back, back-front. Do not let birds touch. Secure with extra long holding forks, or one holding fork per bird. Brush birds with additional butter. Attach spit over medium coals. Roast until done (about 1¼ to 1½ hours), brushing with melted butter every half hour.

Note: Can be roasted in oven if spit is not available.

Yield: 4 servings   Suzanne L. McMillen

Cornish Hens

6 Cornish hens
½ cup butter, melted
½ cup white wine
1 clove garlic, crushed

1½ teaspoons salt
½ teaspoon rubbed sage
Wine gravy (recipe follows)
Wild rice

Preheat oven to 400°. Arrange hens breast side up in pan without rack. Roast about 1 to 1½ hours. Combine butter, wine, garlic, salt, and sage. Mix well and baste hens often. Serve with wine gravy and wild rice.

Wine Gravy:

⅔ cup pan drippings
   from above recipe
3 tablespoons all-purpose flour
½ cup white wine

1 cup currant jelly
1 teaspoon dry mustard
1 teaspoon salt

Return ⅔ cup pan drippings to roasting pan. Gradually add flour and stir until smooth. Add remaining ingredients. Bring mixture to boil; reduce heat and simmer, stirring occasionally until thickened.

Yield: 6 servings   Marie Humphreys O'Neill

Dove Casserole

20 dove breasts
1 cup seasoned flour
Butter
3 chicken bouillon cubes
2 cups water

1 cup chopped celery
1 large onion, chopped
¾ cup chopped parsley
½ cup white wine

Preheat oven to 350°. Dredge doves in seasoned flour. Brown in butter. Dissolve bouillon cubes in water. Place browned doves in 9- x 13-inch ovenproof dish. Add celery, onions, and parsley. Cover with bouillon. Cover and bake 1½ to 2 hours, adding wine last 3 minutes.

Yield: 4 to 6 servings   Carol Smith Hudgens (Mrs. James F.)

Grilled Filet of Duck

Breast filet of Mallard or
   any waterfowl

Italian dressing

Marinate filets in Italian dressing overnight or for several hours. Grill over charcoal approximately 15 minutes per side.

                                                          Joe Congleton

Louisiana Duck Gumbo

1 cup all-purpose flour
1 cup vegetable oil
2 garlic cloves, minced
2 cups finely chopped onions
1½ cups finely chopped celery
1½ cups finely chopped
  green pepper
2 pounds okra, cut in pieces
3 tablespoons bacon drippings
Duck stock (recipe follows)
1 teaspoon thyme
1 teaspoon basil
3 bay leaves

1 teaspoon oregano
1 tablespoon Accent
1 tablespoon Worcestershire sauce
½ teaspoon crushed red pepper
5 dashes Tabasco sauce
1 teaspoon Kitchen Bouquet
10 peppercorns
Salt to taste
1 pound shrimp,
  raw and peeled
1 pint oysters and liquid
¼ cup chopped parsley
2 cups hot cooked rice

In large Dutch oven, make roux by browning flour in oil until dark brown. This takes about 30 to 45 minutes over low heat, stirring often. Be careful not to let flour burn. Add garlic, onions, celery, and green pepper. Sauté uncovered over medium heat about 30 minutes until onions are transparent. In separate skillet, sauté okra in bacon drippings until all ropiness is gone, about 20 minutes. Drain. In large pot, warm stock and slowly stir in roux and vegetable mixture. Add okra and all other seasonings. Simmer covered 1½ hours. Add shrimp, oysters and their liquid, and cook an additional 10 minutes. Stir in parsley and remove from heat. Correct seasoning and serve over hot rice.

Duck Stock:

4 to 6 ducks (use more ducks
  if you like thick soup)
1 gallon water
1 onion, quartered
2 ribs celery

2 carrots
2 bay leaves
3 teaspoons salt
1 teaspoon pepper

Skin ducks and boil in water with remaining stock ingredients 1 hour or until duck meat is tender. Strain, skim all grease, and reserve 3 quarts stock. (Use chicken stock, if needed, to make 3 quarts.) Remove meat and cut into bite-size pieces. Return to stock.

Note: Stock can be prepared day ahead. For thicker gumbo, add more okra. When freezing, omit seafood until after thawing. Better after freezing.

Yield: 10 to 12 servings   Cassandra (Candy) Johnson Brownlow (Mrs. William G.)

Duck Quiche

3 small eggs
1 cup whipping cream
½ cup grated onion or 3
   green onions with tops,
   chopped
¼ cup chopped mushrooms

½ cup cooked duck meat,
   chopped in small pieces
¾ cup grated Gruyère cheese
1 8-inch pie crust
1 tablespoon butter

Preheat oven to 350°. Beat eggs. Add cream, onion, and mushrooms and beat again. Sprinkle duck meat and grated cheese in bottom of pie shell; pour cream mixture over top. Dot with butter and bake 40 minutes.

Yield: 4 servings   Cassandra (Candy) Johnson Brownlow (Mrs. William G.)

Joe's Goose

1 wild goose
6 large apples, cored and
   quartered

3 oranges
1 quart orange juice

Preheat oven to 400°. Stuff cavity of goose tightly with apples and oranges. Truss legs. Place goose, breast side down, in small roaster, preferably with rack on bottom. Add enough orange juice to cover all except 1 inch of goose's back. Cover and cook 45 minutes per pound. After first hour, reduce heat to 325°. To brown breast, place goose breast side up and cook uncovered last 5 minutes of cooking. Discard stuffing.

To serve, thinly slice parallel to breast bone and filet meat from carcass.

Note: This recipe avoids dryness, which is a problem with waterfowl, and is simple for the cook not familiar with wild game cookery. This recipe also works well for duck by reducing the cooking time to 30 to 40 minutes per pound.

Yield: 4 servings   Joe Congleton

Baked Quail

12 to 15 quail
Milk
Flour

4 tablespoons butter
2 cups chicken broth
1 cup wine or sherry

Soak quail in milk all day. Drain and roll in flour. Brown in butter and place in pan, add small amount of flour to pan, and stir in broth and wine. Seal pan tightly and bake 2 hours at 350°.

Yield: 12 to 15 quail   Ann Calhoun McMurray (Mrs. R. F.)

Vegetables

Artichoke Casserole

1 (10¾-ounce) can cream
  of mushroom soup
¼ cup milk
1 (6-ounce) can artichoke hearts,
  drained and sliced

1 (8-ounce) can water chestunuts,
  drained and sliced
½ cup sliced Spanish olives
½ cup grated sharp cheese
Bread crumbs

Grease 1½-quart oven-proof dish. Combine soup with milk and mix together with artichoke hearts, water chestnuts, and olives. Pour into oven-proof dish; top with cheese, then bread crumbs. Bake 30 minutes at 350°.

Yield: 6 servings   Ann Rector Weigel (Mrs. William B.)

Artichoke Bottoms and Spinach

2 (10-ounce) packages frozen
  chopped spinach
½ pound fresh mushrooms
6 tablespoons butter, divided
1 tablespoon all-purpose flour
½ cup milk
½ teaspoon salt

⅛ teaspoon garlic powder
2 (14-ounce) cans artichoke
  bottoms
1 cup sour cream
1 cup mayonnaise
¼ cup lemon juice

Preheat oven to 375°. Cook spinach in saucepan using no additional water; drain. Sauté mushrooms, reserving several to use as garnish, in 2 tablespoons butter. Sauté reserved mushrooms separately in 2 tablespoons butter.

Make cream sauce using remaining 2 tablespoons butter, flour, and ½ cup milk. Add salt, garlic powder, spinach, and mushrooms. Lay artichoke bottoms in 9- x 13-inch pan and fill with spinach mixture.

Combine sour cream, mayonnaise, and lemon juice; spoon over artichoke and spinach mixture. Top with reserved mushrooms. Bake 15 minutes.

Yield: 7 to 14 servings   Geri Carmichael Muse (Mrs. William Scott, Jr.)

Asparagus Sandwich

1 (14-ounce) can asparagus tips,
   drained
1 (8-ounce) package cream cheese
2 hard-cooked eggs, sieved
Juice of one lemon

Seasoned salt to taste
Bread
Mayonnaise
2 tablespoons butter, melted
Parmesan cheese

Combine asparagus, cream cheese, eggs, lemon juice, and salt. Mix until smooth. Spread bread with mayonnaise. Next spread asparagus mixture on bread. Brush melted butter on outside of sandwich and sprinkle with Parmesan cheese. Broil on both sides and slice diagonally.

Yield: 6 to 8 sandwiches
              Ann Lovejoy Browning (Mrs. Louis A., Jr.)

Fresh Asparagus
with Chive-Cream Dressing

Fresh asparagus
⅓ cup sour cream
¼ cup mayonnaise
1½ tablespoons chopped
   fresh chives

1 tablespoon fresh lemon juice
¼ teaspoon salt
¼ teaspoon dry mustard
Lemon slices (optional)
Fresh chives (optional)

Steam asparagus until tender. Combine sour cream, mayonnaise, chives, lemon juice, salt, and mustard. Heat in saucepan until warm, or heat in microwave on high 35 to 40 seconds. Pour dressing over asparagus. Garnish with lemon slices and fresh chives, if desired.

Note: Sauce can be used also as topping for baked potatoes.

Yield: 4 to 6 servings
              Lou Bennett (Mrs. Bill)

Patio Bourbon Baked Beans

4 (16-ounce) cans pork and beans
1 teaspoon dry mustard
½ cup chili sauce
2 tablespoons molasses
½ cup bourbon
½ cup strong black coffee
¾ cup firmly packed
  dark brown sugar
4 to 6 slices bacon

Combine all ingredients except bacon in 11- x 13-inch oven-proof dish and mix well. Refrigerate mixture overnight. The next day, cover beans and bake 1 hour at 350°. Remove cover and top with bacon. Bake uncovered 1 additional hour or until bacon is crisp and brown.

Yield: 6 to 8 servings

Mary Alice Hungate Clarke (Mrs. James L., Jr.)
Rockwood, Tennessee

Triple Bean Bake

8 slices bacon
¼ cup bacon drippings
⅔ cup sugar
2 tablespoons cornstarch
1 teaspoon chili powder
3 to 6 drops Tabasco sauce
¾ cup vinegar
½ cup water
2 (16-ounce) cans cut green
  beans, drained
2 (16-ounce) cans kidney beans,
  rinsed and drained
1 (16-ounce) can garbanzo
  beans, drained

Preheat oven to 350°. Cook bacon in large skillet until crisp. Drain and reserve ¼ cup bacon drippings. Crumble bacon. In same skillet add reserved drippings and remaining ingredients, except beans. Cook over medium heat, stirring until thick and bubbly. Add beans and half crumbled bacon. Toss to coat well. Pour into 2-quart casserole. Bake 25 minutes. Top with remaining bacon and bake an additional 5 minutes.

Yield: 12 servings

Jayne Crumpler Defiore (Mrs. Joseph C.)

Broccoli Nut Casserole

2 (10-ounce) packages frozen
  chopped broccoli
1 (10¾-ounce) can cream
  of mushroom soup
½ cup mayonnaise
1 cup coarsely chopped pecans
2 eggs, well beaten

1½ tablespoons dried
  onion flakes
Salt and pepper to taste
1 cup grated sharp cheese
2 cups crushed Ritz
  crackers, buttered

Preheat oven to 350°. Cook broccoli and drain. Add soup, mayonnaise, and pecans. Mix well. Add eggs and onion flakes. Pour into greased 2-quart oven-proof dish. Sprinkle with salt, pepper, and grated cheese. Top with cracker crumbs. Bake 30 minutes.

Yield: 8 servings   Ann Rector Weigel (Mrs. William B.)

Broccoli with Pimiento

1 bunch broccoli
½ cup sliced whole green
  onions
2 tablespoons margarine
2 canned pimientos, drained
  and chopped

1 teaspoon grated lemon
  peel
2 tablespoons lemon juice
1 teaspoon salt
⅛ teaspoon pepper

Remove leaves and tough portions of broccoli stalks. Wash and split each stalk lengthwise. Place broccoli in saucepan. Add boiling water to measure 1 inch; cook covered 10 minutes, until stalks are tender. While broccoli is cooking, sauté onions in margarine. Remove from heat; stir in remaining ingredients. Drain broccoli; arrange in serving dish. Pour pimiento mixture over top.

Yield: 4 to 6 servings   Suzanne L. McMillen

Cauliflower Au Gratin

6 tablespoons butter
4 tablespoons all-purpose flour
Salt and pepper to taste
2 cups milk
1 cup grated sharp Cheddar
    cheese
4 tablespoons dried parsley
3 whole green onions, chopped
¼ teaspoon monosodium glutamate

Dash lemon pepper
Dash seasoned salt
1 small head cauliflower, cooked,
    or 1 (10-ounce) package
    frozen cauliflower, thawed
Pepperidge Farm herb
    stuffing mix
Paprika

Preheat oven to 375°. Make white sauce with butter, flour, salt, pepper, and milk. Add cheese to hot sauce and stir until melted. Add parsley, onion, and spices. Pour part of sauce in bottom of 1½-quart baking dish. Arrange part of cauliflower over sauce. Repeat layers ending with sauce. Sprinkle stuffing mix to cover casserole. Shake paprika over all and bake 20 to 30 minutes.

Note: Can be frozen.

Yield: 6 to 8 servings   Barbara Leonard Hobson (Mrs. Charles)

Edith's Cauliflower Casserole

1 medium head cauliflower
1 cup sour cream
1 tablespoon all-purpose flour
2 teaspoons chicken bouillon
1 cup grated sharp cheese
1 teaspoon dry mustard

⅓ cup chopped walnuts
¼ cup fine dry bread crumbs
1 tablespoon butter, melted
½ teaspoon onion salt
1 teaspoon dry marjoram

Cook and drain cauliflower. Mix sour cream, flour, chicken bouillon, cheese, and dry mustard to form sauce. Place cauliflower in baking dish and top with sauce. Mix walnuts, bread crumbs, melted butter, onion salt, and marjoram, and sprinkle over top. Bake 20 minutes at 400°.

Yield: 6 to 8 servings   Susan Additon Farris (Mrs. R. Kent)

Easter Carrots

1 pound miniature carrots or
  6 carrots, pared and sliced
½ cup mayonnaise
2 tablespoons horseradish
2 tablespoons grated onion

½ teaspoon salt
½ teaspoon pepper
½ cup stuffing mix
1 tablespoon butter, melted

Preheat oven to 300°. Cook carrots until tender and drain. Combine mayonnaise, horseradish, onion, salt, and pepper; stir into carrots. Put into 1-quart oven-proof dish. Top with stuffing mix and drizzle with butter. Bake 15 to 20 minutes.

Yield: 6 servings
          Priscilla Brandau Siler (Mrs. Tom A.)

Carrots with Orange

3 cups diagonally sliced
  carrots
1 tablespoon grated orange rind
½ to 1 teaspoon salt

¼ cup orange juice concentrate
  plus 1 tablespoon water, or
  juice of 1 orange
4 tablespoons butter
1½ tablespoons chopped parsley

Combine all ingredients. Cook covered until just tender-crisp.

Yield: 4 servings
          Betty Newbill Threadgill

Marsha Roberts' Celery Casserole

4 cups sliced celery
1 (8-ounce) can sliced water
  chestnuts, drained
½ teaspoon basil
1 (10¾-ounce) can cream
  of celery soup

¼ cup chopped pimiento
½ cup soft bread crumbs
½ cup slivered almonds,
  toasted
2 tablespoons melted butter

Preheat oven to 350°. Cook celery in water 5 to 10 minutes until tender-crisp. Drain and mix with water chestnuts, basil, soup, and pimiento. Pour into 2-quart oven-proof dish. Combine crumbs, almonds, and butter. Sprinkle over celery. Bake 35 minutes.

Yield: 6 to 8 servings
          Conni Hanson Collins (Mrs. Townsend S.)

Fresh Corn Pie

½ cup butter, melted
1¼ cups fine soda
  cracker crumbs
2 tablespoons butter
1¼ cups milk, divided
2 cups fresh raw corn

½ teaspoon salt
2 tablespoons all-purpose flour
½ teaspoon onion salt
  (optional)
2 eggs, beaten

Preheat oven to 400°. Combine melted butter and crumbs, reserving ½ cup crumbs for topping. Line 9-inch pie pan with remaining crumbs. Combine 2 tablespoons butter, 1 cup milk, corn, and salt. Bring to boil. Reduce heat and cook 3 minutes. Add flour to remaining ¼ cup milk and mix to a smooth paste. Add slowly to hot milk-corn mixture, stirring constantly. Cook 2 to 3 minutes or until thick. Cool slightly. Add onion salt. Add eggs slowly, stirring constantly. Pour into crumb-lined pie pan. Sprinkle remaining crumbs and bake 20 minutes.

Yield: 6 servings

Ann Dooley

Peggy's Corn Pudding

2 eggs, well beaten
2 cups cooked rice
  (cooked until dry)
1 cup grated Cheddar cheese
1 (17-ounce) can cream style corn

½ cup minced onion
½ cup chopped green pepper
1½ teaspoons salt
⅛ teaspoon pepper

Preheat oven to 350°. Butter 10- x 6-inch casserole. Combine all ingredients in large mixing bowl. Mix lightly but thoroughly. Turn into prepared dish. Bake 45 minutes to 1 hour.

Note: Can be frozen before baking. Thaw completely; then bake as directed.

Yield: 6 servings

Kae Gilmore Lakenan (Mrs. William K., Jr.)

Microwaved Corn on the Cob

Fresh corn, shucked and
   silks removed
½ tablespoon butter per ear

Salt
Pepper

Wash corn and pat dry. Spread each ear with ½ tablespoon butter and sprinkle with salt and pepper. Wrap each ear in wax paper, twisting ends to seal. At this point, corn may be stored in refrigerator 2 to 3 days until ready to cook.

   Microwave on full power 2 minutes per ear, up to 4 ears. When preparing more than 4 ears, microwave approximately 1½ minutes per ear, and turn over halfway through cooking time.

Kae Gilmore Lakenan (Mrs. William K., Jr.)

Eggplant Creole

1 medium eggplant, peeled
Salt to taste
3 tablespoons butter
3 tablespoons chopped onion
3 tablespoons chopped celery
3 tablespoons chopped green pepper

½ teaspoon salt
3 tablespoons all-purpose flour
1¼ cups tomatoes
¼ teaspoon sugar
¼ teaspoon pepper
1 cup butter bread crumbs

Cut eggplant into 1-inch-thick slices. Sprinkle with salt. Arrange in layers, weight down with heavy dish, and let stand 1 hour. Rinse off and cut into 1-inch pieces. Cook about 10 minutes in boiling salted water. Drain and place in greased baking dish. To make creole sauce, melt butter in skillet and brown lightly onions, celery, and green pepper. Add ½ teaspoon salt, flour, tomatoes, sugar, and pepper, and boil 2 minutes. Pour over eggplant. Cover with buttered bread crumbs and bake 15 minutes or until brown on top.

Yield: 6 to 8 servings

Helen Jennings

Eggplant Au Gratin

1 medium eggplant
2 tablespoons butter
2 tablespoons all-purpose flour
1 cup milk
1 cup grated sharp Cheddar
  cheese

¾ cup soft bread crumbs
2 teaspoons grated onion
2 eggs, separated
1 tablespoon catsup
Salt
Pepper

Preheat oven to 350°. Grease 2-quart oven-proof dish. Peel and cube eggplant. Cook until tender; drain and mash. Make cream sauce with butter, flour, and milk. Add remaining ingredients except egg whites. Beat egg whites until stiff and gently fold into eggplant mixture. Pour into prepared dish. Bake 35 to 45 minutes.

Yield: 6 servings

Betty Paxton Galyon (Mrs. L. A.)

Sugar Valley Green Beans

1 pound fresh green beans, washed
  stringed, and broken
1 onion, sliced
1 cup mayonnaise
2 hard-cooked eggs, chopped
1½ heaping tablespoons
  horseradish

1 teaspoon Worcestershire sauce
¼ teaspoon Season-All
¼ teaspoon garlic salt
¼ teaspoon celery salt
2 teaspoons parsley flakes
¼ teaspoon lemon-pepper
Juice of 1 lemon

Cook beans and onion in water slowly 1½ to 2 hours in saucepan. Blend mayonnaise with remaining ingredients and set aside. Place drained beans in serving bowl and top with mayonnaise mixture.

Note: Delicious served cold in tomatoes or on mixed salad.

Yield: 8 to 10 servings

Sissy Law Wilson (Mrs. George Ed, III)

Cheddar Mushroom Casserole

1 pound fresh mushrooms,
  thickly sliced
¼ cup butter
8 slices buttered bread, divided
½ cup chopped onion
½ cup chopped celery
½ cup chopped green pepper
½ cup mayonnaise

¾ teaspoon salt
¼ teaspoon pepper
2 eggs, slightly beaten
1½ cups milk
1 cup grated Cheddar cheese
1 (10¾-ounce) can cream of
  mushroom soup, undiluted

Sauté mushrooms in butter 3 to 5 minutes. Cut 3 slices bread into 1-inch
cubes and place in greased 10-inch oven-proof dish. Combine mushrooms
with vegetables, mayonnaise, salt, and pepper. Spoon mixture on top of
bread cubes. Cover with 3 more slices of bread cut into cubes. Combine eggs
with 1½ cups milk and pour over bread cubes. Refrigerate 1 hour or up to 1½
days. One hour before serving, top with soup and last 2 slices of bread, finely
cubed. Bake 50 to 60 minutes at 325°. Top with cheese the last 10 minutes.

Yield: 8 servings   Wallace Wood Mayo (Mrs. Claxton, Jr.)

Green Pepper Casserole

2 cups finely ground green
  peppers, drained
¼ pound sharp Cheddar cheese,
  grated

14 small soda crackers,
  crumbled
1 (13-ounce) can evaporated milk

Preheat oven to 325°. Combine peppers, cheese, and crackers. Place in
greased 1½-quart casserole. Pour milk over pepper mixture and stir. Bake 30
minutes or until brown.

Yield: 6 servings   Rose "Posey" Stewart Congleton (Mrs. Joseph)

Potatoes Alexandre

8 large baking potatoes
2 tablespoons butter
1 cup sour cream
2 tablespoons chopped
 fresh chives
½ teaspoon nutmeg

Salt and pepper to taste
1 pound caviar
 (Beluga or Sevruga)
8 lemon wedges
Dill or parsley sprigs
 (optional)

Bake potatoes. While hot, slice ¼ inch from tops and remove pulp. Return shells to oven after turning heat off. In saucepan over low heat, mix potato pulp, butter, sour cream, chives, nutmeg, salt, and pepper. Blend well. Add more butter or sour cream, if desired. Stuff warm shells with hot potato mixture. Top each with equal amounts of caviar. Garnish each potato with lemon wedge and sprig of dill or parsley.

Yield: 8 servings   Janey Maddox Sterchi (Mrs. John R.)

Potato Pancakes

4 cups grated raw potatoes
2 large eggs, well beaten
2 tablespoons all-purpose flour
2 tablespoons light cream

2 teaspoons salt
2 teaspoons grated onion
½ cup butter

Combine raw potatoes, eggs, flour, cream, salt, and onion. Blend well. Melt ¼ cup butter in skillet. Drop mixture by tablespoons into butter and fry slowly until golden brown on both sides. Add remaining butter as needed. Keep warm in oven until ready to serve.

Yield: 12 servings   Lillian Astley Rayson (Mrs. Edwin)

Fried Sweet Potato Chips

3 medium sweet potatoes, pared
Vegetable oil

Salt
Confectioners' sugar

Slice sweet potatoes into thin "chips" in food processor. Deep fry in hot oil until golden brown. Drain on paper towels and salt to taste. Before serving, sprinkle with confectioners' sugar. Serve warm or at room temperature.

Note: These may be stored several days in an air-tight container.

Yield: 4 to 6 servings   Pamela Young Richardson (Mrs. Charles Franklin)

Ratatouille

1 medium unpeeled eggplant, cubed
4 medium zucchini, sliced
2 teaspoons salt, divided
Olive oil
2 green peppers, sliced
2 onions, sliced
1 clove garlic, crushed
6 tomatoes, peeled and chopped
½ teaspoon pepper
½ teaspoon sugar
2 tablespoons chopped parsley, divided
Sour cream

Sprinkle eggplant and zucchini with 1½ teaspoons salt and let stand 1 hour. Rinse and dry on paper towels. Preheat oven to 350°. Sauté peppers, onions, and garlic, using more oil. Add tomatoes. Season with remaining salt, pepper, and sugar. Cook until tomatoes are just tender. Place layer of this mixture in bottom of 3-quart oven-proof dish and sprinkle with 1 tablespoon parsley. Layer eggplant and zucchini over tomato layer. Repeat layers, ending with tomato mixture. Sprinkle with remaining parsley. Bake 35 to 40 minutes. Serve cold with dollop of sour cream.

Yield: 8 servings

Suellen Brown Roehl (Mrs. Jay)

Spinach Artichoke Casserole

1 (8-ounce) package cream cheese, softened
½ cup butter, melted
3 (10-ounce) packages frozen spinach, cooked and drained
1 (8-ounce) can sliced water chestnuts, drained
Salt to taste
Dash nutmeg
Parmesan cheese to taste
1 (14-ounce) can artichoke hearts, drained and halved
Bread crumbs (optional)

Preheat oven to 350°. Combine cream cheese with butter and add to spinach. Stir in water chestnuts, seasonings, and Parmesan cheese. Arrange artichoke halves on bottom of lightly greased 1½-quart oven-proof dish. Pour spinach mixture over artichokes and sprinkle generously with Parmesan cheese and bread crumbs. Bake 30 minutes or until bubbly.

Yield: 8 servings

Susan Additon Farris (Mrs. R. Kent)

Spinach Revisited

1 small or medium onion,
    chopped
2 tablespoons butter
1 (3-ounce) package cream
    cheese, softened
1 (10-ounce) package frozen
    chopped spinach, thawed
    and drained
1 egg, beaten

¼ cup bread crumbs or
    prepared stuffing mix
Salt and pepper to taste
Bacon, cooked crisp and
    crumbled (optional)
Sautéed mushrooms (optional)
Paprika
Butter

Preheat oven to 350°. Butter 1-quart oven-proof dish. Sauté onion in 2 tablespoons butter until transparent. Combine onion, cream cheese, spinach, egg, bread crumbs, salt, and pepper in bowl. Add bacon and mushrooms, if desired. Pour into prepared dish, sprinkle with paprika, and dot with butter. Bake uncovered 20 minutes.

Note: May be assembled and refrigerated in advance. Bring to room temperature before baking.

Yield: 3 to 4 servings   Mary Heatherington Lutz (Mrs. John E.)

Snappy Spinach Casserole

3 (10-ounce) packages chopped
    frozen spinach
½ onion, chopped
2 tablespoons butter
2 tablespoons all-purpose flour
1 cup milk

1 (9-ounce) stick hot pepper
    cheese, cubed
½ cup cracker crumbs
3 tablespoons grated Parmesan
    cheese

Preheat oven to 350°. Cook spinach 3 minutes and drain well. Set aside. Sauté onion in butter; stir in flour and add milk to make cream sauce. Add hot pepper cheese and stir until melted. Combine cheese sauce and spinach and pour into 1½- or 2-quart oven-proof dish. Top with crumbs and Parmesan cheese. Bake 20 minutes (30 minutes if refrigerated).

Note: When freezing casserole, add bread crumbs and Parmesan cheese immediately before baking.

Yield: 10 to 12 servings   Donna Dahlen Kerr (Mrs. David)

Microwaved Stuffed Tomatoes

4 unpeeled tomatoes
1 teaspoon salt, divided
4 strips bacon
1 (10-ounce) package frozen
   chopped spinach
⅓ cup soft bread crumbs

¼ teaspoon salt
¼ teaspoon pepper
¼ teaspoon garlic powder
¼ teaspoon grated nutmeg
2 tablespoons melted butter
¼ cup sour cream, divided

Scoop out the pulp of each tomato; salt inside of each with ¼ teaspoon salt per tomato, and drain 1 hour. Microwave bacon on full power until crisp. Open top of spinach box and microwave on full power 3 to 4 minutes. When cooled, squeeze spinach dry. Combine spinach, crumbled bacon, bread crumbs, salt, pepper, garlic powder, and nutmeg. Stuff tomatoes; place in custard cups. Drizzle with melted butter and microwave on full power 4 to 5 minutes, covered with wax paper. Let stand 5 minutes before serving. Serve with 1 tablespoon sour cream on each tomato.

Yield: 4 servings

Suzanne Wood Fletcher

Crêpes Florentine

3 (10-ounce) packages frozen chopped
   spinach, thawed and drained dry
4 tablespoons margarine
6 tablespoons all-purpose flour
3 cups milk
1 medium onion, finely chopped
1 teaspoon salt

¼ teaspoon Tabasco sauce
1 cup Swiss or favorite cheese
1 (4-ounce) can sliced
   mushrooms, drained
24 crêpes
⅓ cup sliced almonds

Preheat oven to 325°. Make white sauce of margarine, flour, and milk. Reserve ¼ of the sauce. Add remaining ingredients except crêpes and almonds. Place ½ cup mixture in each crêpe; roll up. Arrange in 13- x 9-inch oven-proof dish and top with reserved sauce and almonds. Bake 30 minutes.

Yield: 12 servings

Conni Hanson Collins (Mrs. Townsend S.)

Country Club Squash

2½ pounds squash (better
   if ¾ pound is zucchini)
Salt and pepper to taste
2 tablespoons butter
1 chicken bouillon cube
2 tablespoons chopped onion

1 egg, well beaten
1 cup sour cream
½ cup bread crumbs
½ cup grated Cheddar cheese
Dash paprika

Preheat oven to 350° and butter 1½-quart casserole. Cube squash and cook in salted water until tender. Drain excess liquid. Mash and season with salt, pepper, butter, bouillon cube, and onion. Add egg and sour cream. Pour into prepared casserole. Combine bread crumbs, grated cheese, and paprika. Sprinkle on top and bake 30 to 35 minutes.

Note: Can be prepared ahead and refrigerated until ready to bake.

Yield: 8 servings   Nancy Sterchi Montgomery (Mrs. L. L., Jr.)

Two Squash Casserole

1 pound yellow squash,
   cut in ½-inch slices
1 pound zucchini, cut in
   ½-inch slices
1 medium onion, chopped
2 tablespoons bacon drippings

1 (8-ounce) can tomato sauce
1 (3-ounce) can chopped
   green chilies
½ teaspoon salt
1 cup shredded sharp cheese
Bread crumbs

Preheat oven to 350°. Cook yellow squash and zucchini separately in boiling salted water 5 minutes. Drain well. Sauté onion in bacon drippings until tender but not brown. Combine tomato sauce, chilies, and salt. Stir well. Place yellow squash in 1½-quart oven-proof dish. Add onions, spreading evenly. Pour half of sauce over onions. Add zucchini. Pour remaining sauce over top. Sprinkle with cheese and top with bread crumbs. Bake 30 minutes or until bubbly.

Yield: 6 servings   Elizabeth Barton Van Deventer (Mrs. Christopher)

Tomatoes Stuffed with Summer Squash

2 teaspoons salt
1 pound yellow squash, grated
1 pound zucchini, grated
8 small tomatoes
Salt and pepper to taste
Vegetable oil
1 onion, minced

1 clove garlic, minced
2 tablespoons olive oil
2 tablespoons butter
1 cup whipping cream
½ cup grated Gruyère cheese
¼ cup grated Parmesan cheese

Sprinkle 2 teaspoons salt over grated squashes. Drain 30 minutes and squeeze dry. Cut ¾ inch from top of tomatoes. Remove seeds and juice without squeezing tomatoes. Sprinkle with salt and pepper and brush with oil. Invert and drain 30 minutes. Sauté onion and garlic in olive oil and butter and cook 2 minutes. Add cream, salt, and pepper to taste. Cook until cream is absorbed. Stir in cheeses. Stuff tomatoes with mixture and sprinkle with Parmesan cheese. Broil 3 to 4 minutes.

Yield: 8 servings

Betsy Guinn Foster (Mrs. E. Bruce, Jr.)

Yellow Squash Boats with Spinach

12 yellow crookneck squash
2 (10-ounce) packages chopped
    frozen spinach
1 cup sour cream
1 tablespoon butter or margarine

Seasoned salt
Pepper
Bread crumbs
Parmesan cheese

Preheat oven to 325°. Cut squash in halves lengthwise. Scrape out séed portion and cook shells in salted water until tender. Cook spinach as directed on package and drain. Combine spinach, sour cream, butter, and seasonings. Stuff squash shells with mixture and sprinkle with crumbs and cheese. Bake 30 minutes.

Yield: 8 to 10 servings

Anne Walters Pittenger (Mrs. Gaines)

Squash Casserole

6 slices bacon
2 cups yellow squash, cooked
1 tablespoon diced onion

Salt and pepper to taste
1 cup grated Cheddar cheese
½ cup fine bread crumbs

Preheat oven to 350°. Grease 2-quart oven-proof dish. Cook bacon crisp, reserving bacon drippings. Mash squash and combine with crumbled bacon, 2 tablespoons reserved bacon drippings, onion, salt, and pepper. Pour into prepared dish. Cover with cheese and top with bread crumbs. Bake until brown.

Yield: 4 servings

Nancy Whitman Dickson (Mrs. Michael)

Baked Tomatoes

6 firm tomatoes, uniform size
3 tablespoons minced onion
¼ cup Hellman's mayonnaise
1½ cups cooked rice

2 teaspoons salt
1 teaspoon celery salt
1 cup peas, cooked

Preheat oven to 325°. Cut tops from tomatoes; remove and reserve pulp. Sauté onion in mayonnaise. Add rice, salt, celery salt, and peas. Stir in pulp. Fill tomatoes with mixture and bake 20 minutes.

Yield: 6 servings

Lillian Astley Rayson (Mrs. Edwin)

Tomato Pie

1 9-inch pie crust
3 large ripe tomatoes, peeled
Basil to taste
Salt and pepper to taste

½ cup mayonnaise
¾ pound sharp Cheddar
cheese, grated

Preheat oven to 400°. Slice tomatoes ½-inch thick and arrange in crust until full. Sprinkle with basil, salt, and pepper. Combine mayonnaise and cheese. Press mixture on top of tomatoes. Sprinkle again with basil, salt, and pepper. Bake 20 to 30 minutes. Remove from oven and cool 5 to 10 minutes before serving.

Note: Use only vine-ripened tomatoes. To freeze, bake 15 minutes, cool, and freeze.

Yield: 6 to 8 servings

Sandie Kohlhase Bishop (Mrs. Archer)

Stuffed Zucchini

3 large zucchini
½ cup bread crumbs, soaked in
  milk and squeezed dry
¾ cup chopped almonds
¾ cup grated Swiss cheese

3 hard-cooked eggs
2 tablespoons chopped parsley
Salt and pepper to taste
Margarine

Preheat oven to 350°. Halve unpeeled zucchini lengthwise. Scoop out pulp carefully and reserve. Simmer zucchini shells in salted water 5 minutes and drain well. Chop reserved pulp. Combine bread crumbs, almonds, Swiss cheese, eggs, parsley, salt, and pepper; add reserved pulp. Stuff zucchini shells with mixture and dot with margarine. Bake 15 or 20 minutes.

Yield: 6 servings

Rose "Posey" Stewart Congleton (Mrs. Joseph)

Zucchini Milano

A zesty dish from an old family restaurant in Milan. So popular that the recipe was printed and made available for the asking, but only if your I.D. showed you were not from Milan.

7 to 8 medium zucchini,
  cut into ¼-inch slices
1 cup water
2 teaspoons salt, divided
8 slices bacon, diced
1 large onion, chopped
1 large clove garlic, minced
4 slices light or dark
  bread, diced

2 cups Mozzarella or Cheddar
  cheese, shredded
1 teaspoon Italian seasoning
  or combine oregano, basil and
  marjoram to make 1 teaspoon
Dash freshly ground pepper
1 (15-ounce) can tomato sauce
¼ cup grated Parmesan cheese

Preheat oven to 350°. In large saucepan, cook zucchini in boiling water with 1 teaspoon salt until barely tender, about 3 to 5 minutes. Drain. In a skillet, cook bacon until crisp; remove from pan. Add onion and garlic to skillet and sauté until tender. Drain. Add to bacon. Stir onion-bacon mixture into drained zucchini; add bread, cheese, Italian seasoning, remaining salt, pepper, and tomato sauce. Toss lightly until well coated. Spoon zucchini into 13- x 9-inch oven-proof dish. Sprinkle with Parmesan cheese. Bake 20 minutes or until bubbly.

Yield: 10 to 12 servings

Tinque Blakely (Mrs. J. Paul)

Zucchini Bake

1 cup grated sharp Cheddar
  cheese
½ cup cottage cheese
4 eggs, beaten
3 tablespoons minced fresh
  parsley
1½ teaspoons salt (or less)

¼ teaspoon freshly ground
  pepper
2 pounds zucchini, sliced
  ½-inch thick
¾ cup bread crumbs
¼ cup grated Parmesan cheese
¼ cup butter

Preheat oven to 375°. Butter shallow 2-quart oven-proof dish. Combine
Cheddar cheese, cottage cheese, eggs, parsley, salt, and pepper; mix well.
Place layer of zucchini in dish and top with layer of cheese mixture. Repeat,
ending with cheese mixture. Combine bread crumbs and Parmesan cheese
in small bowl. Sprinkle over casserole and dot with butter. Tent with foil
and bake 25 minutes. Remove foil and bake additional 20 minutes or until
top is browned.

Note: Must be assembled just before baking.

Yield: 8 servings

Sue Herrman (Mrs. Milo)
Boggy Bayou, Florida

Zucchini Provençale

1 medium onion, chopped
4 tablespoons vegetable or
  olive oil
4 medium tomatoes, peeled,
  seeded, and chopped
1 green pepper, finely chopped

1 small clove garlic, placed
  on toothpick
Salt and pepper to taste
2 pounds zucchini, peeled
  and cubed
¼ cup snipped parsley
¼ cup grated Parmesan cheese

Sauté onion in oil until soft. Add tomatoes, green pepper, and garlic. Season
with salt and pepper. Simmer over low heat 15 minutes. Remove garlic and
add zucchini. Cover and simmer 15 minutes or until tender. Turn into 2-
quart oven-proof dish. Top with parsley and Parmesan cheese. Bake
covered 15 to 18 minutes at 325°.

Note: May be prepared ahead and refrigerated until ready to bake.

Yield: 4 to 6 servings

Alice Hale Clayton (Mrs. Edward S., III)

Italian Zucchini Pie

4 cups thinly sliced, unpeeled
  zucchini
1 cup coarsely chopped onion
½ cup margarine or butter
½ cup chopped parsley or 2
  tablespoons parsley flakes
½ teaspoon salt
½ teaspoon black pepper
¼ teaspoon garlic powder

¼ teaspoon sweet basil leaves
¼ teaspoon oregano leaves
2 eggs, well-beaten
2 cups (16-ounces) grated Muenster
  or Mozzarella cheese
1 (8-ounce) can refrigerated quick
  crescent dinner rolls
2 teaspoons Dijon or prepared
  mustard

Preheat oven to 375°. In 10-inch skillet, cook zucchini and onion in margarine until tender, about 10 minutes. Stir in parsley and seasonings. In large bowl, blend eggs and cheese. Stir into vegetable mixture. Separate dough into 8 triangles. Place in ungreased 11-inch quiche pan or 6- x 8-inch oven-proof dish. Press over bottom and up sides to form crust. Spread crust with mustard. Pour vegetable mixture into crust. Bake 18 to 20 minutes or until center is done. If crust becomes too brown, cover with foil during last 10 minutes of baking. Let stand 10 minutes before serving.

Yield: 6 servings   Dee Bagwell Haslam (Mrs. James A., III)

Dill Vegetables

2 (10-ounce) packages frozen
  French style green beans
3 carrots
2 small yellow squash

½ basket cherry tomatoes
4 tablespoons butter
1 teaspoon dried dill

Cut frozen beans into thirds. Place in colander and run cold water over beans until thawed. Set aside. Pare carrots and slice diagonally ¼ inch thick. Place in boiling, salted water 2 to 3 minutes; drain and set aside. Cut squash diagonally ¼ inch thick; set aside. Cut cherry tomatoes in half. Melt butter over medium-high heat in large skillet. Add dill, green beans, and squash, stirring until just heated through. Add carrots and stir. Add tomatoes and toss gently to coat with butter mixture. Serve immediately.

Note: Do not overcook. Beans should be crunchy and bright green. They will stay warmer longer if served in heated bowl. May be covered and reheated in microwave 2 minutes at low power.

Yield: 6 servings   Jayne Crumpler DeFiore (Mrs. Joseph C.)

Microwaved Hollandaise Sauce

⅓ cup butter
1 to 2 tablespoons lemon juice
2 egg yolks

¼ teaspoon salt
¼ teaspoon dry mustard
Dash cayenne pepper

Place butter in 4-cup glass measuring cup and microwave at full power 40 to 60 seconds or until melted and hot. Stir in remaining ingredients. Beat with whisk until well mixed. Microwave at medium high 30 seconds to 1 minute, or until thickened. Stir with whisk every 15 seconds while cooking.

Note: If sauce is overcooked and separates, add 1 to 2 tablespoons cold water and beat with whisk until smooth.

Yield: ½ cup

Suzanne Wood Fletcher

Curried Fruit

1 (16-ounce) can peach halves
1 (4-ounce) can sliced pineapple
1 (16-ounce) can pear halves
1 (16-ounce) can sour pitted cherries

⅓ cup butter, melted
¾ cup firmly packed brown
  sugar
3 teaspoons curry powder

Preheat oven to 325°. Drain and dry fruit; arrange in 2-quart oven-proof dish. Combine butter, sugar, and curry. Spoon over fruit. Bake uncovered 1 hour. Refrigerate overnight. When ready to serve, bake 30 additional minutes at 350°.

Yield: 8 to 10 servings

Pamela Young Richardson (Mrs. Charles Franklin)

Pineapple Casserole

½ cup butter
1 cup sugar
4 eggs

1 (20-ounce) can crushed
  pineapple
6 slices white bread, cubed

Preheat oven to 350°. Cream butter and sugar. Add eggs and beat well. Drain pineapple and reserve liquid. Add pineapple and ½ cup reserved liquid. Stir in bread crumbs. Pour into greased 2-quart oven-proof dish and bake 1 hour.

Yield: 6 to 8 servings

Barbara Vought Perkins (Mrs. Alfred)
Maryville, Tennessee

Pound Cake

1 cup butter
3 cups sugar
5 eggs, separated
3 cups sifted all-purpose flour

½ teaspoon soda
Pinch salt
1 cup buttermilk
2 teaspoons vanilla

Preheat oven to 350°. Grease and flour 10-inch tube cake pan. Cream butter and sugar. Add egg yolks one at a time, beating well after each addition. Mix flour with soda and salt. Add dry ingredients to sugar mixture alternating with buttermilk. Add vanilla and fold in stiffly beaten egg whites. Pour into prepared pan and bake 50 to 60 minutes.

Yield: 15 to 20 servings   Melisssa Cooley Gill

Chocolate Pound Cake

1 cup butter or margarine
1 cup granulated sugar
1 cup firmly packed brown sugar
4 eggs
2½ cups all-purpose flour
¼ teaspoon salt
½ teaspoon baking soda
2 (5.5-ounce) cans Hershey syrup

1 cup buttermilk
1 teaspoon vanilla
5 (1.05-ounce) plain milk
    chocolate Hershey bars,
    melted and cooled
Confectioners' sugar (optional)
Chocolate Glaze (recipe follows)

Preheat oven to 350°. Grease and flour 10-inch tube pan. Cream butter and sugars. Add eggs one at a time, beating well after each addition. Mix flour, salt, and soda; add to creamed mixture, alternating with syrup and buttermilk. Add vanilla and melted, cooled Hershey bars. Bake 1 hour and 15 minutes. Top with Chocolate Glaze or dust with confectioners' sugar.

Chocolate Glaze:

1 (4-ounce) bar German's chocolate
1 tablespoon butter
1 egg white

1 cup sifted confectioners'
    sugar
2 to 3 teaspoons water

Melt chocolate with butter. Set aside. Beat egg white until foamy. Gradually add confectioners' sugar, beating until smooth. Add chocolate mixture and 2 to 3 teaspoons water to thin. Adjust amount for desired consistency. Drizzle over warm cake.

Yield: 12 servings   Suzanne Wood Fletcher

Best Ever Chocolate Cake

2 cups all-purpose flour
2 cups sugar
1 cup margarine
¼ cup cocoa
1 cup water
½ cup buttermilk

2 whole eggs
1 teaspoon soda
1 teaspoon vanilla
Pinch salt
Best Ever Chocolate Icing
  (recipe follows)

Preheat oven to 400°. Lightly grease and flour 10- x 15-inch pan. Put flour and sugar in large mixing bowl and set aside. Cook margarine, cocoa, and water just until mixture comes to boil. Cool 1 minute. Pour mixture over flour and sugar while beating with electric mixer. Add buttermilk, eggs, soda, salt, and vanilla. Beat 1 minute more. Pour batter into prepared pan and bake 20 minutes. Frost while hot with Best Ever Chocolate Icing.

Best Ever Chocolate Icing:

½ cup margarine
¼ cup cocoa
3 to 4 tablespoons milk

1 (16-ounce) box confectioners'
  sugar, sifted
1 teaspoon vanilla

Five minutes before cake is done, bring margarine, cocoa, and milk to boil. Add confectioners' sugar and vanilla while beating mixture with electric mixer. Beat until smooth and spread on hot cake.

Yield: 12 to 15 servings

Linnie Graham Davis (Mrs. Charles)

Easy Coconut Cake

This easy dessert tastes as if it were made from scratch.

1 (18½-ounce) box Pillsbury
  Plus white cake mix
2 cups sugar
1 cup milk

12 ounces frozen coconut,
  divided
12 ounces non-dairy whipped
  topping

Prepare cake mix and bake according to package directions for 9- x 13-inch sheet cake. In saucepan, bring milk and sugar to boil. When cake is done, immediately punch full of holes with fork, and spoon half sugar and milk mixture over hot cake. Stir 6 ounces coconut into remaining sugar and milk mixture and spread over cake. Cool completely in refrigerator. Spread whipped topping over cooled cake and sprinkle with remaining coconut. Keep refrigerated. Best after two days in refrigerator.

Julia Bedinger Huster (Mrs. Edwin C., Jr.)

Plum Nut Cake

2 cups self-rising flour
2 cups sugar
1 cup vegetable oil
3 eggs
2 (4¾-ounce) jars baby
  food plums

1 teaspoon cinnamon
1 teaspoon cloves
½ to 1 cup broken pecans
Glaze for Plum Nut Cake
  (recipe follows)

Preheat oven to 350°. Grease and flour 10-inch tube pan or Bundt pan. Mix all ingredients until blended. Pour batter into prepared pan. Bake 45 to 60 minutes. Spread with Glaze for Plum Nut Cake.

Glaze for Plum Nut Cake:

2 tablespoons soft butter
½ cup confectioners' sugar

Juice and grated rind
  of 1 lemon

Combine ingredients and spread on warm cake.

Barbara Reeves McWilliams (Mrs. Hugh)

Fresh Apple Cake

1 cup vegetable oil
2 cups sugar
3 eggs
2½ cups all-purpose flour,
  sifted
1 teaspoon salt

1 teaspoon soda
2 teaspoons baking powder
3 cups chopped apples
¾ cup chopped nuts
  (optional)
Topping (recipe follows)

Preheat oven to 350° and grease a 10-inch tube pan. Beat oil and sugar with electric mixer until thick. Add eggs one at a time and beat well. Sift together flour, salt, soda, and baking powder. Add to egg mixture gradually and beat well. Stir in apples and nuts. Pour into prepared pan and bake 50 to 60 minutes. Cool in pan 10 minutes before removing. Spread Topping on hot cake.

Note: Cake will fall slightly when removed from oven.

Topping:

½ cup margarine
1 cup firmly packed brown sugar
1 (3½-ounce) can coconut

1 teaspoon vanilla
½ cup milk

Combine and cook until thick. Use as directed.

Joyce Julian Whaley (Mrs. Glenn)

Dried Apple Stack Cake

John Craig is known throughout East Tennessee for his stack cake, and he participates annually as a food vendor on Market Square Mall during the Dogwood Arts Festival.

1 pound dried apples
3 cups all-purpose flour
2 teaspoons baking powder
Pinch ginger
Pinch salt
½ teaspoon soda
½ cup buttermilk
½ cup Crisco

1½ cups granulated sugar, divided
1 egg
1 cup firmly packed brown sugar
2 teaspoons cinnamon
½ teaspoon ground cloves
½ teaspoon allspice
½ teaspoon apple pie spice

Soak apples in water overnight; then cook until tender. Preheat oven to 450°. Sift flour, baking powder, ginger, and salt. Combine soda and buttermilk. To flour mixture add Crisco, 1 cup granulated sugar, egg, and buttermilk. Knead well on floured board and work into a 15-inch loaf. Pinch into 5 or 6 equal balls. Roll and pat each to fit greased 9-inch cake pans. Bake 5 minutes. Turn out onto cardboard rounds. To cooked apples, add remaining granulated sugar, brown sugar, cinnamon, cloves, allspice, and apple pie spice; mix well. Invert cake layers and spread apple mixture between layers to form stack cake.

John Craig

Cary Baker's Fruitcake

1 (8-ounce) package chopped dates
½ pound candied pineapple, chopped
½ pound candied cherries, chopped
1 cup sifted all-purpose flour

1 teaspoon baking powder
½ teaspoon salt
½ cup sugar
2 eggs, beaten
1 pound pecans

Preheat oven to 275°. Combine dates, pineapple, and cherries. Combine flour, baking powder, salt, and sugar. Add dry ingredients to fruit mixture. Add eggs and pecans. (Batter will be hard to mix.) Bake in 9- x 5-inch loaf pan 1¼ to 1½ hours.

Note: This fruitcake can be served the next day.

Geri Carmichael Muse (Mrs. William Scott, Jr.)

Regas' Red Velvet Cake

A specialty of Regas Restaurant—this recipe was given to Liberace in 1970 because he patronizes Regas when in Knoxville.

½ cup butter
½ cup shortening
2 cups sugar
4 eggs
2½ cups all-purpose flour
1 teaspoon soda
¼ teaspoon salt

4 tablespoons cocoa
1 cup buttermilk, divided
1 teaspoon vanilla
4 tablespoons red food coloring
Frosting for Red Velvet Cake
   (recipe follows)

Preheat oven to 350°. Grease and flour three 9-inch cake pans. Cream butter, shortening, and sugar. Add eggs one at a time. Combine flour, soda, salt, and cocoa, and gradually add to butter mixture, alternating with buttermilk. Add vanilla and food coloring. Blend well. Pour into pans and bake 25 to 30 minutes. Cool and frost.

Frosting:

1 (16-ounce) box confectioners' sugar
1 cup margarine, softened
1 teaspoon vanilla

4 tablespoons whipping cream
½ cup shredded coconut
Red food coloring

Blend confectioners' sugar, margarine, vanilla, and cream with mixer until smooth and fluffy. Additional cream may be needed to achieve fluffy consistency. Frost layers and assemble. Tint coconut with red food coloring and sprinkle over top.

Note: Sides of this cake are not frosted.

Regas Restaurant
Knoxville, Tennessee

Italian Cream Cake

½ cup margarine
½ cup vegetable shortening
2 cups sugar
5 eggs, separated
2 cups sifted all-purpose flour
1 teaspoon soda

1 cup buttermilk
1 teaspoon vanilla
1 (3½-ounce) can coconut
1 cup chopped pecans
Cream Cheese Icing
(recipe follows)

Preheat oven to 350°. Grease and line with wax paper three 8- or 9-inch cake pans. Cream margarine and shortening; gradually add sugar, beating until light and fluffy. Add egg yolks, one at a time, beating well after each addition. Combine flour and soda; add to creamed mixture alternately with buttermilk. Stir in vanilla, coconut, and pecans. Beat egg whites until they form peaks, and fold into batter. Pour batter into prepared pans. Bake 45 minutes until sides loosen from pans. Set on wire rack to cool before removing. Frost with Cream Cheese Icing.

Cream Cheese Icing:

¼ cup margarine
1 (8-ounce) package cream
cheese, softened

1 (16-ounce) box confectioners' sugar
1 teaspoon vanilla
Chopped pecans

Cream margarine and cream cheese. Add sugar and vanilla and blend well. Spread on cooled cake. Sprinkle top with pecans.

Lane Schreeder Hays (Mrs. Charles, Jr.)

Old Fashioned Buttercakes

1 cup all-purpose flour, sifted
½ cup butter, frozen and sliced

4 tablespoons confectioners' sugar

Preheat oven to 350°. Using steel blade, place flour, sliced butter, and sugar in food processor. Mix until ball is formed. Shape into 6 balls. Press flat into 3-inch rounds. Place on ungreased cookie sheet and bake 15 to 20 minutes or until lightly browned.

Note: Top with sliced fruit and whipped cream.

Yield: 6 servings

Alix Frincke Dempster (Mrs. Donald)

Zucchini Squash Cake

3 cups sugar
1½ cups corn oil
4 eggs, slightly beaten
3 cups grated zucchini
1 cup chopped nuts
3 cups all-purpose flour

2 teaspoons baking powder
1 teaspoon soda
½ teaspoon salt
1½ teaspoons cinnamon
Cream Cheese Icing
   (recipe follows)

Preheat oven to 350°. Grease and flour two 8- or 9-inch cake pans. Beat sugar, oil, and eggs; add squash and nuts. Add remaining ingredients to sugar mixture, beating well. Pour into prepared pans. Bake 30 to 45 minutes. Cool and frost with Cream Cheese Icing.

Cream Cheese Icing:

1 (3-ounce) package cream cheese
¼ cup butter, softened

2 cups confectioners' sugar
1 teaspoon vanilla

Combine all ingredients and beat well.

Yield: 12 servings   Mrs. Fred McCallum

Surprise Cupcakes

1 (8-ounce) package cream cheese
1 egg, beaten
1 tablespoon sugar
⅛ teaspoon salt
1 (6-ounce) package semi-sweet
   chocolate pieces
3 cups all-purpose flour
½ cup cocoa

2 cups sugar
1 tablespoon soda
1 teaspoon salt
2 cups water
2 tablespoons vinegar
⅔ cup vegetable oil
2 teaspoons vanilla

Preheat oven to 350°. Combine cream cheese, egg, sugar, salt, and mix by hand. Stir in chocolate pieces and set aside. Sift flour, cocoa, sugar, soda, and salt together. Add water, vinegar, oil, and vanilla to flour mixture, beating well. (At first it will appear to be unmixable, but keep beating!) Use muffin tins and paper liners, filling half full with cocoa mixture. Drop 1 tablespoon cream cheese mixture on top of each one. Bake about 20 minutes. These freeze successfully.

Yield: 24 cupcakes   Anne Walters Pittenger (Mrs. Gaines S.)

Black Forest Cake

1 cup egg whites
Pinch cream of tartar
2 cups plus 2 tablespoons sugar
1 teaspoon vanilla

1 (4½-ounce) package slivered
   almonds, finely chopped
Chocolate Filling (recipe follows)
Whipped Cream Icing
   (recipe follows)

Preheat oven to 225°. Cut four 9-inch circles from parchment or brown paper. Place on cookie sheets and grease circles. Whip egg whites until foamy and add cream of tartar. Continue whipping until stiff but not dry. Gradually add sugar and vanilla. Fold in almonds. Spread beaten egg whites evenly on paper circles. Cook 2½ hours, turn off oven, and leave meringues in oven 5 to 6 hours or overnight to dry thoroughly. Spread each meringue with Chocolate Filling and refrigerate to cool. Stack meringue circles, spreading with Whipped Cream Icing between layers and on top and sides. Sprinkle top with grated German's Sweet Chocolate (reserved from Chocolate Filling). Store in refrigerator or freezer.

Chocolate Filling:

3 egg whites
¾ cup sugar
3 tablespoons cocoa

1 (4-ounce) bar German's Sweet
   Chocolate, divided
1½ cups butter, softened

Whip egg whites in top of double boiler over hot water. Add sugar and whip until stiff. Add cocoa. Remove from heat and add 3 ounces chocolate. (Reserve remaining chocolate to grate and use as garnish on finished cake.) Fold in softened butter. Chill mixture until of spreading consistency. Use as directed.

Whipped Cream Icing:

3 cups whipping cream
⅓ cup sugar

¾ cup vanilla

Whip cream very stiff. Add sugar and vanilla. Use as directed.

Yield: 12 servings

Cassandra (Candy) Johnson Brownlow (Mrs. William G.)

Chocolate Chip Torte

1 cup chopped dates	4 tablespoons cocoa
1 cup boiling water	½ teaspoon salt
1 teaspoon soda	1 teaspoon vanilla
½ cup vegetable shortening	½ cup chopped nuts
¼ cup margarine	1 (6-ounce) package semi-sweet
1 cup sugar	chocolate chips
2 eggs	Cocoa whipped cream
1¾ cups all-purpose flour	(recipe follows)

Preheat oven to 350°. Grease, flour, and line two 9-inch cake pans with wax paper. Combine dates, water, and soda. Set aside until softened. Cream shortening, margarine, and sugar. Add eggs one at a time, mixing well. Sift together flour, cocoa, and salt. Add flour mixture to creamed mixture alternately with date mixture. Stir in vanilla, nuts, and chocolate chips. Pour into cake pans and bake 25 to 30 minutes. Cool thoroughly and frost with cocoa whipped cream.

Cocoa Whipped Cream:

½ cup sugar	1 pint whipping cream,
¼ cup cocoa	whipped

Sift sugar and cocoa. Add to whipped cream. Frost torte and refrigerate immediately.

Jane Newman Bankston

Raspberry Blitz Torte

1⅓ cups sifted cake flour	4 eggs, separated
1⅓ teaspoons baking powder	5 tablespoons milk
½ cup butter	1 quart raspberries, sweetened
1½ cups sugar, divided	Whipped cream

Grease two 9-inch cake pans. Combine flour and baking powder. Sift together three times. Cream butter and gradually add ½ cup sugar. Beat until light and fluffy. Add egg yolks, one at a time, beating well after each addition. Add flour alternately with milk, beating well after each addition. Spread in pans. Beat egg whites until foamy throughout. Add remaining sugar, 2 tablespoons at a time. Beat after each addition until sugar is blended. Continue beating until mixture will stand in peaks. Spread in equal amounts on top of each layer. Bake 25 minutes at 325°; increase heat to 350° and bake 30 minutes longer. Spread sweetened raspberries between layers and top with whipped cream and raspberries. Cut in wedges to serve.

Yield: 10 to 12 servings   Katherine Spencer McNab (Mrs. R. B.)

Fresh Peach Torte

1 cup all-purpose flour
2 tablespoons sugar
½ cup margarine
1 cup chopped pecans
Cheese Filling (recipe follows)
Sliced fresh peaches

1 teaspoon almond extract
½ (9-ounce) carton non-dairy
  whipped topping; or ½ cup
  whipping cream, whipped
Chopped almonds

Preheat oven to 350°. Blend flour, sugar, margarine, and pecans until crumbled. Press into 9- x 13-inch pan. Bake 15 minutes and cool. Spread Cheese Filling over cooled crust. Cover with peaches and sprinkle with extract. Spread whipped topping over peaches and sprinkle with almonds. Chill and cut into squares to serve.

Cheese Filling:

1 (8-ounce) package cream cheese,
  softened
⅔ cup sugar

½ (9-ounce) carton non-dairy
  whipped topping; or ½ cup
  whipping cream, whipped

Blend cream cheese and sugar. Fold in whipped topping and use as directed.

Note: Peaches will darken if held too long.

Yield: 15 servings

Margie Cooley Jones (Mrs. William W.)

Sunday Special Torte

1 cup butter
1½ cups sugar, divided
5 eggs, separated
2 tablespoons milk
2 teaspoons vanilla, divided
¾ teaspoon salt, divided

½ teaspoon baking powder
2 cups sifted all-purpose flour
1 cup raspberry preserves
1⅓ cups shredded coconut,
  divided
2 cups sour cream

Preheat oven to 350°. Grease three 9-inch cake pans. Cut waxed paper to fit bottoms, place in each pan, and grease paper. Cream butter and ½ cup sugar. Blend egg yolks, milk, 1 teaspoon vanilla, ½ teaspoon salt, and baking powder; add to creamed mixture. Stir in flour and spread into cake pans. Spread ⅓ cup preserves on each layer to within 1 inch of sides. Beat egg whites and ¼ teaspoon salt until stiff. Gradually add 1 cup sugar. Fold in ⅔ cup coconut and 1 teaspoon vanilla. Spread over preserves. Bake 35 to 40 minutes until brown. Cool 15 minutes and remove carefully from pans. Cool completely. Spread mixture of sour cream and ⅔ cup coconut over each layer. Stack layers and chill.

Yield: 10 to 12 servings

Betsy Guinn Foster (Mrs. E. Bruce, Jr.)

Cognac Cheesecake

Crust:

1 cup fine Zwieback crumbs
2 tablespoons butter, melted
2 tablespoons sugar

¼ teaspoon cinnamon
¼ teaspoon nutmeg

Filling:

1¼ cups whipping cream
2 (3-ounce) packages cream cheese, softened
3 eggs
¾ cup sugar

¼ cup Cognac
½ teaspoon grated orange rind
¼ teaspoon salt

For crust, mix all ingredients well and press lightly against sides and bottom of heavily buttered 8-inch spring form pan. Chill.

For filling, combine cream with cream cheese. Set aside. Beat eggs and sugar until light. Add Cognac, orange rind, and salt. Beat until smooth. Combine cheese mixture with egg mixture, beating thoroughly. Pour into chilled crust and bake at 300° about 45 minutes or until set. Turn off oven, open oven door, and let cheesecake cool in oven.

Yield: 8 servings

Karen Brown Henry

Cheesecake Under the Covers

1¼ cups graham cracker crumbs
3 tablespoons sugar
⅓ cup butter or margarine, melted
1 tablespoon cinnamon
½ cup finely chopped walnuts
4 eggs

½ cup sugar
1 teaspoon vanilla
2 (8-ounce) packages cream cheese, softened
2 cups sour cream
4 tablespoons sugar

Preheat oven to 375°. Combine graham cracker crumbs, 3 tablespoons sugar, butter, cinnamon, and walnuts. Press mixture into 9-inch spring form pan. Chill 1 hour. Beat eggs until lemon-colored and thick. Add ½ cup sugar and vanilla. Beat cream cheese into eggs and sugar until well mixed. Pour into pie shell and bake 20 minutes or until set. Cool 10 minutes. Mix sour cream and 4 tablespoons sugar. Gently spoon sour cream and sugar mixture over cake. Increase oven temperature to 400° and bake additional 10 minutes. Remove from oven; cool, cover, and refrigerate at least 6 hours.

Yield: 8 servings

Jane Bradley (Mrs. Charles)
Lebanon, Tennessee

Apple Pizza Pie

1¼ cups all-purpose flour
1¼ teaspoons salt, divided
½ cup vegetable shortening
1 cup grated Cheddar cheese
¼ cup ice water
½ cup powdered non-dairy
   cream substitute
½ cup firmly packed
   brown sugar

½ cup white sugar
⅓ cup sifted all-purpose
   flour
1 teaspoon ground cinnamon
½ teaspoon ground nutmeg
¼ cup butter
6 cups peeled apple slices,
   ½-inch thick
2 tablespoons lemon juice

Preheat oven to 450°. Mix 1¼ cup flour and 1 teaspoon salt; cut in shortening until crumbly. Add cheese. Gradually sprinkle water over mixture and shape into ball. Roll pastry into 15-inch circle on floured surface. Place on baking sheet or pizza pan and turn up edge. Combine powdered non-dairy cream substitute, sugars, ⅓ cup flour, ¼ teaspoon salt, and spices. Sprinkle half mixture over pastry. Cut butter into remaining half of mixture until crumbly. Arrange apple slices, overlapping in circles on crust. Sprinkle with lemon juice and remaining crumbs. Bake 30 minutes or until apples are tender. Watch carefully. Serve warm.

Yield: 12 servings

Linda Jetton Livaudais (Mrs. Denny)

Brown Sugar Pie

1 cup firmly packed brown sugar
1 egg, beaten
⅓ cup all-purpose flour
½ teaspoon soda

1½ teaspoons vanilla
1 cup broken pecans
½ pint whipping cream,
   whipped

Preheat oven to 325° and grease 9-inch pie pan. Combine all ingredients except cream. Pour into prepared pan and bake 25 minutes. Let cook, remove from pan, and crumble into bowl. Fold in cream and return to lightly greased pie pan. Chill in refrigerator until very cold. Serve in small wedges topped with whipped cream.

Yield: 8 to 10 servings

Martha Bacon Hemphill (Mrs. James L.)

Sour Cream Apple Pie

6 tart cooking apples
1 cup sugar
2 tablespoons all-purpose flour
1 teaspoon ground cinnamon
1 teaspoon grated lemon peel
⅛ teaspoon ground cloves
⅛ teaspoon salt
1 (9-inch) sour cream pastry
Cheese Topping (recipe follows)
1 (8-ounce) carton sour cream

Preheat oven to 400°. Peel, quarter, and core apples; thinly slice. Combine sugar, flour, cinnamon, lemon peel, cloves, and salt. Toss apple slices in sugar mixture. Arrange apples, overlapping slices in pastry-lined pan. Sprinkle cheese topping over apples. Bake 40 minutes or until topping and crust are golden brown. Cool on wire rack. Serve warm with generous spoonful of sour cream on each slice.

Cheese Topping:

½ cup all-purpose flour
¼ cup sugar
⅛ teaspoon salt
½ cup grated Cheddar cheese
¼ cup butter, melted

Combine all ingredients and sprinkle cheese crumbs over apples.

Yield: 6 to 8 servings

Sherri Parker Lee

Buttermilk Pie

½ cup margarine
1½ cups sugar
3 eggs
1 tablespoon cornstarch
1 teaspoon vanilla
½ cup buttermilk
1 unbaked 9-inch pie shell

Preheat oven to 325°. Combine all ingredients. Pour into pie shell. Bake 40 to 45 minutes or until knife inserted in middle comes out clean.

Yield: 6 to 8 servings

Preston Pratt Gentry (Mrs. Edgar C., Jr.)

Banana Cream Pie

½ cup sugar
6 tablespoons all-purpose flour
Dash salt
2½ cups milk
2 egg yolks or 1 whole egg
2 tablespoons butter

½ teaspoon vanilla
3 bananas, divided
1 (9-inch) pie crust, baked
1 cup whipping cream,
  whipped and sweetened
Toasted coconut

Mix sugar, flour, and salt in top of double boiler. Gradually stir in milk and cook over boiling water until thickened, stirring constantly. Cover and cook 10 minutes. Beat egg and add small amount of milk mixture to it; return to double boiler and cook 2 minutes over hot water while stirring. Remove from heat and add butter and vanilla. Cool. Slice 2 bananas into pie shell. Pour custard over bananas and chill several hours. Before serving, top pie with whipped cream. Sprinkle toasted coconut on top of cream. Place remaining banana slices around edge of pie.

Yield: 6 to 8 servings

Anne Beall Hillmer (Mrs. Ralph G.)

Banana Liqueur Pie

1 (9-inch) graham cracker crust
1 tablespoon unflavored gelatin
¼ cup cold water
6 egg yolks
1 cup sugar

2 cups whipping cream, whipped
2 tablespoons banana liqueur
2 to 3 bananas, sliced
Glaze (recipe follows)

Prepare pie crust. In saucepan sprinkle gelatin over cold water and let stand 5 minutes. Stir over heat until dissolved and cool. Beat yolks until frothy. Gradually add sugar and continue beating several minutes. Pour gelatin in thin stream into egg mixture, beating constantly. Fold whipped cream into mixture. Add liqueur and mound filling into crust. Chill 30 minutes and decorate top with bananas. Drizzle glaze over top.

Glaze:

⅓ cup apricot preserves

½ teaspoon lemon juice

Heat glaze ingredients and strain.

Yield: 6 servings

Jeanne Holmes Hyatt (Mrs. Hugh C.)

Chess Pie

½ cup butter
1 cup sugar
¼ cup all-purpose flour
½ cup evaporated milk

3 egg yolks, slightly beaten
1½ teaspoons vanilla
⅛ teaspoon salt
1 (9-inch) pastry shell, unbaked

Preheat oven to 325°. Cream together butter, sugar, and flour. Add evaporated milk and blend well. Add egg yolks, vanilla, and salt. Pour into pastry and bake 1 hour or until almost set in center.

Yield: 6 to 8 servings

Martha Bacon Hemphill (Mrs. James L.)

Chocolate Chess Pie

2 (9-inch) pastry shells
2 cups firmly packed light
   brown sugar
1 cup white sugar
2 tablespoons all-purpose flour
4 eggs

1 whole eggshell of milk
2 teaspoons vanilla
3 (1-ounce) squares unsweetened
   chocolate
1 cup butter
Vanilla ice cream

Prebake pastry shells at 400° until just beginning to turn golden. Cool. In large bowl combine brown sugar, white sugar, and flour. Set aside. In another bowl combine eggs, milk, and vanilla, and set aside. Melt chocolate and butter over low heat. (Do not allow this to boil or filling will be bitter.) While chocolate mixture is very hot, pour over sugar mixture and stir well. Add egg mixture and thoroughly blend. Pour into pastry shells and bake 30 to 40 minutes at 325° to 350°. Serve warm or at room temperature with vanilla ice cream.

Note: Freezes well.

Yield: 2 pies

Cheryl Sherling Magli (Mrs. Boyce)
Spring Hill, Tennessee

German's Chocolate Pie

3 egg whites
1 teaspoon vanilla
¾ cup sugar
1 teaspoon baking powder

1 (4-ounce) bar German's chocolate,
  grated, divided
1 cup Ritz crackers, crushed
½ cup chopped nuts
1 cup whipping cream

Preheat oven to 350°. Beat egg whites and vanilla on high, forming soft peaks. Add sugar and baking powder and continue beating until whites form stiff peaks. Add grated chocolate (reserving 1 tablespoon for garnish), crackers, and nuts. Grease 9-inch pie pan and spread mixture over bottom and high on sides. Bake 25 minutes. Cool. Whip cream and spread on top. Garnish with 1 tablespoon grated chocolate. Pie can be prepared and frozen ahead. Add whipped cream before serving.

Yield: 6 to 8 servings   Rose "Posey" Stewart Congleton (Mrs. Joseph)

Chocolate Ice Box Pie

1 graham cracker crust or 12
  pastry tart shells,
  baked and cooled
3 eggs
½ cup butter, softened
1 cup super fine sugar

2 (1-ounce) envelopes pre-melted
  unsweetened chocolate
1 teaspoon vanilla
½ pint whipping cream,
  whipped

Prepare crust. In small mixing bowl, beat eggs one at a time, 5 minutes each. Cream butter and sugar in another mixing bowl. Add eggs, chocolate, and vanilla. Blend well. Pour into crust and refrigerate. (Pie will set in 10 to 15 minutes.) Top with whipped cream before serving.

Yield: 8 to 12 servings   Melissa Cooley Gill

Blackberry Farms' Coconut Pie

1½ cups all-purpose flour
½ cup vegetable shortening
½ teaspoon salt
2 to 3 tablespoons ice water
3 cups milk
½ cup sugar

3 large egg yolks
5 tablespoons cornstarch
1 teaspoon vanilla
7 ounces coconut
Topping (recipe follows)

Preheat oven to 400°. Blend flour, shortening, and salt. Add enough water to make dough stick together, roll out, and line pie plate. Bake about 20 minutes. Cool. Scald milk in double boiler, stirring occasionally. In another pan, combine remaining ingredients except coconut. Add just enough milk to mix. When milk gets hot, add mixture to hot milk in double boiler. Stir occasionally and when thick add coconut. Pour into pie shell and spread topping over filling.

Topping:

½ pint whipping cream
2 tablespoons confectioners' sugar

½ to 1 teaspoon vanilla

Whip cream, adding 1 tablespoon sugar at a time. Add vanilla and spread over pie filling.

Yield: 8 to 10 servings

John Coffey
Blackberry Farms
Blount County, Tennessee

Toasted Coconut Pie

3 eggs, beaten
1½ cups sugar
½ cup margarine, melted
4 teaspoons lemon juice

1 teaspoon vanilla
1 (3½-ounce) can flaked
   coconut
1 (9-inch) pie shell, unbaked

Preheat oven to 350°. Combine eggs, sugar, margarine, lemon juice, and vanilla. Stir in coconut and mix well. Pour filling into unbaked pie shell. Bake 45 minutes or until knife inserted in center comes out clean. Cool before serving.

Yield: 6 to 8 servings   Rose "Posey" Stewart Congleton (Mrs. Joseph)

Surprise Peach Pie

1 (8- or 9-inch) pastry shell
3 fresh peaches, peeled and sliced
1 egg
1 scant cup sugar

⅓ cup all-purpose flour
⅓ cup butter, melted
1 teaspoon vanilla
Dash almond extract

Preheat oven to 350°. Partially bake empty pie shell 5 minutes. Reduce oven to 300°. Place sliced peaches in shell. Combine remaining ingredients and pour over peaches. Bake 1 hour.

Yield: 6 to 8 servings

Margie Cooley Jones (Mrs. William W.)

Easy Pecan Pie

½ cup sugar
¼ cup butter
3 eggs
1½ cups pecans

Pinch of salt
1 teaspoon vanilla
1 cup light corn syrup
1 9-inch pie shell

Preheat oven to 350°. Cream sugar and butter together. Add eggs, pecans, salt, vanilla, and corn syrup. Mix well. Pour into unbaked pie shell. Bake 45 minutes to 1 hour.

Yield: 6 to 8 servings

Susan Cox Watson (Mrs. William Donaldson)

Microwaved Pumpkin Pie

1 (16-ounce) can pumpkin
¾ cup firmly packed
brown sugar
1 tablespoon pumpkin pie spice

½ teaspoon salt
2 eggs
1 cup evaporated milk
1 (9-inch) pastry shell, baked

Combine pumpkin, sugar, and spices in mixing bowl. Beat eggs with milk and stir into pumpkin mixture. Pour into baked pastry shell. Microwave at 60% power 18 to 20 minutes or until set. Turn once during cooking.

Yield: 6 to 8 servings

Suzanne Wood Fletcher

Easy Strawberry Pie

2 quarts fresh strawberries,
  divided
1 cup sugar
3 tablespoons cornstarch
Dash salt
1 tablespoon butter

1 tablespoon lemon juice
1 (9-inch) pie crust, cooked
  and cooled
1 (10-ounce) carton non-dairy
  whipped topping

Crush 1 quart strawberries. Add sugar, cornstarch, and salt. Cook mixture over medium heat until thickened. Add butter and lemon juice. Let mixture cool thoroughly in refrigerator. Place cooled strawberry mixture in pie crust. Top with remaining 1 quart strawberries and non-dairy whipped topping.

Yield: 6 servings   Ann Morgan Iron Bignall (Mrs. Michael)

Mystery Cheesecake Pie

1 (8-ounce) package cream cheese,
  softened
1 egg
⅓ cup sugar
½ teaspoon vanilla
1 (9-inch) unbaked, deep-dish
  pie shell

1 cup pecan halves
2 eggs, slightly beaten
¼ cup sugar
⅔ cup dark corn syrup
¼ teaspoon vanilla

Preheat oven to 375°. In small bowl, combine cream cheese, egg, ⅓ cup sugar, and vanilla. Beat until light and fluffy. Spread over bottom of pie shell. Arrange pecans over cream cheese mixture. Combine 2 eggs, ¼ cup sugar, corn syrup, and ¼ teaspoon vanilla and carefully pour over pecans. Bake 40 to 45 minutes.

Yield: 6 servings   Patti Wasmansdorff Arnold (Mrs. H. Grady)

Chocolate Mousse Pie

3 cups chocolate wafer crumbs
½ cup unsalted butter, melted
1 pound semi-sweet chocolate
6 eggs
2 cups whipping cream

6 tablespoons confectioners' sugar
1 cup whipping cream,
  whipped and sweetened
Chocolate leaves (recipe follows)

Combine wafer crumbs and melted butter; press on bottom and sides of 10-inch springform pan. Chill in freezer.

Soften chocolate in double boiler or in microwave. Let cool to 95°. Add 2 whole eggs and 4 egg yolks, reserving 4 egg whites. Mix until thoroughly blended and set aside. Combine 2 cups whipping cream and confectioners' sugar; whip until soft peaks form. Set aside. Beat reserved egg whites until stiff. Stir a little of the cream and egg whites into chocolate mixture. Fold in remaining cream and egg whites. Turn into crust and chill at least 6 hours or preferably overnight. Loosen crust of pie on all sides and remove spring form. Spread half of sweetened whipped cream over top of mousse; pipe remaining cream around rim of pie. Pipe rosettes in center of pie and arrange chocolate leaves around rosettes as garnish.

Note: This dessert can be frozen and thawed overnight in refrigerator.

Chocolate Leaves:

4 (1-ounce) squares semi-sweet
  chocolate

1½ teaspoons vegetable shortening
Camellia or mint leaves

Melt chocolate and shortening in double boiler or microwave. Using spoon, generously coat undersides of leaves. Freeze until firm. Separate chocolate from leaves, starting at stem of leaf.

Yield: 12 to 14 servings

Suzanne Wood Fletcher

Coffee Toffee Pie

½ (10-ounce) package pie
  crust mix
¼ cup firmly packed brown
  sugar
¾ cup finely chopped walnuts
1 (1-ounce) square unsweetened
  chocolate, grated
1 tablespoon water

1 teaspoon vanilla
½ cup butter, softened
¾ cup sugar
1 (1-ounce) square unsweetened
  chocolate, melted and cooled
2 teaspoons instant coffee
2 eggs
Coffee Topping (recipe follows)

Preheat oven to 375°. Grease 9-inch pie plate. Combine crust mix, brown
sugar, walnuts, and 1 square grated chocolate. Add water and vanilla;
using fork, mix until well blended. Turn into pie plate and press dough
firmly against bottom and side. Bake 10 to 15 minutes and cool on rack. Beat
butter until creamy. Gradually add sugar, beating until light. Blend in
melted chocolate and instant coffee. Add 1 egg, beating 5 minutes. Add
remaining egg, beating 5 minutes longer. Turn filling into baked pie shell.
Refrigerate, covered, overnight. Decorate pie shell with coffee topping,
using pastry bag with #6 decorating tip. Garnish with chocolate curls and
refrigerate 2 hours.

Coffee Topping:

2 cups whipping cream
2 tablespoons instant coffee

½ cup confectioners' sugar
Chocolate curls

Combine cream with instant coffee and confectioners' sugar. Refrigerate,
covered, 1 hour. Beat cream mixture until stiff. Decorate pie.

Yield: 6 to 8 servings

                                        Sheila Prial Jacobstein (Mrs. Richard)

Senate Rum Pie

2 cups milk, divided
¾ cup sugar
Pinch of salt
5 egg yolks
4 tablespoons all-purpose flour
2 tablespoons cornstarch

½ cup butter
2 tablespoons dark rum
1 (9-inch) graham cracker crust
1 cup whipping cream, whipped
Chopped pecans or shaved
   chocolate

Combine 1½ cups milk, sugar, and salt. Bring *almost* to boil. Combine ½ cup milk, egg yolks, flour, and cornstarch. Mix until smooth and add to hot mixture. Cook until thick and clear. Cool to room temperature. Whip in butter and rum. Pour into crust. Chill and top with whipped cream. Garnish with chopped pecans or shaved chocolate.

Yield: 6 to 8 servings   Pamela Young Richardson (Mrs. Charles Franklin)

Amelia Island Mud Pie

2 to 3 cups chocolate ice cream,
   softened
1 tablespoon Sanka coffee grounds,
   perked
2 tablespoons brandy
2 tablespoons Kahlua
2 tablespoons liquid instant
   Sanka coffee

½ pint whipping cream,
   whipped and divided
1 chocolate pie shell
   (recipe follows)
1 (12-ounce) jar Kraft fudge
   topping
¼ cup chopped pecans

Whip ice cream with coffee grounds, liqueurs, and coffee. Fold in 4 tablespoons whipped cream. Pour into prepared shell. Freeze until hard. Cover with thin layer of fudge topping and nuts. Garnish with remaining whipped cream that has been sweetened to taste.

Chocolate Pie Shell:

12 Oreo cookies, without filling,
   crushed
2 tablespoons butter, melted

1 tablespoon Sanka coffee
   grounds, perked

Combine crushed cookies with butter and coffee grounds. Press into pie plate and freeze.

Yield: 6 to 8 servings   Charlsie James Proffitt (Mrs. Douglas)
Tampa, Florida

Frozen Chocolate Pecan Pie

2 cups finely chopped pecans,
  toasted
5 tablespoons plus 1 teaspoon
  firmly packed brown sugar
5 tablespoons butter, chilled,
  cut into small pieces
2 teaspoons dark rum
6 ounces semi-sweet chocolate

½ teaspoon instant coffee
  powder
4 eggs, room temperature
1 tablespoon dark rum
1 teaspoon vanilla
1½ cups whipping cream,
  divided
3 tablespoons shaved
  semi-sweet chocolate

Blend pecans, brown sugar, butter, and rum until mixture holds together. Press into bottom and sides of 9-inch pie pan. Freeze at least 1 hour. For filling, melt chocolate with coffee in top of double boiler. Remove from heat and whisk in eggs, rum, and vanilla until mixture is smooth. Let cool 5 minutes. Whip 1 cup cream until stiff. Gently fold into chocolate mixture, blending completely. Pour into crust and freeze. About 1 hour before serving, transfer pie to refrigerator. Whip remaining ½ cup cream and spoon onto pie. Sprinkle with chocolate shavings.

Note: Pie can be frozen up to 3 months.

Yield: 6 to 8 servings

Nancy Tombras Faulkner

Colonial Innkeeper Pie

1¾ cups vanilla wafer
  crumbs, divided
2 eggs, separated
2 (1-ounce) squares unsweetened
  chocolate
⅔ cup margarine
2 cups confectioners' sugar

1 teaspoon vanilla
½ gallon pecan ice cream,
  softened
Whipped cream (optional)
Maraschino cherries (optional)
Chocolate shavings (optional)

Spread 1 cup crumbs in 9- x 13-inch ungreased pan. Beat egg whites until stiff and set aside. Melt chocolate with margarine. Add sugar, egg yolks, vanilla, and egg whites to chocolate. Spread chocolate mixture on top of crumbs. Freeze 2 hours. Evenly spread softened ice cream over top of chocolate. Sprinkle with ¾ cup crumbs and freeze. To serve, cut in 3-inch squares. Top with whipped cream, maraschino cherries, and chocolate shavings, if desired.

Note: Peppermint or mocha ice cream may be substituted.

Yield: 10 to 12 servings

Betty Newbill Threadgill

Frozen Praline Pie

4 egg whites
½ teaspoon cream of tartar
1 cup sugar
2 quarts vanilla ice cream,
   divided and softened

Butterscotch sauce
   (recipe follows)
1 cup pecan halves
1 cup chopped pecans

Preheat oven to 325°. Grease 10-inch springform pan. Beat egg whites until frothy; add cream of tartar. Beat until stiff. Add sugar slowly, beating until smooth and glossy. Line pan with meringue and mound meringue around sides. Bake 1 hour. Turn off oven and let cool in oven. Spoon 1 quart ice cream into shell and freeze until firm. Pour thick layer of sauce over ice cream and cover with pecan halves. Freeze until firm. Spread remaining ice cream on top of sauce. Freeze until firm. Top with thick layer of sauce and cover entirely with chopped pecans. Cover with foil and freeze. Serve in wedges, pouring more sauce over top.

Butterscotch Sauce:

1¾ cups white corn syrup
2 cups sugar
1 cup butter

2 cups whipping cream,
   divided
1 teaspoon vanilla

Combine corn syrup, sugar, butter, and 1 cup cream. Cook to soft ball stage. Add remaining cup cream to sauce and cook to 218°. Cool, add vanilla.

Yield: 8 servings

Jennifer Brinner (Mrs. Richard)

Southern Ice Cream Pie

1½ cups crushed chocolate
   cookie crumbs
¼ cup butter, melted
1 pint chocolate ice cream

1 quart vanilla ice cream
½ cup crunchy peanut butter
½ cup honey (optional)
½ cup orange liqueur (optional)

Preheat oven to 350°. Combine crumbs and butter. Press into 9-inch pie plate. Bake 10 minutes. Cool. While crust is cooling, remove ice cream from freezer and soften. Scoop chocolate ice cream into crust and spread evenly with knife. Be careful not to disturb crumbs. Place in freezer. Combine softened vanilla ice cream and peanut butter, stirring until well blended. Remove pie from freezer and add vanilla mixture to top of chocolate. Cover and refreeze. Remove from freezer 5 to 10 minutes before slicing. If desired, top with honey and liqueur mixture.

Yield: 6 to 8 servings

Jayne Crumpler DeFiore (Mrs. Joseph C.)

Cream Cheese Tarts

2 (8-ounce) packages cream cheese
2 eggs
2 teaspoons vanilla
½ cup sugar
1½ cups graham cracker crumbs
¼ cup confectioners' sugar
6 tablespoons melted butter

1 teaspoon cinnamon
1 package 2-inch Midget baking
  cups (paper-lined
  foil cups)
1 (20-ounce) can cherry or
  blueberry pie filling or
  fresh strawberry glaze

Preheat oven to 375°. Mix together cream cheese, eggs, vanilla, and sugar in processor. Set aside. Combine graham cracker crumbs, confectioners' sugar, melted butter, and cinnamon to form crust. Put approximately 2 teaspoons crust mixture into each lined cup and press firmly. Place 1 tablespoon cheese filling in each cup. Bake 10 minutes. Chill. Before serving top each with 1 teaspoon pie filling or glaze.

Yield: 40 servings

Carol Smith Hudgens (Mrs. James F.)

Tea-Time Tassies

1 (3-ounce) package cream cheese
½ cup butter, softened
1 cup sifted all-purpose flour
⅔ cup broken pecans, divided
1 egg

¾ cup firmly packed light
  brown sugar
1 tablespoon butter, softened
1 teaspoon vanilla
Dash salt

Make tart shells by combining cream cheese and butter; add flour and mix well. Chill 1 hour. Shape dough into 24 one-inch balls. Place in ungreased miniature 1¾-inch muffin tins. Press bottom and sides to form tart shells. Divide ⅓ cup pecan pieces among pastry-lined cups. Make filling by beating together egg, sugar, butter, vanilla, and salt until smooth. Pour egg mixture into shells and top with remaining pecans. Bake 25 minutes at 325°. Cool and remove from pans. These can be frozen after baking.

Yield: 2 dozen

Diana Carter Samples (Mrs. Robert F.)

Pastry Tarts

1 cup butter or margarine
2 (3-ounce) packages cream
  cheese
¼ teaspoon salt
2 cups all-purpose flour, sifted

7 tablespoons whipping cream
  (approximately)
Jam
Egg white
Sugar

Soften margarine and cream cheese and blend together thoroughly with salt. Cut cream cheese mixture into flour. Add cream until mixture is of pie dough consistency. Refrigerate 3 to 4 hours until dough is set. Preheat oven to 425°. Roll dough thin and cut in 3½- to 4-inch squares. Put 1 teaspoon of jam in center; moisten edges and roll toward one point. To make crescent, curve slightly. Brush tart with slightly beaten egg white, sprinkle with sugar, and bake 15 minutes. Be careful not to overhandle dough.

Yield: 2 dozen

Jeanne Gibbons Fraas (Mrs. Arthur P.)

Easy Pie Crust

1 cup all-purpose flour
½ teaspoon salt

⅓ cup vegetable shortening
3 tablespoons cold water

Preheat oven to 375°. Combine flour and salt. With fork, work in shortening until mixture resembles coarse meal. Sprinkle cold water evenly over surface; stir until all dry particles are moistened. Form into ball, flatten with hands, and roll on lightly floured surface. Place in 9-inch glass pie pan. Prick pastry with fork. Bake 5 minutes at 375°; reduce heat to 350° and bake 15 to 20 minutes longer.

Note: If using food processor, process flour, salt, and shortening until coarsely blended. Add water all at once and process only until it begins to cling to blade.

Yield: 1 9-inch pastry

Anne Beall Hillmer (Mrs. Ralph G., Jr.)

Pêches Cardinale

6 cups water
2¼ cups sugar
2 tablespoons vanilla or
  1 vanilla bean

10 firm fresh peaches,
  pared and halved
Raspberry Purée
  (recipe follows)

Simmer water, sugar, and vanilla until sugar is dissolved. Add peaches and simmer 8 minutes. Remove from heat and let peaches cool 20 minutes in syrup. Drain and chill. Serve with raspberry purée, if desired.

Note: Syrup may be reserved and used for poaching other fruits.

Raspberry Purée:

1 (10-ounce) package frozen
  raspberries, thawed

⅔ cup sugar

Put raspberries through sieve, add sugar, pour in blender and set at top speed 2 or 3 minutes. Chill.

Yield: 8 to 10 servings

Mary Nell Greer Johnson (Mrs. Andrew)

Strawberries Romanoff

1 cup confectioners' sugar
2 pints fresh strawberries,
  washed and hulled

1 cup whipping cream
1 teaspoon almond extract
2 tablespoons Cointreau

Sprinkle sugar over strawberries and gently toss. Refrigerate 1 hour. Whip cream until stiff; add almond extract and Cointreau. Fold into strawberries.

Yield: 6 servings

Mary Ann Durst Cochran (Mrs. Robert B.)

Cherries Jubilee á la Suisse

2 tablespoons butter
2 tablespoons sugar
1 teaspoon grated orange rind
1 teaspoon grated lemon rind
¼ cup fresh orange juice
¼ cup fresh lemon juice

¼ cup Kirsch
3 cups Bing cherries,
  pitted and drained
¼ cup warm brandy
Vanilla ice cream

In skillet melt butter over high heat. Blend in sugar and heat mixture until it bubbles. Stir in orange and lemon rind. Simmer until mixture is light brown. Stir in juices and cook until mixture bubbles. Add Kirsch and cherries. Stir gently until cherries are well saturated. Pour in warm brandy, ignite, and stir sauce until flames die away. Serve over vanilla ice cream.

Yield: 6 servings

Jeanne Holmes Hyatt (Mrs. Hugh C.)

Chocolate Fondue

3 (3-ounce) Toblerone chocolate
  and nougat bars
½ cup whipping cream
2 to 3 tablespoons Cointreau

Bite-size cubes of pound cake,
  marshmallows, cherries, banana
  chunks, fresh pineapple,
  strawberries, etc.

Break chocolate into pieces. Combine with cream in small saucepan over low heat until chocolate melts or use microwave oven. Stir in Cointreau; keep warm. Spear cake and fruit on forks and dip into fondue.

Yield: 6 to 8 servings

Kaye McIntyre Littlejóhn

Round Chocolate Éclairs

¾ cup water
6 tablespoons butter or margarine
¾ cup all-purpose flour

3 eggs
Cream Filling (recipe follows)
Chocolate Glaze (recipe follows)

Preheat oven to 425°. Bring water to boil in saucepan, add butter and continue boiling until butter melts. Quickly add flour all at once. Beat with wooden spoon until mixture forms ball that leaves sides of pan. Remove from heat and cool slightly. Add eggs to mixture, one at a time, beating well after each addition. (Mixture will separate as each egg is added; beat until smooth again.) Spoon batter by heaping tablespoons onto greased cookie sheet. Bake 20 minutes. Reduce heat to 325° and bake 30 minutes longer. Remove éclair shells to wire rack and cool thoroughly. Cut off tops, remove moist webbing inside, fill with Cream Filling, replace tops, and spread with Chocolate Glaze.

Cream Filling:

1 (5½-ounce) package vanilla
  instant pudding and pie
  filling mix
2 cups milk

1½ cups non-dairy
  whipped topping
1 teaspoon vanilla

Combine pudding mix and milk; stir until smooth. Fold in whipped topping and add vanilla. Use as directed.

Chocolate Glaze:

4 ounces semi-sweet chocolate   ¼ cup butter

Melt chocolate and butter over hot water. Stir well. Use as directed.

Note: Make these one day ahead or early same day as these are best cold.

Yield: 8 servings

Margie Cooley Jones (Mrs. William W.)

Apple Pudding

¾ cup margarine
2 cups sugar
2 eggs
2 cups all-purpose flour
1 teaspoon soda

1 teaspoon salt
1 teaspoon vanilla
2 teaspoons cinnamon
3 apples, cored, pared, and
   thinly sliced

Preheat oven to 350°. Cream margarine and sugar. Add eggs and mix thoroughly. Add flour, soda, salt, vanilla, and cinnamon, and mix well. Stir in apples. Put in 3-quart oven-proof dish and bake 45 minutes.

Yield: 12 servings

Catherine Daughtery Cifers (Mrs. Ed)

English Plum Pudding

This has been a family recipe for over 160 years.

1 (10-ounce) package currants
1 (15-ounce) package seedless
   raisins
1 pound candied fruit
1 rounded "saucer full of
   all-purpose flour"
1 cup coarse bread crumbs
½ teaspoon salt
1 cup sugar

1¾ teaspoons baking powder
½ teaspoon ground cloves
1 teaspoon ground cinnamon
1½ teaspoons allspice
½ pound beef suet
   from kidneys
3 eggs
Brandy

Put currants, raisins, and candied fruit in large bowl. Add flour, crumbs, salt, sugar, baking powder, cloves, cinnamon, and allspice. Set aside. Run suet through grinder, using small blade. Add suet to fruit mixture. Add eggs; mix to moisten all ingredients. If too dry, add brandy, milk, or wine until bonded together.

Flour large square of clean sheet, put pudding in center, pull up all corners of sheet, hold tight, and form round shape. Tie loosely with cord to allow expansion of pudding. Slowly lower pudding into large kettle of boiling water. Keep water gently boiling 4 hours. Add water as needed. Remove cloth, place on serving platter, with holly wreath as garnish. Scoop 1 tablespoon pudding from top center. Fill with warm brandy, light, and serve flaming. Serve with whipped cream.

Note: If made ahead, resteam before serving.

Lillian Astley Rayson (Mrs. Edwin)

Microwaved Plum Pudding

3 slices bread, torn in pieces
¾ cup prepared mincemeat, drained
⅓ cup milk
2 slightly beaten eggs
¾ cup firmly packed brown sugar
3 tablespoons brandy
3 ounces (¾ cup) finely
   chopped beef suet
¾ teaspoon vanilla
¾ cup all-purpose flour

¾ teaspoon soda
½ teaspoon salt
1½ teaspoons ground cinnamon
¾ teaspoon ground cloves
¾ teaspoon ground mace
1 cup chopped candied lemon peel
¾ cup raisins
⅓ cup toasted slivered almonds
Brandied Hard Sauce
   (recipe follows)

Heavily grease a 6-cup microwave ring mold. In a bowl combine bread, mincemeat, and milk. Beat and stir in eggs, brown sugar, brandy, suet, and vanilla. Set aside. Thoroughly combine flour, soda, salt, cinnamon, cloves, and mace. Add candied lemon peel, raisins, and almonds. Stir into bread mixture. Mix well and pour into mold. Microwave at 50% power 11 to 12 minutes, turning twice during cooking. Microwave at full power 2 minutes. Cool 10 minutes in mold. Remove from mold and serve warm with Brandied Hard Sauce.

Brandied Hard Sauce:

½ cup butter
1 cup confectioners' sugar, sifted

2 tablespoons brandy
½ teaspoon vanilla

Soften butter in microwave at 10% power 2 minutes. Beat with mixer and slowly add confectioners' sugar. Add brandy and vanilla. Beat until smooth and chill.

Yield: 12 servings

Suzanne Wood Fletcher

Desserts

231

Microwaved Boiled Custard

1 quart whole milk
3 eggs
1 egg yolk
⅔ cup sugar

Pinch salt
1 tablespoon vanilla
Grated nutmeg

Pour milk in 2-quart casserole and cook in microwave at 80% power (medium high) until milk is scalded. Should reach 190° in 8 to 10 minutes. Meanwhile, place eggs and yolk in bowl and beat slightly. Gradually add sugar and salt to eggs. When milk is scalded, slowly add to egg and sugar mixture. Return to 2-quart casserole and cook in microwave at 80% power (medium high) 2½ to 3 minutes or until mixture coats a metal spoon. Stir once or twice during cooking. Add vanilla and chill. Garnish with grated nutmeg to serve.

Suzanne Wood Fletcher

Yield: 4 to 5 cups

Angel Toffee Roll

1 (18½-ounce) Duncan Hines
   angel food cake mix
Confectioners' sugar

13 ounces non-dairy whipped
   topping
8 Heath bars, crushed

Preheat oven to 375°. Line two 10- x 15-inch jelly-roll pans with waxed paper. Mix cake according to package directions. Spread batter evenly in the two pans. Place on oven rack positioned 4 or 5 inches from bottom of oven. Bake one at a time 11 to 13 minutes or until top is golden brown. Turn out onto a towel dusted with confectioner's sugar. Peel off waxed paper and roll cake up in towel. Repeat with second roll. Let cool.

Mix whipped topping with crushed candy. Unroll cake, fill with topping mixture, re-roll, and refrigerate. Can garnish with whipped cream rosettes, strawberries, or flowers.

Note: To crush Heath bars, freeze, then break up with hammer or mallet while candy is still in wrapper.

Jeanne Holmes Hyatt (Mrs. Hugh C.)

Yield: 16 servings

Chocolate Angel Food Dessert

2 (6-ounce) packages semi-sweet
   chocolate chips
4 eggs, separated
2 tablespoons sugar

1 pint whipping cream, whipped,
   or 2 (1.5-ounce) envelopes
   Dream Whip
1 (13-ounce) prepared angel food
   cake, broken into pieces

Melt chocolate over hot water and cool. Place 4 egg yolks in large bowl and add chocolate. Beat egg whites until stiff, gradually adding sugar. Fold egg whites into chocolate mixture. Fold in whipped cream. Line 9- x 13-inch pan with half of cake pieces. Pour half of chocolate mixture over cake. Repeat layers with remaining cake and chocolate. Chill 24 hours. Serve with additional whipped cream on top.

Note: Can be frozen.

Yield: 16 servings   Kathleen McAuliffe Farnham (Mrs. William J.)

Angel Cake Sherry Dessert

1 envelope unflavored
   gelatin
¼ cup cold water
4 eggs, separated

1 cup sugar, divided
½ cup sherry
½ pint whipping cream
1 large angel food cake

Line botom of tube pan with foil. Soak gelatin in cold water. Mix egg yolks, ½ cup sugar, and sherry; cook in double boiler over hot water, stirring constantly, until thick. Add gelatin to egg yolk mixture and blend thoroughly. Remove from hot water. Whip egg whites, adding ½ cup sugar, until stiff. Whip cream. Fold together egg whites, whipped cream, and sherry mixture to form custard. Break cake into small chunks and layer cake pieces in bottom of prepared pan. Pour some of custard mixture over top. Repeat layers,ending with custard layer. Chill 3 to 4 hours and serve cold. Can be served with dollop of whipped cream and strawberry on top.

Yield: 8 servings   Ena Taylor Kirkpatrick (Mrs. David M.)

Authentic Spanish Flan

1 cup sugar, divided
2 cups milk
3 eggs

2 teaspoons vanilla
Pinch salt

Preheat oven to 300°. In small, heavy skillet, melt ½ cup sugar, stirring constantly until caramel-colored. Pour caramelized sugar into bottom of 1½-quart oven-proof dish or eight 6-ounce custard cups. Set aside. Scald milk and set aside. Beat eggs and add remaining ½ cup sugar, vanilla, and salt. Add this mixture to milk; pour into mold, place in pan of warm water, and bake 2 hours or until knife inserted in center comes out clean. (If using custard cups, bake 1 hour.) Chill. To serve, invert on serving dish.

Yield: 8 servings

Cheryl Sherling Magli (Mrs. Boyce)
Spring Hill, Tennessee

Burnt Crème

½ cup sugar
4 egg yolks, beaten

1 pint whipping cream
1 teaspoon vanilla

Preheat oven to 350°. Add sugar to egg yolks. Scald cream and pour in steady stream into egg mixture while beating with whisk. Add vanilla. Pour into 8 custard cups. Place cups in pan with boiling water ½ to 1 inch deep. Bake 45 minutes. Remove from water and chill. Sprinkle each cup with sugar. Place on top oven rack under broiler and broil until sugar is caramel color. Refrigerate before serving.

Yield: 8 servings

Ann Calhoun McMurray (Mrs. R. F.)

Pots de Crème

1 (6-ounce) package semi-sweet
   chocolate chips
2 tablespoons sugar
¾ cup milk, scalded

1 egg
1 teaspoon vanilla
Whipping cream, whipped

Warm blender by rinsing in boiling water. Put chocolate chips and sugar in warm blender. Pour in hot milk and blend at high speed. Add egg and vanilla and blend. Pour into demitasse cups or champagne glasses. Chill. Serve with dollop of whipped cream. This dessert is rich and servings are small.

Yield: 8 servings

Ellen Hardwick Tipton (Mrs. Joseph Mangham)

Coeur á la Crème

2 (8-ounce) packages cream cheese
1 cup cottage cheese
½ cup confectioners' sugar
2 teaspoons vanilla
2 cups whipping cream, whipped

2 (10-ounce) packages frozen
   raspberries, thawed
4 tablespoons Kirsch
2 tablespoons sugar

Beat together cream cheese, cottage cheese, confectioners' sugar, and vanilla. Fold in whipped cream and spoon into 6 molds or sherbet glasses. Chill overnight. Before serving, purée raspberries in blender and strain. Add Kirsch and granulated sugar to raspberries. Spoon raspberry mixture over mold immediately before serving.

Yield: 12 servings

Conni Hanson Collins (Mrs. Townsend S.)

Eggnog-Walnut Bavarian

1 cup walnuts
3 tablespoons unflavored gelatin
½ cup milk
1 quart dairy eggnog
⅛ teaspoon salt

⅓ cup brandy or 2½ teaspoons
  brandy flavoring
2 egg whites, stiffly beaten
¾ cup whipping cream, whipped
Caramel Sauce (recipe follows)

Toast walnuts in 350° oven in shallow pan until crisp (about 20 minutes). Finely chop ¾ cup walnuts; set aside. In saucepan soak gelatin in milk and add 1 cup eggnog. Heat, stirring until gelatin is dissolved. Do not boil. Add remaining eggnog, salt, and brandy. Cool until mixture begins to thicken. Fold in egg whites, whipped cream, and ground walnuts. Pour into lightly greased mold and chill several hours. Unmold; drizzle with Caramel Sauce and sprinkle with remaining walnuts.

Yield: 8 to 10 servings

Caramel Sauce:

1½ cups firmly packed
  light brown sugar
¾ cup light corn syrup

4 tablespoons butter
½ cup half and half cream

Cook brown sugar, corn syrup, and butter in double boiler to soft ball stage. Add cream and continute to cook briefly.

Yield: 1½ cups

Ena Taylor Kirkpatrick (Mrs. David M.)

Chocolate Soufflé

3 tablespoons butter
¼ cup all-purpose flour
¼ teaspoon salt
1 cup milk
2 (1-ounce) squares unsweetened
  chocolate, cut up

4 eggs, separated
½ cup sugar
¼ teaspoon cream of tartar
Grand Marnier Sauce
  (recipe follows)

Preheat oven to 325°. In saucepan, melt butter and blend in flour and salt. Add milk all at once. Cook and stir until mixture is thickened and bubbly. Remove from heat, add chocolate, and stir until melted. Separate eggs, reserving egg whites. Beat egg yolks until thick and lemon-colored. Gradually beat sugar into yolks and add to chocolate mixture. Beat reserved egg whites with cream of tartar until stiff. Carefully fold egg whites into chocolate mixture. Pour mixture into ungreased 5-cup soufflé dish. Bake about 1 hour and 10 minutes. Serve with Grand Marnier Sauce. Lacking the time and inclination for the Grand Marnier Sauce, serve with melted vanilla ice cream for sauce.

Grand Marnier Sauce:

¼ cup sugar
1 tablespoon cornstarch
¾ cup orange juice

¼ cup Grand Marnier
¼ cup slivered almonds

Combine sugar and cornstarch in small saucepan. Stir in orange juice and heat to boiling point, stirring constantly. Remove from heat and add Grand Marnier and almonds.

Yield: 5 to 6 servings

Anne Walters Pittenger (Mrs. Gaines Sherman)

Cold Lemon Soufflé

10 eggs, separated
2 cups sugar, divided
1 cup unstrained lemon juice
Grated rind of 4 lemons

2 tablespoons unflavored gelatin
¼ cup water
¼ cup light rum
2 cups whipping cream, whipped

Brush oil on waxed paper and fold to form collar around 6-cup soufflé dish. Tie with string tightly. Beat egg yolks with mixer until thick. Slowly add 1 cup sugar. When thick, add lemon juice and rind. Heat mixture, stirring until back of spoon is coated. Dissolve gelatin in water. Add rum and let stand until clear. Add to lemon mixture. Chill. Beat egg whites until foamy. Add 1 cup sugar, 1 tablespoon at a time. Beat egg whites and sugar. Add egg whites to lemon mixture. Fold in whipped cream. Pour into soufflé dish and refrigerate.

Note: Prepare at least 24 hours ahead.

Yield: 8 servings

Jean L. Nichols Alsentzer (Mrs. John S.)

Peppermint Mousse

½ pound red and white peppermint
   candies, finely crushed
½ cup half and half cream
2 teaspoons unflavored gelatin

1 tablespoon cold water
1½ cups whipping cream, whipped
Red food coloring
Crème de menthe

Stir crushed candies into half and half cream in top of double boiler and heat over simmering water until candy dissolves. Sprinkle gelatin over cold water to soften and stir into peppermint mixture until gelatin dissolves. Cool mixture and fold in whipped cream. Add a few drops of red food coloring and pour into 4-cup mold or bowl. Chill until firm. Unmold on chilled serving dish and spoon crème de menthe on each serving.

Yield: 4 servings

Jeanne Holmes Hyatt (Mrs. Hugh C.)

Chocolate Grand Marnier Mousse

½ pound Baker's semi-sweet
   chocolate
½ cup sugar
½ cup prepared coffee
½ cup Grand Marnier

5 eggs, separated
1 teaspoon vanilla
½ cup warm milk
Whipped cream

Melt chocolate in double boiler over medium heat. Put sugar, coffee, and Grand Marnier in sauce pan and bring to boil. As soon as chocolate becomes soft, add Grand Marnier mixture. Continue to cook and stir constantly until satin-smooth. Pour into large mixing bowl and cool. Beat egg yolks and vanilla together until light in color. Combine egg yolk mixture and chocolate. Add warm milk and stir well. (Consistency should be semi-fluid.) Beat egg whites until stiff; fold into chocolate mixture until all lumps are broken and chocolate looks speckled. Pour into individual sherbet or champagne glasses and refrigerate at least 1 hour. Top with whipped cream to serve.

Yield: 8 servings

William Allen
The Orangery Restaurant

Bisque Tortoni

3 eggs, separated
¼ cup sugar
12 macaroon cookies, divided
   and crumbled
2 tablespoons Grape Nuts cereal

1 tablespoon Maraschino cherry
   juice
¼ teaspoon almond extract
½ cup chopped pecans
1 cup whipping cream, whipped

Combine egg yolks and sugar, beating until thick. Stir in 9 crumbled cookies, cereal, cherry juice, almond extract, and pecans. Beat egg whites until stiff and fold into macaroon mixture. Fold in whipped cream. Spoon mixture into paper baking cups set in muffin tins. Sprinkle with 3 crumbled cookies. Freeze until firm.

Yield: 12 servings

Mary Nell Greer Johnson (Mrs. Andrew)

Frosty Apricot Delight

¼ cup chopped unsalted
  almonds, toasted
1⅓ cups crushed vanilla
  wafers
2 tablespoons melted margarine

1 teaspoon almond extract
½ gallon softened vanilla
  ice cream
1 (12-ounce) jar apricot
  preserves

Combine almonds, vanilla wafer crumbs, margarine, and almond extract.
Mix well. Reserve ½ cup of mixture for topping. Put half of remaining crumb
mixture in 9- x 12-inch oven-proof dish. Layer half of ice cream and half of
preserves on crumb mixture. Repeat layers. Sprinkle reserved crumbs on
top. Freeze.

Yield: 9 to 12 servings

Marion Burton Webb

Frozen Toffee Dessert

12 ladyfingers, split
2 tablespoons instant coffee
1 tablespoon boiling water
5 (1⅛-ounce) Heath bars, frozen

1 quart vanilla ice cream,
  softened
½ cup whipping cream
2 tablespoons creme de cacao

Line bottom and sides of 8-inch springform pan with ladyfingers, cutting to
fit sides. Dissolve coffee in boiling water and cool. Crush 4 candy bars with
flat side of a mallet. Combine crushed candy with vanilla ice cream and
dissolved coffee. Spoon mixture into springform pan and freeze until firm.
Whip cream with creme de cacao until stiff. Spread over frozen ice cream.
Crush remaining candy with mallet and sprinkle over whipped cream layer.
Freeze until firm. To serve, cut in wedges.

Yield: 8 to 10 servings

Nancy Tombras Faulkner

Jane's Boiled Custard Ice Cream

4 tablespoons all-purpose flour
8 eggs, beaten well
4 cups sugar

2 quarts milk
1 quart whipping cream
4 teaspoons vanilla

Combine flour, eggs, and sugar. Bring milk to boil in double boiler. Add sugar mixture and stir over low heat until bubbles disappear. Cool. Add whipping cream and vanilla. Pour into 1-gallon freezer and freeze according to directions.

Yield: 12 servings

Cordy Wiley Arnold (Mrs. Arch V., III)

Royal Stuart Ice Cream

2½ cups sugar
4 cups whipping cream
4 cups half and half cream
1 (14-ounce) can sweetened
    condensed milk
½ cup milk

¼ cup evaporated milk
1 (1-ounce) bottle vanilla
¼ teaspoon rose water
¼ teaspoon mace
¼ teaspoon salt
¼ teaspoon nutmeg

Combine all ingredients and freeze in hand-turn or electric freezer.

Yield: About 2½ quarts

Grace (Teedee) Garland Nystrom (Mrs. Hugh)

Peach Ice Cream

4 to 5 cups sliced peaches
2 tablespoons sugar
5 eggs
1 pint whipping cream
1½ cups sugar

1 tablespoon vanilla
1 (15-ounce) can sweetened
    condensed milk
1 quart whole milk

Mash peaches with 2 tablespoons sugar. Set aside. Beat eggs until pale yellow. Stir into remaining ingredients, adding peaches last. Pour into ice cream freezer and freeze until firm.

Yield: 1 gallon

Julia Bedinger Huster (Mrs. Edwin C., Jr.)

Fresh Strawberry Ice Cream

1 (14-ounce) can sweetened
  condensed milk
2 cups whole milk

1 quart ripe strawberries,
  crushed and sweetened

Combine ingredients and chill. Freeze in 2-quart ice cream freezer.

Yield: 2 quarts

Marie Fowler Alcorn (Mrs. W. R., Jr.)

Raspberry Ice Cream

2 cups sugar
3 tablespoons lemon juice
1 cup sour cream

2 (10-ounce) packages frozen raspberries, thawed and mashed
1 quart half and half cream
Milk

Combine sugar, lemon juice, and sour cream. Set aside. Combine mashed raspberries and half and half cream. Blend two mixtures together and pour into 1-gallon ice cream freezer. Add milk to fill ⅔ full. Freeze according to type of freezer.

Note: If made with frozen unsweetened strawberries, reduce sugar by ½ cup.

Yield: 1 gallon

Anne Keller Walters (Mrs. Charles M.)

Pineapple Sherbet

1 quart milk
2 cups sugar

1 (8-ounce) can crushed pineapple
Juice of 4 lemons

Combine all ingredients and mix well. Freeze in ice cream freezer.

Yield: ½ gallon

Ellen Clarke Spitzer (Mrs. James M.)

Creamy Lime Sherbet

1 (3-ounce) package lime-flavored
 gelatin
1 cup hot water
1½ cups sugar

Juice of 2 lemons
3 cups milk
1 cup whipping cream
Creme de menthe

Dissolve gelatin in hot water. Add sugar. When cooled, add lemon juice.
Combine milk and cream and add to gelatin mixture, beating vigorously.
Pour into ice cube tray and freeze. When serving, drizzle creme de menthe on
top.

Yield: 6 to 8 servings

Mary Alice Hungate Clarke (Mrs. James L., Jr.)

Christmas Cookies

1½ cups sugar
⅔ cup vegetable shortening
2 eggs, unbeaten
4 teaspoons milk
3⅔ cups sifted all-purpose flour

2½ teaspoons baking powder
½ teaspoon salt
½ teaspoon mace
1 teaspoon vanilla

Cream sugar and shortening. Add eggs and milk and beat well. Add dry
ingredients and chill, preferably overnight. Preheat oven to 325°. Roll out
dough on floured pastry cloth until very thin. Cut with decorative cookie
cutters and sprinkle with colored sugar, if desired. Bake until lightly
browned.

Note: May be frosted after baking, if preferred.

Yield: 3 to 4 dozen

Melissa Cooley Gill

Lemon Cookies

½ cup butter
½ cup vegetable shortening
1 cup sugar
1 egg
2 teaspoons fresh lemon juice

½ teaspoon lemon rind
2⅛ cups all-purpose flour
¾ teaspoon baking powder
¼ teaspoon salt

Preheat oven to 400°. Cream butter and shortening; add sugar, egg, lemon juice, and rind. Sift together flour, baking powder, and salt; add to butter mixture. Mix well. Drop by teaspoons onto cookie sheet. Stamp flat with bottom of glass covered with wet cloth. Bake 5 to 7 minutes until brown around edges.

Yield: 3 to 4 dozen

Judith Stephens Frost (Mrs. Robert B.)

Scotch Shortbread

1 cup butter
1½ cups confectioners' sugar,
    sifted before measuring,
    divided

2 cups all-purpose flour,
    sifted before measuring
¼ cup granulated sugar

Preheat oven to 300°. Soften butter just to workable stage. Work in ¾ cup confectioners' sugar and flour with hands. Chill. Roll out on floured cloth into preferred shape. Place on ungreased cookie sheet. Bake 10 minutes or until delicate brown. Sift remaining ¾ cup confectioners' sugar and ¼ cup granulated sugar. Dust cookies with mixture immediately after taking from oven.

Yield: 18 large cookies

Lillian Astley Rayson (Mrs. Edwin)

Whole Wheat Sugar Cookies

1 cup sugar
1 teaspoon baking powder
½ teaspoon salt
½ teaspoon soda
½ teaspoon nutmeg
½ cup butter, softened
2 tablespoons milk

1 tablespoon grated orange
  or lemon peel
1 teaspoon vanilla
1 egg
2 cups whole wheat flour
Topping (recipe follows)

Preheat oven to 375°. Combine sugar, baking powder, salt, soda, nutmeg, butter, milk, peel, vanilla, and egg in large bowl. Blend well. Stir in flour. Shape dough into 1-inch balls. Place on ungreased baking sheet, 2 inches apart. Flatten slightly. Sprinkle topping over cookies and bake 8 to 10 minutes or until golden brown.

Topping:

2 tablespoons sugar   ½ teaspoon cinnamon

Combine topping ingredients and use as directed.

Yield: 3 dozen

Lucie Carlson Polk (Mrs. Robert H.)

Peanut Butter Blossoms

½ cup smooth peanut butter
½ cup sugar + additional sugar
½ cup butter
½ cup firmly packed brown sugar
1 egg
1 teaspoon vanilla

½ teaspoon salt
1 teaspoon soda
1¾ cups all-purpose flour
1 (9-ounce) package solid
  milk chocolate kisses

Preheat oven to 375°. Cream peanut butter, sugar, butter, and brown sugar. Add egg and vanilla. Sift salt, soda, and flour together. Combine with peanut butter mixture. Shape into balls and dip in additional white sugar. Bake 8 minutes, remove from oven, and press chocolate kiss into each cookie. Return to oven and bake an additional 2 to 5 minutes.

Yield: 3 to 4 dozen

Nancy Whitman Dickson (Mrs. Michael)

Kathleen Weigel's Pecan Delights

1 cup firmly packed brown sugar
2 egg whites, stiffly beaten
1 teaspoon vanilla

1 cup whole pecans
½ cup chopped pecans
½ cup chopped almonds

Preheat oven to 250° and lightly grease cookie sheet. Combine sugar with beaten egg whites until smooth. Add remaining ingredients. Drop by teaspoons onto cookie sheet. Bake approximately 1 hour or until firm and golden brown.

Yield: 2 dozen

Emily Pryor Browning (Mrs.Louis A.)

Twice-Baked Pecan Squares

½ cup butter or margarine,
  softened
½ cup firmly packed dark
  brown sugar
1 cup all-purpose flour
2 eggs
1 cup firmly packed light
  brown sugar

1 cup coarsely chopped pecans
½ cup flaked coconut
2 tablespoons all-purpose flour
1 teaspoon vanilla
Pinch salt
Confectioners' sugar

Preheat oven to 350°. Grease 13- x 9- x 2-inch baking pan. Combine butter and dark brown sugar, creaming until light and fluffy. Add 1 cup flour and mix well. Press evenly into greased pan and bake 20 minutes.

Beat eggs until frothy; gradually add light brown sugar, beating until smooth and thickened. Combine pecans, coconut, and flour; add to egg mixture. Add vanilla and salt. Mix well and spread over crust. Bake 20 minutes at 350°. Cool and sprinkle with confectioners' sugar. Cut into squares.

Yield: 36 squares

Marie Fowler Alcorn (Mrs.W.R., Jr.)

Mint Meringue Cookies

2 egg whites
½ teaspoon mint or peppermint
   extract
½ cup sugar

6 drops green food coloring
   (optional)
1 (6-ounce) package semi-sweet
   chocolate chips

Preheat oven to 200° and butter cookie sheets. Combine egg whites and extract; beat until frothy. Gradually add sugar, 1 tablespoon at a time, beating until glossy and stiff peaks form. Beat in food coloring, if desired. Do not overbeat. Fold in chocolate chips. Drop by rounded teaspoons onto cookie sheet. Bake 1 hour or until dry and set. Cookies should not brown. Cool.

Yield: 2½ dozen

Julia Bedinger Huster (Mrs. Edwin C., Jr.)

Aunt Jo's Brownies

2 eggs
1 cup sugar
⅓ cup vegetable oil
¾ cup all-purpose flour
½ teaspoon baking powder

1 heaping tablespoon cocoa
1 teaspoon vanilla
½ cup chopped pecans
Confectioners' sugar

Preheat oven to 350°. Flour and grease 8- x 8-inch pan. Beat eggs. Add sugar, oil, flour, baking powder, and cocoa. Mix well and add remaining ingredients. Bake 30 to 35 minutes. Dust with confectioners' sugar.

Note: Recipe can be doubled.

Yield: 16 brownies

Martha Bacon Hemphill (Mrs. James L.)

Marshmallow Fudgkins

3 (1-ounce) squares unsweetened
  chocolate
1 cup butter
4 eggs
2 cups sugar
1½ cups all-purpose flour

1 teaspoon baking powder
1 cup chopped nuts
2 teaspoons vanilla
1 (6-ounce) package miniature
  marshmallows
Topping (recipe follows)

Preheat oven to 350°. Melt chocolate and butter in top of double boiler or in microwave oven. In large mixing bowl beat eggs until foamy. Add sugar and beat well. Add all other ingredients and combine with chocolate mixture. Blend well and spread in 11- x 13-inch pan. Bake 30 minutes. Immediately cover with marshmallows and pour hot topping over all.

Topping:

½ cup butter
3 (1-ounce) squares unsweetened
  chocolate
1 (13-ounce) can evaporated milk

1 cup sugar
1 pound box confectioners' sugar
1 teaspoon vanilla

Melt butter and chocolate. Add milk and sugar. Cook until blended. Beat in confectioners' sugar and vanilla. (Mixture will be thin.)

Yield: 24 squares

Betty Newbill Threadgill

Peanut Butter Brownies

3 eggs, well beaten
1½ cups sugar
½ cup vegetable oil
1 cup all-purpose flour
½ teaspoon salt

½ teaspoon baking powder
½ cup peanut butter
1 (6-ounce) package semi-sweet
  chocolate chips
½ cup chopped nuts

Preheat oven to 350°. Grease and flour 7- x 11-inch baking pan. Combine eggs, sugar, oil, flour, salt, baking powder, and peanut butter. Beat until smooth. Stir in chocolate pieces and nuts. Spread mixture into prepared pan. Bake 30 to 35 minutes. Cool and cut into squares.

Yield: 2½ dozen

Kane Watson McAfee (Mrs. Joe M.)

Microwaved Layered Brownies

2 (1-ounce) squares unsweetened
  chocolate
⅓ cup butter
1 cup sugar

2 eggs
1 teaspoon vanilla
⅔ cup all-purpose flour, unsifted
¼ teaspoon salt
Frosting (recipe follows)
Glaze (recipe follows)

Place chocolate and butter in glass bowl. Microwave at full power until melted (2½ or 3 minutes). Add sugar, eggs, and vanilla. Beat mixture 2 minutes. Stir in flour and salt until blended. Pour into greased 8-inch square dish. Microwave at full power about 4 or 4½ minutes, turning dish after 2 minutes. Remove from oven and cool. Frost and glaze.

Frosting:

¼ cup butter
2 cups confectioners' sugar, sifted

2 tablespoons milk
½ teaspoon vanilla

Place butter in 1-quart glass bowl. Cover with wax paper and microwave at full power 5 minutes or until golden brown. Blend in confectioners' sugar, milk, and vanilla. Spread over brownies.

Glaze:

1 (1-ounce) square semi-sweet
  chocolate

1 tablespoon butter

Place chocolate and butter in 1-cup glass measuring cup. Microwave at full power 2 minutes or until melted. Cool slightly and drizzle over frosted brownies. Refrigerate until frosting and glaze are set.

Yield: 20 squares

Gale Cifers Pettit (Mrs. Michael)

Turtle Cookies

2 cups all-purpose flour
1 cup firmly packed brown sugar
½ cup butter, softened
2 cups whole pecans

Topping (recipe follows)
1 cup milk chocolate or semi-sweet chocolate chips

Preheat oven to 350°. Mix flour, brown sugar, and butter at medium mixer speed 2 to 3 minutes. Pat onto bottom of ungreased 9- x 13-inch pan. Sprinkle pecans over mixture. Pour hot topping over all and bake 18 to 22 minutes or until bubbly. Immediately sprinkle chocolate chips over top and swirl.

Topping:

⅔ cup butter

½ cup firmly packed brown sugar

Cook butter and sugar over medium heat, stirring constantly, until entire surface begins to boil. Boil 1 minute, stirring constantly.

Note: Can be chilled to harden chocolate for easier cutting. Freezes well.

Yield: 24 to 32 cookies

Genia Vookles

Caramel Morsel Bars

1 (14-ounce) bag Kraft caramels
3 tablespoons water
5 cups crisp rice cereal
1 cup peanuts

1 (6-ounce) package semi-sweet chocolate morsels
1 (6-ounce) package butterscotch morsels

Melt caramels with water in saucepan over low heat or in microwave. Stir frequently until sauce is smooth. Pour over cereal and nuts; toss until well-coated. With greased fingers, press mixture into greased 9- x 13-inch pan. Sprinkle chocolate and butterscotch morsels on top. Place in 200° oven 5 minutes or until morsels soften. Remove from oven and spread softened morsels over top to form frosting. Cool and cut into squares.

Yield: 3 dozen squares

Marsha Kinard Selecman (Mrs. William D.)
Crossville, Tennessee

Cheesecake Cookies

1 cup all-purpose flour
¼ cup firmly packed light
   brown sugar
1 cup finely chopped pecans
½ cup butter, melted
2 (8-ounce) packages cream cheese

1⅓ cups granulated sugar,
   divided
2 teaspoons vanilla, divided
3 eggs
2 cups sour cream

Preheat oven to 350°. Combine flour, brown sugar, pecans, and butter. Press in bottom of 9- x 13-inch oven-proof baking dish. Bake 10 to 15 minutes or until brown.

Combine cream cheese, 1 cup sugar, and 1 teaspoon vanilla. Add eggs, and beat well. Pour onto crust and bake 20 minutes.

Combine sour cream, remaining sugar, and remaining vanilla. Pour over baked filling and bake 3 to 5 minutes. Cool and refrigerate before cutting.

Yield: 48 squares

Beverly Lamb
Kenner, Louisiana

Favorite Lemon Squares

½ cup butter
1 cup all-purpose flour
¼ cup confectioners' sugar
2 tablespoons fresh lemon juice
1 lemon rind, grated

2 eggs, beaten
1 cup sugar
2 tablespoons all-purpose flour
½ teaspoon baking powder
Frosting (recipe follows)

Preheat oven to 350°. Combine butter, 1 cup flour, and confectioners' sugar. Press mixture into 9-inch square oven-proof dish. Bake 10 minutes and cool. Combine lemon juice, lemon rind, eggs, sugar, 2 tablespoons flour, and baking powder. Pour over crust and bake 25 minutes. Cool and frost.

Frosting:

¾ cup sifted confectioners' sugar
1 teaspoon vanilla
1 tablespoon butter, softened

1 tablespoon milk
¾ to 1 cup shredded coconut

Combine ingredients and spread over filling. Cut into small squares and serve.

Note: These are also good without coconut.

Yield: 2 dozen squares

Martha Bacon Hemphill (Mrs. James L.)

Chess Squares

1 (18.5-ounce) package yellow
  cake mix
4 eggs, divided

½ cup butter, melted
8 ounces cream cheese, softened
1 (1-pound) box confectioners' sugar

Preheat oven to 350°. Combine cake mix, 1 egg, and butter; press into 9- x 13-inch pan. Combine softened cream cheese, confectioners' sugar, and remaining eggs. Pour over cake mixture. Bake 35 to 40 minutes.

Yield: 36 squares

Jan Spitzer Frey (Mrs. David M.)

Pumpkin Bars

4 eggs
1⅔ cups sugar
1 cup vegetable oil
1 (16-ounce) can pumpkin
2 cups all-purpose flour
2 teaspoons baking powder

2 teaspoons cinnamon
1 teaspoon salt
1 teaspoon soda
Cream Cheese Icing
  (recipe follows)

Preheat oven to 350°. Beat eggs, sugar, oil, and pumpkin until light and fluffy. Add remaining ingredients and mix thoroughly. Spread batter in ungreased 15- x 10-inch jelly-roll pan. Bake 25 to 30 minutes. Cool, frost with Cream Cheese Icing, and cut into bars.

Cream Cheese Icing:

1 (3-ounce) package cream cheese,
  softened
½ cup butter or margarine, softened

1 teaspoon vanilla
2 cups sifted confectioners' sugar

Cream together cream cheese and butter. Stir in vanilla. Gradually add confectioners' sugar, beating well, until mixture is smooth.

Yield: 2 dozen bars

Wanda H. Schmitz
Cincinnati, Ohio

Fruit Bars

1 cup butter
2 cups sugar
3 eggs
1 teaspoon soda
2 teaspoons water
1 (8-ounce) package chopped dates
3 cups all-purpose flour

1 teaspoon cinnamon
1 teaspoon ground cloves
¼ teaspoon nutmeg
Dash of salt
1 cup chopped English Walnuts
  or pecans
2 tablespoons sugar

Cream butter and 2 cups sugar; add eggs. Combine soda and water, blend, and add dates. Sift flour, cinnamon, cloves, nutmeg, and salt. Add to creamed mixture; add nuts. Chill overnight. On lightly floured board, shape into rolls 10 x ¾ inches. Place 2 rolls on cookie sheet and flatten until ¼-inch thick. Sprinkle with sugar. Bake 15 to 18 minutes at 350°. While still hot, cut into diagonal slices. Cool.

Yield: 5 to 6 dozen   Judith Stephens Frost (Mrs. Robert B.)

Raspberry Oatmeal Squares

1½ cups all-purpose flour
1 cup firmly packed brown sugar
1 cup quick-cooking oatmeal
½ teaspoon cinnamon
½ cup butter, melted
1 teaspoon vanilla

2 (10-ounce) packages frozen
  raspberries, thawed
½ cup sugar
1½ tablespoons cornstarch
2 tablespoons water
Whipped cream

Preheat oven to 325°. In large bowl combine flour, brown sugar, oatmeal, and cinnamon. Add butter and vanilla; combine until mixture crumbles. Drain raspberries, reserving liquid. Add enough water to raspberry liquid to measure 1 cup and pour into saucepan. Add sugar and cornstarch dissolved in 2 tablespoons water to the raspberry liquid. Cook and stir over moderately high heat until thick and clear. Add raspberries. Press 2 cups oatmeal crumbs into a 9- x 9-inch dish. Spread with raspberry filling and top with remaining crumbs. Bake 55 minutes to 1 hour or until top is light brown. Let cool on rack 10 minutes. Cut into 3-inch squares and serve with whipped cream.

Yield: 9 servings   Jeanne Holmes Hyatt (Mrs. Hugh C.)

Buckeyes

1 cup creamy peanut butter
½ pound whipped butter
1½ pounds confectioners' sugar
1½ teaspoons vanilla

2 tablespoons vegetable shortening
1 (12-ounce) package semi-sweet
  chocolate chips

In food processor or by hand, cream peanut butter, butter, sugar, and vanilla. Roll into balls about the size of large marbles. Chill. Melt shortening and chocolate in top of double boiler. Spear each ball with toothpick and dip in chocolate mixture to coat. Cool on waxed paper. Store tightly covered in refrigerator. Keeps almost indefinitely.

Yield: 4 to 5 dozen

Melissa Cooley Gill

Daddy's Candy

16 (1-ounce) squares semi-sweet
  chocolate

1 (15-ounce) can sweetened
  condensed milk
2 cups chopped pecans

Melt chocolate squares in double boiler. Add milk and nuts. Remove from heat, stirring until thick and the consistency of dough. Drop on 3 separate pieces of wax paper and roll up log style. Chill. Slice just before serving.

Yield: 3 logs

Melissa Cooley Gill

Maple Pecan Pralines

1 cup firmly packed brown sugar
2 cups white sugar
1 cup water
1 tablespoon butter

¼ teaspoon salt
1 teaspoon maple extract
1½ cups pecan pieces or
  3 cups pecan halves

Line baking sheets with waxed paper. In saucepan combine sugars and water. Stir over medium heat until melted. Bring to boil; boil to soft ball stage (236°). Remove from heat and stir in butter, salt, and maple flavoring. Beat until syrup starts to become creamy. Stir in pecans. Drop by teaspoon onto baking sheets.

Note: If candy becomes too hard to drop from spoon, place pan over hot water and stir a few drops of hot water into mixture until soft.

Yield: 2 dozen

Barbara Leonard Hobson (Mrs. Charles)

Margaret's Toffee Candy

2 cups butter
2 cups sugar
2 (2¾-ounce) packages slivered
  almonds

1 pound milk chocolate Hershey bars
2 (2¾-ounce) packages sliced
  almonds

Melt butter in heavy saucepan. Add sugar and cook until dissolved. Add slivered almonds and cook over medium heat stirring constantly until mixture becomes caramel color and pulls away from sides of pan, or until 290° is reached on candy thermometer. Pour onto ungreased cookie sheet and cool. Melt chocolate candy in top of double boiler. When toffee is cool, pour half chocolate over toffee and spread thin. Sprinkle with half sliced almonds. Place in refrigerator 10 minutes to harden. Flip candy over and repeat process with remaining chocolate and sliced almonds. When cooled, break into pieces.

Note: Make this candy on a cool, dry day.

Yield: Approximately 5 pounds

Nancy Powell Wilson (Mrs. Grover)

Microwaved Texas Turtles

1 (14-ounce) package caramels
1 tablespoon milk
1¾ cups chopped pecans

1 (12-ounce) package semi-sweet
  chocolate chips
1 tablespoon vegetable shortening

Place caramels in 2-quart casserole and microwave on full power 1 to 1¼ minutes, stirring often. Add milk and microwave on full power 1½ to 2 minutes, stirring every 30 seconds. Stir until smooth. Add pecans and stir well. Drop by teaspoonfuls on buttered wax paper. Set aside to cool. Cover and chill.
  Combine chocolate chips and shortening in 4-cup oven-proof dish. Microwave on medium power 3 to 4 minutes, stirring well. Dip caramel centers into chocolate mixture. Return to wax paper. Chill. Store candy in refrigerator.

Yield: Approximately 2 dozen

Gale Cifers Pettit (Mrs. Michael)

Divinity Candy

2½ cups sugar
⅓ cup white corn syrup
½ cup hot water
¼ teaspoon salt

2 egg whites
1 teaspoon vanilla
½ cup broken pecans

Combine sugar, syrup, hot water, and salt in saucepan. Cook over medium heat, stirring constantly until sugar is completely dissolved. Cover pan and boil 5 minutes. Uncover and continue cooking to hard ball stage. Remove from heat. Beat egg whites until foamy. Add hot syrup in thin stream while beating with mixer. Continue beating 3 to 5 minutes until candy thickens and loses gloss. Add vanilla while beating. Stir in pecans. Drop quickly by teaspoons onto waxed paper.

Yield: 50 to 60 pieces

Cornelia Grace Hickman (Mrs. J. H., Jr.)

Butterscotch Sauce

1½ cups light brown sugar
⅓ cup butter
¾ cup light corn syrup

⅛ teaspoon salt
1 cup half and half cream
   or evaporated milk

Heat sugar, butter, syrup, and salt, stirring constantly until sugar is dissolved. Slowly add cream, stirring until syrup thickens (approximately 226°). If sauce is not of proper consistency, remove from heat and add more cream. A quick whirl in blender while sauce is still lukewarm will smooth it out. Keeps indefinitely in refrigerator.

Yield: 2 cups

Jean Slayden (Mrs. Paul)

Hot Fudge Sauce

6 tablespoons unsalted butter
½ cup water
3 ounces unsweetened chocolate

1 cup sugar
2 tablespoons light corn syrup
1 teaspoon vanilla

Melt butter in water in small heavy saucepan over medium heat. Bring to boil, stirring constantly. Add chocolate, stirring until melted. (Do not be alarmed if lumps develop.) Add sugar and corn syrup. Let come to soft boil and boil gently 5 minutes. Add vanilla when bubbles disappear. Serve hot.

Yield: 1½ cups

Ena Taylor Kirkpatrick (Mrs. David M.)

Microwaved Hot Chocolate Sauce

1 (4-ounce) package German's Sweet
   Chocolate
1 tablespoon water
4 tablespoons butter
1 cup sugar

Dash salt
1 tablespoon light corn syrup
¾ cup whipping cream
2 tablespoons Grand Marnier

Melt chocolate with water in 4-cup oven-proof dish 3 to 4 minutes at 60% power, stirring once. Add butter and stir until melted. Add sugar, salt, and corn syrup. Mix well and microwave at full power 2½ to 3 minutes or until sugar is dissolved, stirring once. Add cream and microwave at 80% power 2 to 3 minutes. Remove and stir in Grand Marnier.

Note: Thickens when cooled. Good on ice cream or as dessert sauce on cream puffs.

Yield: 2 cups

Suzanne Wood Fletcher

Poached Plum Sauce

½ cup sugar
1 cup water
Rind from 1 lemon, cut
   in strips
1 teaspoon vanilla

Dash nutmeg
1 pound red plums, pitted and
   quartered (about 2 cups)
1 tablespoon cornstarch
1 tablespoon water

In saucepan, combine sugar, 1 cup water, lemon rind, vanilla, and nutmeg. Bring to boil. Reduce heat, cover, and simmer 5 minutes. Add plums and simmer 4 to 5 minutes or until plums are slightly soft. Remove plums and set aside. Discard lemon rind. Combine cornstarch with 1 tablespoon water. Add to liquid and cook, stirring, until sauce thickens and bubbles. Return plums to sauce. Serve over ice cream.

Yield: 2⅓ cups

Lou Bennett (Mrs. Bill)

Pickles
Relishes
Preserves

Kosher Dills

Chow-Chow

Blueberry Jam

Bread and Butter Pickles

1 gallon small cucumbers,
   thinly sliced
6 medium onions, thinly sliced
2 green peppers, cut in
   thin strips
½ cup salt
Ice

5 cups sugar
5 cups vinegar
½ teaspoon ground cloves
2 tablespoons mustard seed
1 teaspoon celery seed
2 teaspoons turmeric

Layer cucumbers, onions, and green peppers. Sprinkle with salt and cover with ice. Repeat layers, using plenty of ice. Let stand 3 hours. Drain vegetable mixture and rinse well. Combine sugar, vinegar, cloves, mustard seed, celery seed, and turmeric. Heat to boiling. Add drained vegetables and bring to simmer. Seal in sterilized jars.

Yield: 8 to 10 pints   Caroline Siler Hill (Mrs. Robert E.)

Yellow Cucumber Pickles

4 quarts yellow cucumbers
1 green pepper or 1 red
   sweet pepper, chopped
3 medium onions, chopped
3 cloves garlic, chopped
3 cups vinegar

5 cups sugar
1½ tablespoons celery seed
1½ tablespoons turmeric
2 tablespoons salt
5 tablespoons mustard seed

Peel, remove seeds, and cut cucumbers into chunks. Put cucumbers and chopped vegetables in bowl with ice. Let chill at least 3 hours in refrigerator. Drain well. Boil vinegar, sugar, and spices 1 minute or until well dissolved. Add vegetables and cook 15 to 20 minutes or until cucumbers are transparent. Put in sterilized jars and seal.

Note: These pickles are made from cucumbers that are large and yellow and look overripe. Don't throw them away—they make delicious, unusual pickles.

Yield: 8 pints   Carolyn Dew Pearre (Mrs. Courtney N.)

Lime Pickles

gallons medium cucumbers,
 sliced
cups lime
gallons water
ce water
 quarts white vinegar

5 pounds sugar
1 tablespoon salt
1 tablespoon whole cloves
1 tablespoon pickling
 spices
1 tablespoon celery seed

Soak cucumbers in lime water 24 hours *only.*Rinse cucumbers thoroughly
and soak in ice water 2 hours. Combine vinegar, sugar, salt, and the spices
tie cloves, pickling spices, and celery seed in cheesecloth bag). Stir well.
Drain pickles and add to vinegar mixture. Let stand overnight. Remove
spice bag. Heat on medium just until cucumbers are heated through, since
overcooking makes soft pickles. Pour into sterilized jars and seal.

Yield: 13 pints

Scott Davis Wilson (Mrs. Don)

Pickled Okra

4 pounds okra
5 to 7 cloves garlic
5 to 7 hot red peppers
5 to 7 teaspoons dill seed

5 to 7 teaspoons mustard seed
1 quart white vinegar
1 cup water
½ cup salt

Wash okra and trim stems without cutting too close. In bottom of each
sterilized jar, place 1 clove garlic and 1 hot pepper. Firmly pack okra in jars,
adding 1 teaspoon dill and 1 teaspoon mustard seed per jar. Bring vinegar,
water, and salt to boil; simmer 5 minutes. Pour boiling solution over okra.
Place lids on jars. Lids will seal as jars cool. (Jars which are not sealed
should be kept in refrigerator.) Let stand several weeks before using. Serve
chilled.

Yield: 5 to 7 pints

Marti Schmitz Hobson (Mrs. Leonard)

Pickled Peaches

7 pounds peaches
3 pounds sugar
1 scant quart vinegar

2 sticks cinnamon
2 tablespoons whole cloves

Peel peaches. Combine sugar, vinegar, and spices. Cook until mixture boils well. Add fruit and cook until tender. Put peaches in sterilized jars and fill with hot syrup.

Yield: 3 quarts

Mary Culver Spengler (Mrs. Joseph

Bell Pepper Relish

12 large red bell peppers,
   seeded
12 large green bell peppers,
   seeded
6 small hot peppers
6 medium onions

1 quart white vinegar
2 cups sugar
¼ cup salt
1 teaspoon mustard seed
1 teaspoon celery seed

Finely chop peppers and onions. Cover with boiling water and let stand 20 minutes. Drain thoroughly. Combine vinegar and seasonings in 5-quart pan. Bring to boil. Stir in drained vegetables and simmer 15 minutes. Put in hot sterilized jars and put on lids. Lids will seal as jars cool. Jars which are not sealed should be kept in refrigerator. Store in cool, dark place.

Note: Serve with beans or meat. Glorifies hot dogs and hamburgers. Good with Cheddar cheese as an appetizer.

Yield: 6 to 7 pints

Alice Ann Hale Clayton (Mrs. Edward S., III)

Pickled Squash

quarts yellow squash,
cut in round slices
medium onions, chopped
₂ cup salt
cups white vinegar

3 cups sugar
4 green peppers, chopped
2 hot red peppers, chopped
1 teaspoon mustard seed
1 teaspoon celery seed

Sprinkle squash and onions with salt and mix thoroughly. Let stand at
least 1 hour. Bring vinegar and sugar to boil; add green and red peppers,
mustard seed, and celery seed, and cook until peppers are tender. Drain salt
water from squash. Do not wash. Add squash and onions to vinegar mixture
and boil until squash is tender. Do not overcook. Pour into sterilized jars and
seal.

Yield: 6 to 8 pints   Scott Davis Wilson (Mrs. Don)

Green Tomato Relish

2 quarts chopped green tomatoes
¾ cup salt
1 teaspoon pepper
1½ teaspoons dry mustard
1½ teaspoons cinnamon
½ teaspoon allspice
1½ teaspoons ground cloves

1 tablespoon celery seed
¼ cup mustard seed
1 quart cider vinegar
2 red or green peppers,
chopped
1 large onion, chopped
3 cups sugar

Combine tomatoes and salt. Cover and let stand 24 hours. Drain tomatoes
and rinse several times. Add all ingredients to tomatoes and bring to boil.
Simmer mixture 15 minutes. Put into sterilized jars and top with lids.

*Note: Lids will seal as jars cool. Jars which are not sealed can be kept in
refrigerator indefinitely.*

Yield: 4 pints   R. S. Schmitz
                                                          Gulf Shores, Alabama

Pear Relish

8 large or 22 small hard pears, pared and cored	2 cups water
2 quarts onions	5 cups sugar
8 large bell peppers	8 tablespoons all-purpose flour
½ cup salt	4 tablespoons Coleman's mustar_
3 pints vinegar	2 tablespoons turmeric
	4 dill pickles, chopped

Put pears, onions, and peppers through food grinder. Cover mixture with ? cup salt and leave overnight. The next morning squeeze out all water. Pu vinegar and water in large pan and heat. Meanwhile, mix sugar, flou_ mustard, and turmeric. Add enough vinegar mixture to dry ingredients t make smooth paste. Then add paste to hot vinegar mixture and cook stirring constantly, until mixture is cream sauce consistency. Then ad_ ground pear mixture and cook approximately 30 minutes. Add chopped di_ pickles during last few minutes of cooking. Pour into sterilized jars. Sea while hot.

Yield: 6 pints

Mary Neal Slatery Culver (Mrs. Robert

Wilson Red Devil (Tomato Relish)

1 peck ripe tomatoes	1 teaspoon ginger
4 medium onions, chopped	1 teaspoon allspice
4 cups sugar	1 teaspoon celery salt
1 quart cider vinegar	6 to 8 hot red peppers,
1 tablespoon salt	chopped
1 teaspoon cinnamon	

Scald, peel, core, and chop tomatoes into coarse pieces and combine with onions, sugar, vinegar, and spices in heavy pan. Cook at rolling boil, stirring occasionally until reduced to half volume (about 3 to 4 hours). Add hot peppers halfway through cooking time. Seal in sterilized jars. Delicious on hamburgers and meat loaf.

Note: Recipe can be doubled.

Yield: 6 pints

Scott Davis Wilson (Mrs. Don)

Apple-Mint Jelly

large bunches fresh mint
½ cups water
cup cider vinegar
cup apple juice

7 cups sugar, divided
1 (6-ounce) box liquid
  fruit pectin

Wash mint and shake dry. Place on cutting board and crush with rolling
pin. In 3-quart saucepan, place water, vinegar, and apple juice. Bring to boil.
Add mint and bring to boil again. Cover, remove from heat, and let stand 10
minutes. Strain and measure 1¾ cups of mint infusion. In another large
saucepan, combine infusion with 3½ cups sugar. Place over high heat, stir
well, and bring to full rolling boil. Stir in 1 (3-ounce) pouch of pectin. Boil
hard 1 minute, stirring constantly. Remove from heat and skim off foam.
Pour into 4 hot jelly glasses and seal. Repeat process with remaining
infusion, sugar, and pectin.

Yield: 8 half-pints   Jane Crumpler DeFiore (Mrs. Joseph C.)

Green Pepper Jelly

4 large green peppers
1½ cups cider vinegar
1 small hot red pepper
6½ cups sugar

1 (6-ounce) bottle liquid
  fruit pectin
8 drops green food coloring

Seed and chop peppers. Put peppers and vinegar in blender and purée 30
seconds. Combine green pepper mixture, red pepper, and sugar in large
kettle. Bring mixture to boil, stirring constantly, and boil 10 minutes.
Remove from heat and allow to stand 15 minutes. Return to heat and boil 2
minutes. Pour through strainer lined with damp cheesecloth. Place pepper
liquid in kettle, add fruit pectin, and bring quickly to boil. Boil hard 1
minute, stirring constantly. Remove from heat, skim off foam with metal
spoon, and add food coloring. Pour into hot sterilized jelly glasses and seal.

Yield: 4 cups   Ellen Clarke Spitzer (Mrs. James M.)

Mom's Blackberry Jelly

1 gallon blackberries
1 quart water

4 cups sugar
Juice of 1 lemon

Boil berries in water 10 to 15 minutes. Strain through cheese cloth. Boil
cups blackberry juice 10 minutes. Add sugar and lemon juice. Coo
additional 7 to 10 minutes or until mixture sheets off metal spoon. Pour in
sterilized jars. When cool, seal with paraffin.

Yield: 4 half-pints   Mary Alice Hungate Clarke (Mrs. James L., J

Blackberry Jam

2 quarts fresh blackberries   6 cups sugar

Wash blackberries and cook in saucepan over medium heat until berries are
soft and juice begins flowing. Strain through food mill to obtain juice and
pulp. Measure 4 cups juice and pulp and return to saucepan. Add sugar and
cook over medium heat about 30 minutes or until candy thermometer
reaches 221°. Pour into sterilized jars and seal.

Yield: 6 half-pints   Marti Schmitz Hobson (Mrs. Leonard)

Christmas Jam

1 (1-pound, 14-ounce) can pineapple
   chunks, cut in half
1 (8-ounce) jar maraschino
   cherries, quartered

3½ cups water
1 (11-ounce) package dried
   apricots, quartered
6 cups sugar

Drain pineapple and cherries, reserving liquid. Combine pineapple,
reserved liquid, water, and apricots. Let stand 1 hour or longer to soften
apricots. Cook over medium heat until apricots are tender (approximately 5
minutes). Add sugar and cook over medium heat until thick and clear or
until reading of 216° is reached on candy thermometer. Add cherries. Cook
and mix thoroughly. Pour into hot sterilized jars and seal with paraffin.

Note: Makes a good jam when fresh fruits are out of season.

Yield: 6 half-pints   Ellen Brown Adams (Mrs. Elliott D.)

Fresh Peach Preserves

ipe peaches

emons

Sugar (¾ cup to each cup of fruit)

ip fruit into boiling water *briefly* to remove skins. Peel and cut into ngthwise slices. Measure peach slices and pour into large bowl or Dutch ven. Add ¾ cup sugar for each cup of fruit. Stir and let stand 2 hours. leasure 4 to 5 cups of peach mixture and pour into large, deep pot. Do not ook more than 5 cups at a time. Add juice of 1 lemon. Simmer 25 to 35 ninutes, stirring occasionally. Mixture is ready when thick and trans-arent. Pour into hot sterilized jars and seal.

ield: 4 quarts of sliced peaches usually yield 8½ to 9 pints preserves.

Anne Beall Hillmer (Mrs. Ralph G., Jr.)

Lucy Templeton's Strawberry Preserves

This is an East Tennessee favorite!

4 cups strawberries

3 cups sugar

Wash and hull strawberries. Put 1½ cups sugar on berries and let stand approximately 20 minutes. Bring to boil slowly in 5-quart Dutch oven. Boil 5 minutes and add remaining sugar. Cook at rolling boil 10 to 20 minutes or until syrup sheets off metal spoon. Skim foam off as it boils. Pour into crock, cover, and let stand at room temperature 24 hours. Pack in sterile jars and seal with paraffin. Be sure to cook *only* 4 cups of berries at one time.

Yield: 4 to 5 half-pints

Index

267

Index

269

Index

273

Index

275

Index

277

Index

BIBLIOGRAPHY

Ginders, James, *A Guide to Napkin Folding,* 1978, Reprint Edition (Boston: CBI Publishing Co., Inc., 1979)

Walsh, Marie T., "How to Entertain and Enjoy Yourself," *Family Circle Great Ideas,* Volume 7, No. 4 (New York: Family Circle, Inc., May, 1981)

White: Joseph R., *Secrets of Napkin Folding,* 1976, Revised Edition (Joseph R. White, 1975)